THE
National ◆SABR◆ Pastime

Steel City Stories

Edited by Cecilia M. Tan

◆SABR◆ **Published by The Society for American Baseball Research**

THE NATIONAL PASTIME

Copyright © 2018 The Society for American Baseball Research

Editor: Cecilia Tan
Design and Production: Lisa Hochstein
Cover Design: Lisa Hochstein
Fact Checker: Clifford Blau
Copy Editor: King Kaufman

Front cover: Photo of PNC Park by J.C. Sullivan/Flickr.
Images of players: Honus Wagner: Library of Congress, Bain Collection;
Roberto Clemente, Willie Stargel: Courtesy of the Pittsburgh Pirates.

ISBN 978-1-943816-67-5 print edition
ISBN 978-1-943816-66-8 ebook edition

Society for American Baseball Research, Inc.
Cronkite School at ASU
555 N. Central Ave. #416
Phoenix, AZ 85004

Web: www.sabr.org
Phone: (602) 496–1460

Contents

Note from the Editor

SABRen, welcome to "The Burgh," home to some truly significant episodes in baseball history, being not only the home to the great Negro Leagues teams the Homestead Grays and Pittsburgh Crawfords, but to a major league team who came by their name honestly—no pun intended—for what others called the "piratical" practice of poaching players.

The articles in this volume are arranged roughly chronologically, starting from the opening of Forbes Field in 1909 and carrying through to the annual ritual that takes place every October at the section of the Forbes Field outfield wall that still stands today. Fans re-live the magic of Game Seven of the 1960 World Series on the very spot where Bill Mazeroski's home run flew like David's stone into the head of Goliath. Sounds like nearly as much fun as the annual ritual known as the SABR National Convention, which brings us to a different city every year, and thus a different theme for *The National Pastime*.

The greats are here of course: Honus Wagner, Josh Gibson, Roberto Clemente, Wille Stargell, but as usual for a SABR publication we look for the angles and storylines in history that aren't in Baseball History 101. So we'll look at Honus Wagner's election bid for sheriff, pitcher Mudcat Grant's singing career in the time of Jim Crow, and the exploits of a Guy named Bush. It wouldn't be SABR without a little number-crunching, so enjoy the retroactive analysis of Honus Wagner "five-tool player" and the conclusion that the Cubs' greatest rivals are none other than the Pirates. If you're at the convention, you may get to debate that point with the author, perhaps over libations. If you're not at the convention, it's not to late to join SABR (anyone may join) and be a part of the fun next year!

— Cecilia M. Tan, Publications Director
June 2018

Forbes Field

Ahead of Its Time in 1909

Robert C. Trumpbour

Many people regard Pittsburgh's Forbes Field, home of the Pirates from 1909 to 1970, as a quaint, simple ballpark. Some might even consider Forbes Field's design reflective of an old-fashioned and bygone era. Nevertheless, its construction was very much rooted in embracing modernity. Forbes Field inspired other sports entrepreneurs to embrace more permanent, luxurious, and ambitious projects. This led to the rise of increasingly opulent sports facilities throughout the nation.

Forbes Field and Philadelphia's Shibe Park, both christened in 1909, were built to be permanent ballparks. Philadelphia Athletics owner Benjamin Shibe and Pittsburgh Pirates owner Barney Dreyfuss were the first major league owners to fully plan, design, and engineer ballparks that abandoned wooden construction in favor of facilities that were built entirely of fireproof steel and masonry. Forbes Field was the first ballpark to require a million-dollar investment, as well. However, it was not the first venue to embrace luxurious amenities.

In the 1880s, sporting goods entrepreneur and team owner Albert Spalding entertained Chicago White Stockings fans at White Stocking Park, offering well-heeled patrons enclosed private spaces that overlooked the field. These precursors to luxury suites included comfortable armchairs. Spalding even installed a telephone in his own private box. Ballpark historian Michael Benson described the facility as "the finest in the world" at the time. But it was a wooden structure, and like many nineteenth-century parks, it closed less than a decade after opening.[1]

Cincinnati's Palace of the Fans opened in 1902 and continued a trend of hastily constructed opulence, as did New York's legendary Polo Grounds, built in 1890. The Polo Grounds was then a wooden ballpark, while Cincinnati incorporated fireproof materials, masonry, and steel for much of the structure. Its Corinthian columns, palatial architecture, and opera-style private boxes looked impressive, but its uneven construction quality led to its demise in 1911, a mere 10 years after its unveiling.[2]

Philadelphia's Baker Bowl is often called the first fireproof major league ballpark. Constructed largely of wood in 1887, it was quickly reconstructed of brick and masonry after extensive fire damage in 1894. However, some platforms in the rebuilt venue retained wooden support materials.[3] As such, Shibe Park, also in Philadelphia, could be considered America's first carefully engineered, fully fireproof baseball venue. Nevertheless, it contained wooden seats, as did other ballparks of the era. Produced at a cost of $315,248.69, Shibe Park was described as the finest American ballpark when it opened on April 12, 1909. It featured French Renaissance flourishes and was designed with an intended permanence not previously found in other American ballparks.[4]

Nevertheless, the scope and scale of Forbes Field's construction dwarfed the highly touted project in Philadelphia. Forbes Field needed almost three times more structural steel and, with its million-dollar price tag, cost over three times more to build. In February, as work was underway, the *Pittsburgh Post* asserted that 537 large freight cars of materials would be required to finish the project.[5] Forbes Field actually required approximately double that early estimate, including

Forbes Field on Opening Day in 1909. The ballpark was named for the British army general, John Forbes, who captured Fort Duquesne and named the city Pittsburgh.

carload totals of 40 for ornamental iron, 70 for seats, 110 for cement, 130 for structural steel, and 650 for sand and gravel.[6]

To ensure that Forbes Field avoided the short life-span of other ballparks, Dreyfuss solicited engineering and architectural expertise beyond what had been used elsewhere. On December 15, 1908, the Pirates announced that "numerous architects" had submitted plans for the proposed venue.[7] After sifting through proposals, Dreyfuss hired Charles Wellford Leavitt Jr., a respected New York architect and civil engineer, to supervise the design. Leavitt worked on major projects for municipalities and wealthy clients, with his entry into sports having come through horse racing, with New York's famed Belmont and Saratoga racetracks as clients.[8] These venues featured large grandstands with opulent flourishes intended to attract wealthy patrons, making Leavitt's transition to Pittsburgh's ballpark design desirable.

C.E. Marshall, a Leavitt employee, provided further engineering expertise. Marshall's years of site work at the Panama Canal shaped the early stages of that complex undertaking. Specifically, his knowledge of retaining wall construction and drainage was touted as construction began. Such a focus was likely by design, as Exposition Park, the Pirates' home at the time, experienced numerous drainage and water-related problems.[9]

Site work began on December 23, 1908, shortly after the Nicola Building Company was announced as lead contractor. Before that, steel magnate and confidant Andrew Carnegie assisted Dreyfuss in property acquisition. As work began, Dreyfuss emphasized that although the ballpark was not located near Pittsburgh's central business district, "We have not made any mistake in choosing the best site," in part because the location was in an emerging upscale neighborhood, and, in part because the site afforded transportation options, including nearby trolley stations, that Dreyfuss said "are better than any other part of the city."[10]

Forbes Field was unique in the level of publicity it received. Such attention reached beyond the predictably enthusiastic drumbeat of local newspapers. In one example, *Harper's Weekly* offered a national feature that included panoramic photographs with coverage that emphasized its million-dollar cost while highlighting the location in "the Schenley district, one of the city's most prominent residential sections."[11] Newspaper reporting was widespread, too. An Iowa newspaper, for example, explained that enthusiasm at the June 30, 1909, opening game was so intense that many of Pittsburgh's downtown businesses "declared a half holiday," while asserting police presence was required to quell "riots" caused by large crowds.[12]

The scale of the Forbes Field project and its focus on opulent modernity helped it to stand out among other ballparks. Even before planning and building Forbes Field, Dreyfuss was a baseball pioneer. He was an early proponent of postseason interleague play, with his Pirates facing the Boston Americans in the 1903 "World's Championship Games." He was an early adopter of the use of a canvas tarpaulin to keep Exhibition Park's easily water-soaked infield dry, and he fabricated an even larger protective cover for Forbes Field. The Pirates were the first team to maintain a fully equipped training facility in the south, too.[13] Subsequently, these strategies were emulated elsewhere.

Forbes Field's innovations were numerous. As its grand opening approached, reporter James Jerpe asserted that "every detail at Forbes Field is many years ahead of the so-called modern effects and innovations elsewhere." For example, Dreyfuss installed public telephones for use on all floors, a first for a major league-venue. He also created a separate entrance for "holders of season box admission tickets."[14]

Luxury seating was not new, but Dreyfuss was the first to install elevators to comfortably transport patrons to their posh seating locations on the exclusive third tier. This precursor to modern skyboxes was described as "boxes for

COURTESY OF THE PITTSBURGH PIRATES

Aerial view of Forbes Field, circa 1960.

the true lovers of the game who are willing to spend a little extra money to not only obtain a fine view of the field, but to be able to secure a quiet and comfortable time." For other visitors, ramps replaced stairways, allowing more convenient and efficient entry and exit.[15]

Less than six months after the first Ford Model T rolled out of a Detroit assembly plant, Dreyfuss planned for the installation of an expansive parking area underneath the ballpark.[16] As the concrete was being poured, a *Pittsburgh Post* story explained that this part of the park "will be the finest automobile garage in Pittsburgh."[17]

Dreyfuss also worked to astutely cultivate his most loyal customers. In one example, he installed brass identification plates on the private boxes of season ticket-holders.[18] Additionally, men's and ladies' restrooms were more modern and comfortable than was available in other ballparks. Dreyfuss added private areas for umpires, too, as well as a separate entrance for players. The visiting team had access to locker rooms with similar space and amenities as the home team, including on-site laundry equipment. Electricity and lighting were installed, with early plans discussed for night baseball, even though such a game did not occur in Pittsburgh until 1940.[19]

Nevertheless, the lighting, electricity, and other amenities made Forbes Field a highly versatile all-purpose venue. In its opening week, Dreyfuss provided fans with baseball in the daytime, but after the game was over, a new group of patrons paid up to a dollar to watch evening fireworks while listening to a patriotic military band.[20] When the team was on the road, events were scheduled, including a heavily touted extravaganza called the Hippodrome, a mix of circus acts, vaudeville, and popular culture.[21] Football, boxing, and other entertainment took place, too.

Many considered Dreyfuss's investment in Forbes Field foolish and overly extravagant, suggesting that he might never fill his cavernous new ballpark.[22] The detractors were wrong, and the ballpark's opening game unfolded in front of a massive crowd that exceeded capacity. Forbes Field attracted strong interest for the remainder of the 1909 season as the Pirates advanced to the World Series, and, in storybook fashion, beat the Detroit Tigers to be crowned world champions.

Barney Dreyfuss's investment, persistence, and vision helped baseball to retain its stature as the national pastime at a time when the entertainment landscape was rapidly changing. Recently opened nickelodeons showcased films and relatively new commercial

Baseball under the lights at Forbes Field. The Pirates began to play night games in 1940.

amusement parks such as nearby Kennywood Park in West Mifflin provided consumers with a broader array of leisure options than in previous generations.[23] This uncertain environment presented unique challenges to sports entrepreneurs such as Dreyfuss.

The opulence that Forbes Field initially projected helped to attract numerous customers and, while doing so, altered the nature of the sporting experience in subtle and unexpected ways. Pirates shortstop Honus Wagner asserted that with a classier atmosphere, players needed to "stop cussing" during games, while Giants pitcher Christy Mathewson joked about the potential to lose fly balls because of shimmering diamonds in the stands.[24]

Of greater significance, rival baseball owners worked to emulate the success achieved at Forbes Field, with Albert Spalding boasting in 1911 that "there is nothing that can equal such baseball palaces as have been built in Philadelphia, Chicago, Cleveland, Pittsburgh, and other cities, to say nothing of the improvement contemplated in New York."[25] As other cities committed to new construction, New York rebuilt a fireproof version of the Polo Grounds in 1912, erected Ebbets Field in Brooklyn in 1913, and wrapped up baseball's first concrete-and-steel era with the completion of cavernous Yankee Stadium in 1923.

For those unfamiliar with Pittsburgh's baseball legacy, Forbes Field might not evoke the awe-inspiring, heart-pounding excitement of the much-ballyhooed Yankee Stadium, or perhaps one of today's more modern twenty-first-century ballparks. But after Dreyfuss died in 1932, National League President John Heydler recognized the transformative nature of Forbes Field. He displayed a picture of the crowded ballpark's inaugural game directly opposite his office desk, and its careful positioning ensured that it would be an image that he would see every day. Neatly written below this large photograph was: "Forbes Field. June 30, 1909. Attendance, 30,332."[26] Forbes Field's cultural and commercial success in 1909 paved the way for not only the House That Ruth Built, but numerous other majestic ballparks that would be unveiled throughout the twentieth century and beyond. ■

Notes

1. Michael Benson, *Ballparks of North America* (Jefferson, NC: McFarland, 1989), 82–83.
2. Robert Trumpbour, *The New Cathedrals* (Syracuse: Syracuse University Press, 2007), 75.
3. Michael Gershman, *Diamonds: The Evolution of the Ballpark* (New York: Houghton Mifflin, 1993), 57–59.
4. Rich Westcott, *Philadelphia's Old Ballparks* (Philadelphia: Temple University Press, 1996), 106.
5. "Construction of New Ball Park at Pittsburgh Will Tax the Capacity of 537 Large Freight Cars," *Pittsburgh Post*, February 28, 1909.
6. Gershman, Diamonds, 88.
7. "Plans Arrive for Park," *Pittsburgh Post*, 7 December 15, 1908.
8. "Charles W. Leavitt, Park Designer, Dies," *The New York Times*, April 24, 1928.
9. "Workmen are Busy at New Ball Park," *Pittsburgh Post*, January 3, 1909.
10. "Grading of New Baseball Grounds to Be Finished Within Sixty Days," *Pittsburgh Post*, December 23, 1908.
11. "Pittsburg's Million-Dollar Baseball Park" *Harper's Weekly*, May 22, 1909.
12. "New Ball Park Opened," *The Burlington* (IA) *Hawkeye*, July 1, 1909.
13. "Fifteen Hundred Tons of Steel for Grandstand at Pirate Park," *Pittsburgh Post*, January 29, 1909.
14. James Jerpe, "Forbes Field, the World's Finest Baseball Grounds," *Pittsburgh Post*, June 27, 1909.
15. "New Ballpark Will Surpass Expectations," *Pittsburgh Post*, March 7, 1909.
16. "Major League Schedule Makers to Meet in Cleveland Tomorrow," *Pittsburgh Post*, January 17, 1909.
17. "Two Shifts Will Work on New Baseball Park," *Pittsburgh Post*, March 28, 1909.
18. "Pirates to Depart for Cincinnati," *Pittsburgh Post*, May 9, 1909.
19. "Baseball Games by Electric Light Are Planned for New Pirate Park," *Pittsburgh Post*, April 4, 1909.
20. "Fireworks at Forbes Field," advertisement, *Pittsburgh Post*, July 4, 1909.
21. "Pittsburgh's Hippodrome Is a Real Open-Air Circus," *Pittsburgh Post*, August 6, 1909.
22. John Kieran, "The Passing of Barney Dreyfuss," *The New York Times*, February 6, 1932.
23. "Season Opens Today at Kennywood Park," *Pittsburgh Post*, May 2, 1909.
24. Dennis DeValeria and Jeanne Burke DeValeria, *Honus Wagner: A Biography* (New York: Henry Holt and Company, 1996), 213.
25. Albert Spalding, *America's National Game* (New York: American Sports Publishing, 1911), 505.
26. Kieran, "The Passing of Barney Dreyfuss."

Honus Wagner
Baseball's Prototypical Five-Tooler?

Herm Krabbenhoft

The highly regarded "five-tool" label is a relatively modern term in baseball's lexicon, usually traced to Leo Durocher proclaiming the greatness of his star player of the early 1950s, Willie Mays.[1] The five tools are: hit for average, hit with power, run with speed and prowess (particularly on the basepaths), catch the ball, and throw the ball (with accuracy and high velocity). *Sports Illustrated* called Mays "The prototypical five-tool player," i.e., the first or original.[2] Assuredly, however, each of these five diamond skills has been important since day one of major league baseball—and therefore it does not seem unreasonable that there could have been five-tool players who preceded the Say Hey Kid. This article describes the results of my effort to objectively investigate this matter.

RESEARCH PROCEDURE

The connotation of the "five-tool player" term is *sustained outstanding performance in each of the five talents*. Since "outstanding performance" does not necessarily mean "the best performance," I decided to zero in on those players who achieved multiple top-five rankings in each of the metrics employed to evaluate relative performance in each of the five tools.[3] For the domain of players in this study, I chose all Hall of Fame players (except pitchers) whose major-league careers commenced before Mays began his 22-year National League career (May 25, 1951, through 1973, with 1953 missed because of military service). Thus, all the Hall of Famers from Cap Anson (1876–97) through Mickey Mantle (April 17, 1951, through 1968) are included. For additional comparison, those Hall of Famers who began their big-league careers within a few years after Mays's debut and were contemporaries of Mays for at least 15 years are also included. Thus, players such as fellow outfielders Al Kaline (1953–74), Hank Aaron (1954–76), Roberto Clemente (1955–72), and Frank Robinson (1956–76) are also included. Altogether, the domain consists of 116 players. Using the *Spalding*, *Reach*, and *Sporting News* baseball guides, the baseball encyclopedias utilizing Pete Palmer's database of baseball statistics—i.e., *Total Baseball* (Thorn and

Palmer) and *The ESPN Baseball Encyclopedia* (Gillette and Palmer)—and the Baseball-Reference.com and Retrosheet websites, I ascertained the number of times a player excelled in each of the five tools. From this information, I was able to construct tables (organized according to the principal fielding position of each player) that summarize on a career basis the five-tool accomplishments of each player.[4] These tables are provided in the Appendix, which is available on the SABR website.

RESULTS AND DISCUSSION

The "hit for average" tool is a vital skill because it indicates how proficiently a player gets on base (via base hits), the first requirement for the main offense objective, scoring runs. However, after nearly a century of relying solely on batting average (BA) to gauge a player's ability to get on base, the importance of measuring a player's skill in getting on base via walks (and by being hit by pitched balls) became appreciated as a valuable strategy and on-base average (OBA) emerged—thanks to the innovative research and statistical analysis of Allan Roth, coupled with the input and strong endorsement of Branch Rickey.[5] Indeed, on-base average, or on-base percentage (OBP), as it's often called, is now generally regarded to be more

Honus Wagner: Was he baseball's prototypical five-tool player?

useful than the traditional BA. Therefore, in my evaluation of a player's performance for the "hit for average" tool I utilized both the classic BA and the relatively modern OBP. Continuing, the "hit with power" tool demonstrates how well a player enhances the advancement of both himself and any teammates already on base around the basepaths to home plate—the ultimate goal—with extra-base hits. To assess a player's ability to hit with power I utilized two metrics: the classic slugging average (SLG) and the modern isolated power (ISO).[6] With that introduction, let's first focus on those players who excelled in BA, OBP, SLG, and ISO.

During his journey to Cooperstown, Mays achieved the following yearly top-five performances:

- 7 in BA (including one first place)

- 10 in OBP (two firsts)

- 14 in SLG (five firsts)

- 12 in ISO (five firsts)

This impressive record was deemed to be the threshold for a player to be considered as a five-tool player prior to Mays. That is, a player had to at least come reasonably close to Mays's accomplishments. Table 1, culled from the tables in the Appendix, presents a list of those players who qualified in these four statistical departments, the qualification requirements being (a) at least six top fives in BA or eight top fives in OBP *and* (b) at least 12 top fives in SLG *or* at least 10 top fives in ISO. Table 1 also provides information on the base stealing performance achieved by these players (discussed below). Also included in Table 1, irrespective of their record, are the 11 Hall of Famers who played primarily for the Pittsburgh Pirates: center fielders Lloyd Waner and Max Carey; right fielders Roberto Clemente and Paul Waner; left fielders Willie Stargell, Ralph Kiner, and Fred Clarke; second baseman Bill Mazeroski; third baseman Pie Traynor; and shortstops Arky Vaughan and Honus Wagner.

Inspection of Table 1 reveals that, in addition to Mays, only 14 other players satisfied the admission requirements: Mantle, Tris Speaker, Ty Cobb, Frank Robinson, Aaron, Mel Ott, Babe Ruth, Sam Crawford, Stan Musial, Ted Williams, Jimmie Foxx, Lou Gehrig, Rogers Hornsby, and Wagner.

Let's now address the running tool, which manifests itself in both offense and defense: Speed and effectiveness in running give the player an advantage to beat out scratch hits, take extra bases, and steal bases while his team is batting and to run down flyballs hit to the outfield gaps or reach grounders hit to the infield holes while his team is in the field. Probably the most expedient metric for assessing a player's running speed is his base-stealing performance. Three different metrics have been employed to evaluate base-stealing: (1) stolen bases (SB), which were first recorded officially in 1886; (2) base-stealing runs (BSR); and (3) stolen-base percentage (SBP).[7] The BSR and SBP metrics utilize caught stealing (CS) numbers, which regrettably are not available officially for all seasons. For the American League, CS stats are available for only 1914–16 and 1920 forward; for the National League, CS stats are available for only 1913, 1915–16, 1920–25, and 1951 forward. Thanks, however, to the phenomenal efforts of the volunteers who contribute to the Retrosheet database of baseball information, *unofficial* CS statistics are available for the 1926–50 NL seasons (although these CS stats may not be complete for all players since game play-by-play accounts have not yet been ascertained for all teams and all seasons from 1926 through 1940). Inspection of Table 1 reveals that of the 14 players (besides Mays) with excellent performance records in both "hitting for average" and "hitting with power," only six produced base-stealing stats at least reasonably in line with those achieved by the Say Hey Kid: center fielders Mantle, Speaker, and Cobb, right fielders Robinson and Aaron, and shortstop Wagner. With Mantle, Robinson, and Aaron being contemporaries of Mays, only Speaker, Cobb, and Wagner remain as possibilities for being the genuine prototypical five-tooler, depending on how each stacks up with Mays in the two fielding tools.

For the two fielding tools, I have utilized two sets of fielding metrics to evaluate a player's performance:

1. The classic metrics of putouts-per-game (PO/G) for catching the ball and assists-per-game (A/G) for throwing it; in addition, the traditional fielding average (FA) was also included in the evaluation. These metrics were used only for the outfielders and the shortstops.

2. The modern metrics developed by Pete Palmer: fielding runs (FR), fielding range (RNG), and fielding throwing (THR).[8] These metrics were used for all the players.

Because only one player at most can qualify for a fielding title for each position from each team, I tightened the ranking requirement from a top five to a top two. The pertinent fielding information for Mays, Speaker, Cobb, and Wagner is provided in Table 2. (See page 14.)

Table 1. Players with (a) 6 Top 5s in BA or 8 Top 5s in OBP & (b) 12 Top 5s in SLG or 10 Top 5s in ISO.

		Number of Top-Five Rankings (#1 Ranking)						
		Hit for Average		Hit with Power		Run with Speed and Prowess		
HOF Center Fielders	Years	BA (#1)	OBP (#1)	SLG (#1)	ISO (# 1)	SB (#1)	BSR (#1)	SBP (#1)
Willie Mays	1951–1973	7 (1)	10 (2)	14 (5)	12 (5)	7 (4)	6 (4)	7 (4)
Mickey Mantle	1951–1968	6 (1)	12 (3)	11 (4)	11 (3)	3 (0)	6 (0)	7 (2)
Joe DiMaggio	1936–1951	4 (2)	3 (0)	10 (2)	10 (2)	0 (0)	1 (0)	0 (0)
* Lloyd Waner *	1927–1945	1 (0)	0 (0)	0 (0)	0 (0)	0 (0)	0 (0)	0 (0)
* Max Carey *	1910–1929	0 (0)	1 (0)	0 (0)	0 (0)	15 (10)	* 11 (7) *	* 9 (6) *
Tris Speaker	1907–1928	13 (1)	15 (4)	12 (1)	9 (0)	5 (0)	* 1 (0) *	* 0 (0) *
Ty Cobb	1905–1928	17 (11)	16 (7)	15 (8)	10 (5)	15 (6)	* 2 (2) *	* 1 (1) *
HOF Right Fielders	Years	BA (#1)	OBP (#1)	SLG (#1)	ISO (# 1)	SB (#1)	BSR (#1)	SBP (#1)
Frank Robinson	1925–1945	6 (1)	11 (2)	11 (4)	14 (2)	3 (0)	4 (1)	4 (2)
* Roberto Clemente *	1955–1972	10 (4)	2 (0)	2 (0)	0 (0)	0 (0)	0 (0)	1 (0)
Hank Aaron	1954–1976	11 (2)	7 (0)	14 (4)	13 (2)	3 (0)	6 (1)	5 (2)
Mel Ott	1926–1947	0 (0)	11 (4)	12 (1)	15 (2)	0 (0)	0 (0)	1 (0)
* Paul Waner *	1926–1945	8 (3)	7 (0)	5 (0)	1 (0)	1 (0)	0 (0)	2 (0)
Babe Ruth	1914–1935	8 (1)	16 (10)	15 (13)	14 (12)	0 (0)	* 0 (0) *	* 0 (0) *
Sam Crawford	1899–1917	7 (0)	4 (0)	11 (0)	11 (3)	0 (0)	* 0 (0) *	* 0 (0) *
HOF Left Fielders	Years	BA (#1)	OBP (#1)	SLG (#1)	ISO (# 1)	SB (#1)	BSR (#1)	SBP (#1)
* Willie Stargell *	1962–1982	0 (0)	2 (0)	6 (1)	6 (1)	0 (0)	0 (0)	0 (0)
* Ralph Kiner *	1946–1955	2 (0)	3 (1)	6 (3)	7 (4)	0 (0)	0 (0)	0 (0)
Stan Musial	1941–1963	17 (7)	15 (6)	13 (6)	11 (2)	0 (0)	1 (0)	0 (0)
Ted Williams	1939–1960	12 (6)	12 (12)	13 (9)	13 (6)	0 (0)	0 (0)	0 (0)
* Fred Clarke *	1894–1915	3 (0)	5 (0)	4 (1)	2 (1)	1 (0)	* 0 (0) *	* 0 (0) *
HOF Infielders	Years	BA (#1)	OBP (#1)	SLG (#1)	ISO (# 1)	SB (#1)	BSR (#1)	SBP (#1)
Harmon Killebrew	1954–1975	1 (0)	5 (1)	10 (1)	11 (4)	0 (0)	0 (0)	0 (0)
Jimmie Foxx	1925–1945	6 (2)	11 (3)	11 (5)	12 (3)	0 (0)	1 (0)	2 (0)
Lou Gehrig	1923–1939	9 (1)	11 (5)	12 (2)	13 (2)	0 (0)	0 (0)	0 (0)
* Bill Mazeroski *	1956–1972	0 (0)	0 (0)	0 (0)	0 (0)	0 (0)	0 (0)	0 (0)
Rogers Hornsby	1915–1937	12 (7)	12 (9)	14 (9)	11 (5)	0 (0)	* 0 (0) *	* 0 (0) *
* Pie Traynor *	1920–1937	1 (0)	0 (0)	0 (0)	0 (0)	1 (0)	1 (0)	3 (0)
* Arky Vaughan *	1932–1948	4 (1)	5 (3)	2 (1)	1 (0)	0 (0)	2 (0)	2 (0)
* Honus Wagner *	1897–1917	12 (8)	10 (4)	12 (6)	14 (5)	9 (5)	* 0 (0) *	* 0 (0) *

NOTES: (1) Players whose names are listed in boldface and bracketed with asterisks indicates that they played primarily with the Pittsburgh Pirates. (2) Ranking entries shown in boldface indicates that the ranking equaled or surpassed the ranking achieved by Willie Mays. (3) Entries in the BSR and SBP columns that are bracketed with asterisks indicates that the rankings are incomplete due to the unavailability of CS statistics for almost all seasons prior to 1920.

Table 2. Top-Two Fielding Rankings Achieved by Mays, Speaker, Cobb, and Wagner.

Player	PO/G (#1)	A/G (#1)	FA (#1)	FR (#1)	RNG (#1)	THR (#1)
Willie Mays	**7 (2)**	**6 (2)**	**3 (0)**	**9 (3)**	**9 (3)**	**7 (3)**
Tris Speaker	**9 (6)**	**10 (7)**	**8 (7)**	**14 (6)**	**11 (8)**	**15 (9)**
Ty Cobb	**7 (4)**	**7 (5)**	**7 (2)**	7 (3)	7 (3)	5 (4)
Honus Wagner	**9 (4)**	3 (3)	**5 (4)**	3 (2)	3 (2)	**9 (4)**

From inspection of the fielding analytics given in Table 2 we can see that by the classic fielding metrics, Speaker, Cobb, and Wagner generally outperformed Mays. With Palmer's modern fielding metrics, Speaker surpassed Mays in each, while Mays outfielded Cobb in each; Wagner and Mays split the three metrics, with Mays getting the lion's share.

It is worth noting that comparing the relative fielding performances of center fielder Mays with shortstop Wagner is an apples and oranges situation. Another modern analytical technique for assessing relative fielding performance is Defensive Regression Analysis (DRA), developed by Michael Humphreys.[9] According to Humphreys, the top center fielder of all time is Andruw Jones, followed by Mays, Speaker, Paul Blair, Gary Pettis, and Richie Ashburn. No other Hall of Famers were included in Humphreys' "Top Forty Center Fielders of All Time." At the shortstop position, Humphreys came up with Mark Belanger as number one, followed by Rey Sanchez, Ozzie Smith, and Joe Tinker. Wagner did not make Humphreys' list. "Honus was only a solid-to-good, not great, fielder at shortstop," Humphreys wrote. "He was clearly among the better-fielding shortstops of his time, just not an all-time great." Bill James, though, in his *New Historical Baseball Abstract*, wrote, "Wagner was among the greatest defensive players in the history of baseball." James's top five defensive shortstops of all time were, in order, Wagner, Smith, Bill Dahlen, Rabbit Maranville, and Pee Wee Reese. James adds that this list "includes Win Shares earned at other positions, as well as shortstop; if you base the rankings only on Defensive Win Shares at shortstop, Ozzie is first."[10]

CONCLUDING REMARKS

Based on the information collected in Tables 1 and 2, it's reasonable to consider Speaker, Cobb, and Wagner to have been true five-tool players. Therefore, based on the facts and figures assembled in this report, Willie Mays may not be the prototypical (i.e., original) five-tooler, as claimed in *Sports Illustrated*. It appears that The Grey Eagle, The Georgia Peach, and (perhaps) The Flying Dutchman may have preceded The Say Hey Kid. Being recognized as "the ultimate five-tool player" is part of the legacy of Willie Mays.[11] But he wasn't the first. ∎

Acknowledgments

It is a pleasure to express my tremendous gratitude to Bill Deane, Gary Gillette, and Pete Palmer for the input and guidance they provided to me. I should also like to thank the following people for their very valuable help in providing me with important information (including scans of articles) on the origin and use of the "five-tool" term: Bruce Berger, Adrian Fong, Chuck Hildebrandt, Wayne McElreavy, Rod Nelson, Dave Newman, Cliff Otto, and Dennis VanLangen.

Notes

1. Lou Smith, "Lou Smith's Notes," *The Cincinnati Enquirer*, June 6, 1954. See also: Jean Hoffman, "Durocher People's Choice to Manage Giants," *The Los Angeles Times*, July 19, 1960.
2. Bill Syken, "Alltime Best," *Sports Illustrated*, November 24, 2003.
3. The Appendix—available on SABR.org (https://sabr.org/node/50353)—provides complete details with regard to the requirements to qualify for a top-five ranking in the BA, OBP, SLG, ISO, and SBP metrics (and for a top-two ranking in the fielding metrics).
4. Baseball America and the Baseball Hall of Fame, *The National Baseball Hall of Fame Almanac* (Durham, North Carolina: Baseball America, 2017).
5. Branch Rickey, "Goodby to Some Old Baseball Ideas," *Life*, August 2, 1954.
6. The present-day definition of isolated power (ISO) is "slugging percentage minus batting average," which can be expressed equivalently as: $ISO = (SLG - BA) = (D + 2T + 3HR)/AB$ which is identical to the formula for extra base power developed in the 1950s by Branch Rickey and Allan Roth; see Note 5.
7. John Thorn & Pete Palmer, *The Hidden Game of Baseball* (New York: Doubleday, 1984). Base stealing runs (BSR), also called stolen base runs (SBR), was devised by Palmer and used in *The Hidden Game of Baseball*. In emails between Palmer and Krabbenhoft February 7 and 9, 2018, Palmer wrote, "Another way of doing it would be to rank players on SB minus 2 x CS. A stolen base is worth about .22 runs and a caught stealing is minus .35 runs, which works out to a 63% success rate to break even. So, $SBR = .22 \times SB - .35 \times CS$. Using 2 to 1 is an approximation which makes the calculation easier. The run values are based on the change in expected runs to be scored before and after the event." It is pointed out in emails February 7 and 9, 2018, between Bill Deane and Krabbenhoft that an analogous metric, adjusted stolen bases (ASB), was concocted by Deane "around 1983, before *Hidden Game* came out." The formula for ASB is: $ASB = SB - 2(CS)$. Finally, the formula for stolen base percentage is: $SBP = 100 \times SB/(SB + CS)$.
8. Gary Gillette and Pete Palmer, *The ESPN Baseball Encyclopedia* (New York: Sterling, 2008).
9. Michael A. Humphreys, *Wizardry: Baseball's All-Time Greatest Fielders Revealed* (New York: Oxford University Press, 2011).
10. Bill James, *The New Bill James Historical Baseball Abstract* (New York: Free Press, 2001).
11. Matt Doeden, *Willie Mays* (Minneapolis: Twenty-First Century Books, 2011).

Honus Wagner, *Spring Fever*, and *Two* Three Stooges

Rob Edelman

NOTE: The following is excerpted from "Lost (and Found) Baseball," first published in 2011 in *Base Ball: A Journal of the Early Game*.[1] It was reprinted the following year online in Our Game.[2] Special thanks to John Thorn and Gary Mitchem.

A gloomy fact of film history is that more than half the movies made during the silent film era (pre-1927) are lost—vanished into the mists of the passing generations. Yet a smattering of materials related to the early motion pictures do exist, and occasionally, their origins are cloaked in mystery.

For example, in 2004, Robert Edward Auctions sold a set of five lobby cards from *Spring Fever*, a Honus Wagner short that the auction house reported as being released in 1919. Wagner appears on three of the five, identified as "Hans Wagner." Filmgraphs is cited as the film's releasing company, but the company name is an addition, a photographed overlay. The cards were part of the Hall of Famer's estate and were put up for auction by his granddaughter, Leslie Blair Wagner.[3]

To be sure, *Spring Fever* is a curio, and not just because it features Wagner in a rare screen appearance. As described in the auction catalog:

In *Spring Fever* Honus Wagner teaches a young boy the skill of batting. Incredibly, the young boy in the film was Moses Horowitz [sic], who later became very well known as Moe Howard, of the Three Stooges.[4] The cast of *Spring Fever* also included Moe's brother, Shemp Howard. Now really, we must pause for a moment, to contemplate the fact that the great Honus Wagner actually starred in a movie with two future members of the Three Stooges, long before this comedy team's formal debut.

The opening bid for the set was $500. The sale price: $1,495.[5]

The whereabouts of any existing print of *Spring Fever*, knowledge of the actual year in which it was made, and the possibility that it was originally released under a different title remain unanswered questions—much like the rest of Wagner's screen career.[6] Moe Howard died in 1975 at the age of 77, and apparently, late in life, he claimed to have appeared with Wagner in 12 short films. All supposedly were made in the early 1920s, a "fact" that is casually noted in a number of Three Stooges histories. "Besides stage work," reads *The Three Stooges Scrapbook*, written by Jeff and Greg Lenburg and Moe's daughter, Joan Howard Maurer, "Moe also appeared in 12 two-reel shorts with baseball great Hans Wagner."[7] However, in a 2005 post on a Three Stooges forum, a user named BeAStooge wrote: "In the early '90s at one of the Philadelphia (Three Stooges) Conventions, Joan Howard told me she did not know where the Lenburgs got that information; as co-author, it did not come from her, and she was not aware of anything in her father's papers that may have sourced the information."[8]

In T*he Three Stooges, Amalgamated Morons to American Icons: An Illustrated History*, Michael Fleming reported that a "series of twelve two-reel silent sports comedies (were) filmed outside Pittsburgh. The result: it's a good thing Wagner could hit a curveball. He won five batting titles for Pittsburgh but was not Oscar material. 'I think,' said Moe, 'that perhaps they made banjo picks out of the (films)'."[9] No detailed production information is cited in either book, and no record of their existence is found in the standard film history sources. (For the record, Wagner copped *eight* batting crowns.)

The Wagner/Three Stooges connection remains an enigma to Three Stooges experts. "It has been written in the past that Moe and Shemp starred with Honus Wagner in the *Spring Fever* short and that Moe starred with him in 12 shorts," wrote Wil Huddleston of C3 Entertainment, which owns the Three Stooges brand and sponsors the group's official website. "As to which ones, I am not sure. Unfortunately, I do not have any way of confirming this because we do not have those shorts available to us."[10]

Regarding *Spring Fever*, other sources—for example, the first edition of *Total Baseball* and Arthur D. Hittner's

Two of the five *Spring Fever* lobby cards.

Honus Wagner: The Life of Baseball's "Flying Dutchman"—report that Wagner made the film in 1909 for the Vitagraph Studios. According to *Total Baseball*, "The movie showed Honus Wagner teaching a little boy the art of batting." Hittner noted that the film "featured the famous ballplayer delivering batting tips to a young boy, played by Moses Horwitz." Lending this credence is the fact that Horwitz/Howard was born in 1897; by 1919, he was no longer a "little" or "young" boy. Furthermore, the Vitagraph studio was located in Brooklyn, and the Horwitz brothers were born and raised in Brooklyn.

As listed in *The American Film Institute Catalog, Film Beginnings, 1893–1910*, Vitagraph released over 175 short films in 1909. None is titled *Spring Fever*, and most are long-lost. So perhaps the *Spring Fever* lobby cards are connected to the film's retitling for re-release. Adding to the confusion is another 1919 short with the same title, this one a Harold Lloyd comedy. But the existence of the lobby cards is proof positive that Wagner did appear in a movie that at one time was marketed under the title *Spring Fever*. ∎

Notes

1. Rob Edelman, "Lost (and Found) Baseball," *Base Ball: A Journal of the Early Game* 5, no. 2 (2011): 23–37.
2. Rob Edelman, "Lost (and Found) Baseball," Part 2, Our Game, September 28, 2012, https://ourgame.mlblogs.com/lost-and-found-baseball-part-2-12163c87037b.
3. 1919 Honus Wagner in Spring Fever Lobby Cards (5), Robert Edward Auctions, Spring 2004, http://www.robertedwardauctions.com/auction/2004/ spring/328/1919-honus-wagner-spring-fever-lobby-cards.
4. Moe's and Shemp's birth name was in fact Horwitz, rather than Horowitz. Shemp later appeared opposite Dizzy and Paul Dean in *Dizzy & Daffy* (1934, Warner Bros.), a two-reel comedy in which he plays a half-blind hurler who quips, "The only Dean I ever heard of is Gunga."
5. 1919 Honus Wagner in *Spring Fever* Lobby Cards.
6. According to the Internet Movie Database, Wagner also appeared as himself in *Al You Know Me* (1915), a comedy short penned by Ring Lardner, and *The Baseball Review of 1917*, a documentary. Then in the IMDB summary for *In the Name of the Law* (1922), he "expanded his entertainment repertoire by catching baseballs dropped from the top of the ten-story city-county building in Pittsburgh while hundreds of people watched and cameras rolled. Pittsburgh Police Superintendent and former professional ball player John C. Calhoun dropped three balls more than 150 feet to a waiting Wagner who was able to snare the first and third 'pitches.' The film of the stunt was later shown at the Carnegie Theatre as a prologue entitled 'In the Name of the Law.'" http://www.imdb.com/name/nm0905929.
7. Jeff Lenburg, Joan Howard Maurer, Greg Lenburg, *The Three Stooges Scrapbook* (Secaucus, NJ: Citadel Press, 1982), 20.
8. BeAStooge, "Re: Missing Moe Solos?" The Kingdom of Moronica forum, November 3, 2005, http://moronika.com/forums/index.php?topic=782.0
9. Michael Fleming, *The Three Stooges: An Illustrated History, From Amalgamated Morons to American Icons* (New York: Doubleday, 1999), 11.
10. Wil Huddleston, email to author, May 10, 2011.
11. John Thorn and Pete Palmer, eds., *Total Baseball: The Official Encyclopedia of Major League Baseball* (New York: Warner Books, 1989), 409.
12. Arthur D. Hittner, *Honus Wagner: The Life of Baseball's "Flying Dutchman"* (Jefferson, NC: McFarland, 1996), 243.
13. *The American Film Institute Catalog, Film Beginnings, 1893–1910* (Metuchen NJ: Scarecrow Press, 1995), 239.

Honus Wagner's Short Stint as Pirates Skipper in a Forgettable Final Season

Gregory H. Wolf

onus Wagner, or Hans as he was almost universally called, was relieved the season was over. His 20th campaign in the big leagues and 17th with the Pittsburgh Pirates had been physically and emotionally draining. The 1916 season had been troublesome even before it started and had only gotten worse. Many had predicted Wagner would take the managerial reigns of the club in '16 following the retirement of longtime Pirates skipper Fred Clarke, who had guided the Bucs to 14 consecutive first-division finishes (1900–13) and four pennants; however, the soft-spoken Wagner adamantly refused the job. "I would not be a manager," he said, "because I would not want to leave the ball field and take my worries and troubles home with me."[1]

Jimmy Callahan accepted the job with a two-year contract, but the results were disastrous. The Pirates finished in sixth place with their worst winning percentage since 1914. The 42-year-old Wagner suffered through a myriad of injuries to his hands and hip, and was no longer the "Flying Dutchman." He had lost more than a few steps and played in 92 games at shortstop, the fewest since moving to that position full-time in 1903, though he also made 23 starts at first base.

Wagner wasn't sure if he'd be back with the Pirates in 1917. He concluded the season with the worst slump of his career, managing just 11 hits in his last 77 at-bats and scoring just one run in his final 23 games. His struggles intensified speculation that he would finally hang up his spikes. He hadn't batted .300 since 1913, it was increasingly difficult for him to get into and stay in condition, and his days as an everyday shortstop were over. On the other hand, he was the most visible person in the Smoky City. Pittsburgh sportswriter Henry Keck called him "probably the most beloved man in baseball," admired and praised by fans and press across the country as much for his accomplishments as for his upstanding character.[2] There wasn't much more he could do: He was a World Series champion, had collected the most hits (3,359) and runs (1,724) in big-league history, and was the active leader in home runs (101).

Cognizant of his eroding skills, Wagner needed a rest and also wanted to spend more time with 26-year-old Bessie Smith, a local Pittsburgher and his companion of eight years. Although he was an avowed bachelor who had pledged to remain one as long as he played baseball, Wagner's attitude shifted that offseason after the sudden death of his oldest brother, Charley, from complications of pneumonia on October 31, 1916. The two siblings had been very close; Charley and his wife, Olive, and three children provided Hans a semblance of domestic life. Long known as an intensely shy man who shunned the spotlight, Wagner pulled off the biggest surprise of his life on December 30 when he married Smith in a private ceremony in his childhood parish, St. John Evangelical Lutheran Church in Carnegie, a small coal-mining and steel mill community six miles southwest of Pittsburgh, where Wagner grew up and still lived. The wedding was such a secret that Wagner's brother Al, who served as best man, found out just hours before the ceremony, after which the newlyweds traveled to the bride's house to inform her parents. "Honus Wagner Caught at 'Home' by Dan Cupid," reported the *Pittsburgh Gazette-Times* playfully on the front page

A career .328 hitter, Wagner led the National League in batting average eight times.

the following day, adding confidently, "His retirement from baseball is not yet in sight."[3]

While Wagner embarked on a care-free honeymoon vacation in warmer climates in the south and west, Pirates owner Barney Dreyfuss brooded. The shrewd German-born businessman, upset about high player salaries coupled with poor results on the field, embarked on a policy of financial retrenchment, as did owners throughout baseball. He slashed contract offers, in some cases by half, and expected holdouts, reported sportswriter Charles J. Doyle of the *Gazette-Times*, but players had few options and no leverage.[4]

Among the highest paid players in baseball, earning a reported $10,000 annually, Wagner had his salary reduced significantly, according to Arthur Hittner in his groundbreaking biography *Honus Wagner: The Life of Baseball's "Flying Dutchman,"* and might have been slashed to as low as $5,400.[5] Ralph S. Davis, a sportswriter with the *Pittsburgh Press*, attempted to defuse the growing public perception that Wagner was in a salary dispute with Dreyfuss and had retired, suggesting that Wagner's reluctance to sign had more to do with his expanding girth (he had gained a reported 20–30 pounds).[6]

By the first week of February 1917, the great Wagner wait was on. While Pittsburgh sportswriters reported every rumor, Wagner himself remained silent about his future. Wagner "still has a lot of baseball left in him," said former Pirates skipper Fred Clarke.[7] Wagner uncharacteristically stepped into the limelight on February 25 when the Hot Stove Club of Pittsburgh put on a gala celebration for the player's 43rd birthday at the luxurious William Penn Hotel, where he was roasted by local politicians, industrial magnates, and big-league players. Dreyfuss described his long-time star as a model player and the one "with whom no one ever had any trouble," according to sportswriter Ed F. Balinger.[8] Those laudatory remarks seemed to diffuse, at least momentarily, any sign of a feud between the two kingpins of Pirates baseball and instilled confidence that Wagner would play in 1917.

Wagner was not with the Bucs when they departed on March 9 to Columbus, Georgia, for spring training. "Is Hans dissatisfied in his relations with the Pirates club?" asked beat reporter Harry Keck. "Or is he afraid that he will not be able to finish the season a regular? Does he see the dread shadow of the bench trailing in his wake?"[9] Dreyfuss publicly denied that Wagner was a "hold-out" because of a salary dispute but also added that "I do not know what he will do."[10]

Questions swirled around not only Wagner's future, but the entire 1917 baseball season. On April 6 the United States declared war on Germany, thereby expanding the scope of the world war and raising discussions about canceling the season. Baseball commenced as planned, but for the first time since the previous century, Wagner was not on the Pirates' roster when they opened the season on April 11 in Chicago. "As far as I know," said Dreyfuss a few days later, Wagner "has quit the game as he told me he thought of doing."[11] While the Pirates played 28 of their first 35 games of the season on the road, sportswriters deliberated if Wagner retired on his own accord or if he was forced out by the miserly Dreyfuss's contract offer. "Whichever is correct," declared Davis, "Wagner quit."[12]

As Wagner gradually faded from the headlines in May, Balinger dropped a bomb in the *Pittsburgh Post* on June 3: "Hans Wagner's baseball days may not be over after all," began the sportswriter in an article that initiated a frenzied few days.[13] Wagner's return, if it happened, continued the scribe, would be as a coach. Pittsburghers woke four days later to read "Wagner Signs Pirates Contract" emblazoned on the front page of the sports section of the *Post*.[14] The previous evening Wagner had accepted a contract calling for a reported $10,000 salary. Dreyfuss issued a statement suggesting the inevitability of Wagner's return. "He has been a fixture for so many years that he has come to be almost a part of the club, like the grandstand or the pitcher's box."[15]

Less than a day after signing his contract, Wagner was in uniform as the lowly Pirates, with major league baseball's worst record (14–27), took on the Brooklyn Robins at Forbes Field on June 7 in front of an "unusually large" crowd [estimated at 4,000] for a midweek game.[16] "It was evident that something would have to be done to revive interests," Davis quipped about the legend's return to the moribund team.[17] Playing first base and batting fifth, Wagner put on a "classy performance" (Balinger) and "played in oldtime style" (Davis), singling in four at-bats and driving in a run, but the Pirates lost yet again.[18] Visibly overweight and out-of-shape, Wagner hadn't trained, let alone played baseball, since ending the 1916 season in a month-long slump; nonetheless, in his fourth game, he took over third base, a position he'd played just 18 times since 1901. After his first eight games in 1917, he had managed nine singles, four of which came in one game, in 33 at-bats, while the Bucs won just twice. It was clear that the Flying Dutchman was no elixir to the Bucs woes.

Wagner's return for his 21st season was akin to a grand farewell tour. In the first contest of a three-game series in St. Louis, Wagner was "center of attraction for the fans," opined the *Press*.[19] That was just prelude to "Wagner Day" on June 22, when Pittsburgh celebrated its favorite citizen's return to baseball by staging a grand fête and 200-car parade with a "distinct military atmosphere," reflecting the country's wartime status.[20] Hailed as a "national institution through baseball," Wagner, flanked by mayor Joseph G. Armstrong, passed by immense crowds from Liberty Street and Fifth Avenue to Forbes Field. The festivities were even greater at the ballpark, where Wagner was presented various gifts while an estimated 1,000 soldiers drilled. "Hans Wagner was the hero of one of the most public demonstrations in the history of the diamond," gushed Balinger.[21] The 43-year-old lined an RBI single in his first at-bat in the Bucs' eventual victory in 10 innings over the Chicago Cubs. Still, Pirates fans had little to cheer other than Wagner, who ended his slump one day after those festivities by pounding out 13 hits in his next 21 at-bats over a five-game stretch to lift his batting average from .236 to .342 on June 28.

By that time, reports circulated that Callahan, on the hot seat for weeks, had been fired and that Wagner would take the reins of the club. Ralph S. Davis attempted to quash those rumors, reminding readers that Wagner had refused the job when Clarke retired. "He is even more determined now that he will not be manager of the Pirates," wrote Davis, adding that Wagner "is evidently too wise to attempt to bring order out of chaos that exists."[22] Pittsburgh sportswriters seemed concerned about Wagner's reputation and how it could be tarnished by taking over a club described by Balinger as comprising "considerable inferior material" and by Davis as a "mistfit aggregation of minor leaguers" and "disgruntled" veterans.[23]

Callahan was removed as manager on June 29, leading to "all sorts of weird guesses" about his successor, wrote Davis.[24] The new manager, he reported, was supposedly from "out west" and had "considerable experience." Among those tossed around by sportswriters as the next manager included Harry Wolverton, the recently fired skipper of the San Francisco Seals, who was supposedly in Pittsburgh to discuss the matter with Dreyfuss; former NL MVP Larry Doyle, captain of the Cubs, who was rumored to have been acquired in a trade for flychaser Max Carey; and even Dreyfuss himself.

Defying expectations of the Smoky City sportswriters, Wagner was named Pirates interim manager the day Callahan was fired. "Just how long Wagner will remain at the helm appears to be indefinite," wrote

Wagner was a longtime coach for the Pirates and a member of the inaugural class of the Baseball Hall of Fame, in 1936.

Balinger, noting that Wagner "would be afforded ample opportunity to show what he might do in the role of a real pilot."[25] Providing a different perspective, Davis reported that Wagner "requested that he be relieved of the duties as soon as possible. Evidently, the veteran does not care to shoulder the responsibility for a tail end club."[26]

While spreading the news about Wagner, Davis offered yet another twist by suggesting that Hugo Bezdek, a "professional friend" of Dreyfuss, might be the hitherto unidentified westerner and yet another managerial candidate. Bezdek was a well-known college football coach who had guided the University of Arkansas to an undefeated season in 1909 and was coming off a Rose Bowl victory as head coach of the University of Oregon. He had also served as head baseball coach at those two institutions and was a Pirates scout on the West Coast. Unimpressed with those credentials, Davis opined that Bezdek "can probably be secured on the cheap."

On his first day calling the shots for what Davis called "one of the cheapest [teams] in the major leagues and…just where it belongs in the standings," manager Wagner made all the right moves while first baseman Wagner supplied some timely hitting for the last-place Bucs' 5–4 win against skipper Christy Mathewson's Cincinnati Reds.[27] Wagner led off the second with a double and then scored on Chuck Ward's two-bagger to tie the game, 1–1. In the sixth, Wagner's two-run single knotted the game, 3–3. Wagner's batting average improved to .354, but declined steadily thereafter.

Notwithstanding his reputation as one of the greatest players in history, Wagner was in an untenable position as both player and interim manager. His return, predicated on Dreyfuss's acquiescence to his salary demands, fueled dissension among the players, most of whom weren't in the big leagues during the Flying Dutchman's heyday. The *Pittsburgh Press* noted that some players were upset by what they felt was Wagner's special treatment by Dreyfuss and "became more sullen and discontented than ever, and, instead of helping matters, the situation became worse than ever."[28] To some teammates, Wagner was part of the problem, not a solution.

Fresh off his first, and what proved to be his only, victory as manager, Wagner and the Pirates traveled to Cincinnati for a doubleheader the next day. Wagner "was not forgotten by his thousands of faithful friends at Redland" Field, gushed Queen City sportswriter Jack Ryder about the large crowd, estimated at 18,000 strong, on hand for "Wagner Day" at the park.[29] Reds players and officials celebrated the living legend and showered him with gifts in ceremonies before the first and second games. Reds hurler Fred Toney stole the show, however, as he started both games of the twin bill, tossing consecutive complete-game three-hitters. Wagner collected one safety in each contest, extending his hitting streak to nine games.

Accompanying the Pirates on their one-day whirlwind tour to Cincinnati was Dreyfuss, who met with Bezdek, who'd arrived from Oregon. The reason for the meeting was unclear, but to Pittsburgh sportswriters, it appeared as though an intrigue were brewing. Harry Keck of the *Post* defended Wagner, writing that he "will lose no prestige if he doesn't improve" the team, and that he doubted Wagner would remain much longer as skipper because he lacks the tough-edged personality needed to discipline the players.[30] Ralph S. Davis thought Wagner "appears to be defeated before he starts," considering the Pirates' below-average talent.[31]

Dreyfuss, Wagner, and Bezdek traveled back to the Smoky City separately from the players. Following the Bucs' 6–4 loss to the Cardinals at Forbes Field on July 2, details of their meeting emerged. Balinger reported that Wagner and Bezdek "will work together," with the former in charge of "playing" and the latter taking care of "business affairs" in a potentially awkward responsibility-sharing situation.[32] "The team needs much more than a new manager before it will become a menace to the other seven clubs in the league," wrote the *Press*.[33]

On Tuesday evening, July 3, following the Pirates' fourth straight loss, Wagner resigned from his position as interim manager. "You couldn't coax him back on the job with a battle ax as a persuader," joked Davis in the *Press*.[34] The 34-year-old Bezdek was named the new skipper for the rest of the season and was in the

dugout as the club hosted the Redbirds for a Fourth of July doubleheader. The Bucs dropped both games, but Wagner, noted Balinger, "played first base without being bothered by the cares and worries of a tail-end ball club."[35]

So ended Wagner's inglorious five-game, four-day career as Pirates skipper. Liberated from a task he never really wanted, Wagner was able to settle into his role as the grand old man of the national pastime and continue his farewell tour. On July 6 the Pirates kicked off an eastern road swing in Philadelphia, where the Phillies celebrated Wagner Day at the Baker Bowl by presenting the player with a leather traveling bag in a pre-game ceremony.[36] Six days later, it was the Brooklyn Robins' turn with Wagner Day at Ebbets Field, where the club's namesake, skipper Wilbert Robinson, presided over a ceremony at home plate.[37]

A chance for a fairy-tale ending to Wagner's illustrious career was abruptly snatched away two days later when he was spiked on the right ankle by the Robins' Casey Stengel in the second game of a doubleheader in Brooklyn.[38] The injury, initially diagnosed as slight, became infected and derailed Wagner's season. Batting a robust .313 at the time, he had trouble pivoting on the foot and started only 24 more games the rest of the year. He was shelved for Wagner Day at Braves Field in Boston on July 19, but delighted fans the next afternoon at Coogan's Bluff by pinch-hitting against the New York Giants on yet another Wagner Day, at the Polo Grounds. A hobbling Wagner managed just 3 hits in his final 30 at-bats of the season and batted a paltry .202 (20-for 99) after the spiking.

In an interview with *Baseball Magazine* in March 1918, Wagner admitted, "I had firmly made up my mind to quit [following the 1916 season]. I was getting old for a player and the end was clearly in sight. ...But when the season rolled around and the boys began to take their swing and the pitchers started loosening up I couldn't get over the idea that I would like one more try at it."[39] Wagner had the same thoughts again that spring, but knew better than to try another comeback. ∎

Sources

In addition to the sources cited in the Notes, the author also accessed Retrosheet's World Wide Web site, Baseball-Reference.com, SABR.org, and *The Sporting News* archive via Paper of Record.

Notes

1. Dennis DeValeria and Jeanne Burke DeValeria, *Honus Wagner. A Biography* (New York: Henry Holt, 1995), 267.
2. Harry Keck, "Sporting Chit Chat," *Pittsburgh Post*, June 21, 1917.
3. "Honus Wagner Caught At 'Home' by Dan Cupid," *Pittsburgh Gazette-Times*, December 31, 1916.

4. Charles J. Doyle, "Carmen Hill Released to Birmingham in Grimes' Deal," *Pittsburgh Gazette-Times*, January 7, 1917.

5. Arthur D. Hittner, *Honus Wagner. The Life of Baseball's "Flying Dutchman*," (Jefferson, NC: McFarland, 1996).

6. Ralph Davis, "Ralph Davis' Column," *Pittsburgh Press*, February, 5, 1917.

7. "Hans Wagner Praised by His Former Pilot," *Pittsburgh Press*, February 11, 1917.

8. Ed F. Balinger, "Wagner Night Howling Success," *Pittsburgh Post*, February 25, 1917.

9. Harry Keck, "Sporting Chit-Chat," *Pittsburgh Post*, March 13, 1917.

10. "Wagner Not a 'Hold-Out,' Says Barney," *Pittsburgh Post*, March 16, 1917.

11. "Wagner Has Not Signed A Contract," *Pittsburgh Press*, April 15, 1917.

12. "Ralph Davis, "Ralph Davis' Column," *Pittsburgh Press*, April 21, 1917.

13. Ed F. Balinger, "Wagner May Come Back. See Phils Down Bucs. Confers With Callahan," *Pittsburgh Post*, June 3, 1917.

14. Ed F. Balinger, "Hans Wagner Signs Pirates Contract," *Pittsburgh Post*, June 7, 1917.

15. DeValeria and DeValeria, *Honus Wagner*, 272.

16. Ralph S. Davis, "Baird Goes To Bench," *Pittsburgh Press*, June 8, 1917.

17. Ralph. S. Davis, "Brooklyn-Pittsburgh Ball Game Today Postponed," *Pittsburgh Press*, June 6, 1917.

18. Davis, "Baird Goes To Bench."

19. "Pepper Shown By Pirates," *Pittsburgh Press*, June 19, 1917.

20. "Thousands Will Honor Honus Wagner Today," *Pittsburgh Gazette-Times*, June 22, 1917.

21. Ed F. Balinger, "Bigbees's Long Blow and Big Bill's Rap End Fray in 10th," *Pittsburgh Post*, June 23, 1917.

22. Ralph S. Davis, "Dreyfuss Seeking Successor to Jimmie Callahan. Wagner Refuses The Job," *Pittsburgh Press*, June 29, 1917.

23. Ed F. Balinger, "New Buccaneer Leader May Succeed Callahan With Next Few Days," *Pittsburgh Post*, June 29, 1917; Davis, "Dreyfuss Seeking Successor."

24. Ralph S. Davis. "Guessing As To Identity of New Buccaneer Manager," *Pittsburgh Press*, June 30, 1917.

25. Ed F. Balinger, "Hans Wagner Chosen Pilot of Buccaneers in Callahan's Place," *Pittsburgh Post*, July 1, 1917.

26. Ralph S. Davis, "Honus Wagner In Command," *Pittsburgh Press*, July 1, 1917.

27. Davis, "Honus Wagner In Command."

28. Ralph S. Davis. "Callahan's Successor in Tough Tome. New Policy Is Needed," *Pittsburgh Press*, July 1, 1917.

29. Frank Ryder, "Toney Wins Both Ends of Double-Header," *Cincinnati Enquirer*, July 2, 1917.

30. Harry Keck, "Sporting Chit Chat," *Pittsburgh Post*, July 2, 1917.

31. Ralph S. Davis, "Bezdek Will Not Supplant Wagner Just Now, 'Honus' Still On The Job," *Pittsburgh Press*, July 2, 1917.

32. Ed F. Balinger, "Hans Wagner Comes First On Pilot Job," *Pittsburgh Post*, July 3, 1917.

33. Ralph S. Davis, "Wagner Can't Make 'Em Win," *Pittsburgh Press*, July 3, 1917.

34. Ralph S. Davis, "Big Job For News Manager," *Pittsburgh Press*, July 5, 1917.

35. Ed F. Balinger, "Hans Wagner Resigns And Managerial Reins Are Given To Bezdek," *Pittsburgh Press*, July 5, 1917.

36. Jim Nasium, "Phils Lacked Punch When Men Were On," *Philadelphia Inquirer*, July 7, 1917.

37. Ed F. Balinger, "Dodgers Donate Stein To Wagner, Game To Pirates," *Pittsburgh Post*, July 13, 1917.

38. Ed F. Balinger, "Dodgers Again Take Twin Bill Off The Bezdeks," *Pittsburgh Post*, July 15, 1917.

39. "Twenty-One Years In The Major Leagues," *Baseball Magazine*, March 1918: 395.

Wagner for Sheriff

Honus Runs into the Coolidge Tax Cut

Mark Souder

Pittsburgh Pirate Honus Wagner is the greatest shortstop of all time. Baseball guru Bill James ranks Wagner as the second greatest baseball player in history, behind only Babe Ruth. He was a longtime hero in Pittsburgh. So how did the beloved Pirate get routed in the 1925 race for sheriff of Allegheny County? He ran into presidential politics in Pennsylvania.

But that is not how most baseball historians have recorded his history. Wagner biographer Arthur Hittner writes the consensus view: "Despite the support of several newspapers, Wagner's half-hearted campaign fell short of the mark."[1] The Associated Press wrote in 1925 that "in sport parlance it might almost be said that Mr. Wagner hit weakly to the infield."[2] Others loved analogies to striking out. The prevailing view, however, is very wrong.

The complexity of the interaction of politics and Honus Wagner sheds much insight into how politics actually works.

Republicans had long been touting Wagner for office. In 1917 the *New York Sun* headlined, "Honus Wagner for Sheriff: Famous Pirate Is Logical Candidate of Pittsburg Republicans." Leaders of the machine-led Republican Party were touting Wagner for sheriff of Allegheny County, which includes Pittsburgh.[3] The boss-picked county coroner called him the "ideal man": "The old Pirate standby is popular and would win in a walk. I feel sure that I am voicing the opinion of the great majority of Republican voters in Allegheny County when I say that he is the logical man for the job."[4]

Wagner may have been able to hit almost any kind of pitched ball with a baseball bat, but when he finally did run for sheriff eight years later, he was completely shut down by the political dealmaking necessary to pass the Calvin Coolidge/Andrew Mellon tax cut. It remains the most celebrated tax cut in American politics, touted by Ronald Reagan in promoting his own administration's cuts and compared in a *Washington Post* headline to the 2017 tax-cut bill.[5] No former baseball player was going to stand in the way.

Germans were still struggling with acceptance by the WASP establishment during Wagner's life. Honus is a variation (Hah-nus) of Johann or Johannes. He was a German who liked his strong drink. Debates over beer, Sunday baseball, and the rowdiness at games were proxy battlegrounds for the extended political controversies of the era. Pennsylvania was on the front line of the national debates. Barney Dreyfuss, who had worked in his family's Kentucky whiskey business, cashed in his share to buy control of the Louisville team and move it to Pittsburgh. His most important decision was to bring Wagner with him from Louisville to Pittsburgh. Honus fit well with the German wet population in Pittsburgh.

Prohibition was coming when the first "run, Honus, run" political rumors began in 1917 and was in place during his actual campaign in 1925. Known to like his beer, sometimes too much, Honus was presumably not the teetotaler candidate to run the Pittsburgh sheriff's office. A leader of the then-powerful Women's Christian Temperance Union specifically denounced him as a candidate because his election could lead to an "open county and Sunday athletics." She said that Wagner "may be a good ball player, but he would not be a good sheriff."[6]

The issue was extra intense in Pittsburgh because "revenuers" were part of the Department of Treasury run by native Andrew Mellon, who was part of the Pittsburgh Republican establishment. He designated his nephew to chair the state GOP as well as coordinate Pittsburgh politics during the period of Wagner's campaign.

Nor was Honus Wagner going to be mistaken for a classic western-style sheriff in the Clint Eastwood mode. Jan Finkel, in his SABR biography of Wagner, does not describe someone who sounds like the slick political candidates of today. He was "awkward-looking" and had huge hands that "made it difficult to tell whether he was wearing a glove." "His one weakness in the field stemmed from his oversized feet, which sometimes got in the way." "He tore around the bases with his arms whirling like a berserk freestyle swimmer." When he lost, even a small-time newspaper in Iowa reprinted this line: "Someone says Pittsburgh refused to elect Honus Wagner sheriff because a crook could get away through Honus' bow legs. Baseballs didn't." So Wagner's looks weren't going to carry his campaign.[7]

Nor was Wagner much of a public speaker. His four-minute speeches to help sell World War I Liberty Bonds were possibly the longest speeches he ever gave. He wasn't going to wow the voters with his words.

But he did have political assets. He was the hometown sports hero who helped make Pittsburgh a worldwide name beyond just its industry. Pittsburgh was the city of smoke and grime. Honus Wagner besting Ty Cobb and the Detroit Tigers to win a World Series in 1909 had helped every Pittsburgher's self-image. Wagner loved people and they loved him. That tends to be important in politics. Wagner had interests similar to those of the common man and he developed his business interests around those personal interests. To a political boss trying to win an election, Wagner was a magnet for the average laborer. He also had other "common man" interests:

- He loved to tinker with automobiles, which were just emerging at the time. So he started a garage where he sold cars and gas. His only problem was that he was not a good salesman and admitted to buying about half the gas he sold to use for his personal touring.

- He loved to fish, so he started the Honus Wagner Sporting Goods Store. He and fellow Pirates star Pie Traynor signed autographs, chatted with folks, and got fishing and hunting gear wholesale. They lost their investment but had a good time doing so.

- He loved sports, so he played on a top local basketball team in the offseason and later headed local youth sports leagues. He was always out mixing with the "folks," as voters are often called by politicians.

- He liked to drink pretty well so he partnered in the creation of a distillery. It failed, but the discounts were nice. And most men weren't teetotalers.[8]

Was running for sheriff a "last-minute" thought by Wagner? This is a common assertion in any comments that go beyond the basic "and he lost." Wagner flirted

Two baseball sages: John McGraw and Honus Wagner.

with the idea in 1910 when he was asked, possibly in jest, by a congressman to run for sheriff. The Republican Party, at least segments of it, clearly pushed him to run by going public in 1917. That year was not an easy one for the GOP. Nationally, it was coming off two straight Woodrow Wilson presidential victories after Teddy Roosevelt's Bull Moose Party had carved up the Republican vote in 1912. In Pennsylvania, there was still bitter infighting between progressive Republicans and regulars. Having the most popular Pittsburgher as a candidate for sheriff, the most visible candidate spot other than mayor, would have been a big asset in 1917. But Wagner didn't file. In 1925, when he did run, he filed just before the deadline. In 1929 he filed to run for sheriff again, but then withdrew his name before he was locked on the ballot.

While this could suggest a lack of serious commitment, I tend to think it reflects not only a dogged interest in being sheriff but also someone who is making a calculation about other job options, personal financial need, and some chance of electoral success. When you're the biggest name in town, people always whisper sweet nothings in your ear about how you should run for this or that.

The fact that Wagner accepted a political appointment to the Fish & Wildlife Commission from Pennsylvania Governor John Tener in 1914 is instructive. Tener, a former baseball player, was elected in 1910 with the support of the Republican political bosses. Much later, in 1942, Wagner briefly accepted a post as sergeant-at-arms of the Pennsylvania legislature, again a patronage post controlled by the Republican political bosses.

Many baseball writers point out that Wagner was also made a deputy sheriff in 1940. That post obviously wasn't very taxing, since one month after receiving the appointment, Wagner took leave and left for Florida to help coach the Pirates in spring training. Memoirs suggest that Deputy Sheriff Wagner mostly hung around the judge's office talking with his old friend and former Pirates star Deacon Phillippe, who was a bailiff. The position did indicate his ongoing interest in police work. A photograph exists showing Wagner as an old man with a gun in each hand. It fits the profile of a person who was attracted to law enforcement his whole life, as Wagner clearly was.[9]

Wagner obviously liked guns, because in the biography *Honus Wagner: Life of Baseball's Flying Dutchman* he is always off hunting or fishing. Probably even more importantly, and seldom noted, is that his wife's father was a police detective.[10] So Wagner was the son-in-law of a police detective; he was a potential sheriff's candidate three times, running once; he was later a sergeant-at-arms and a deputy sheriff; and he loved guns. I don't think his interest in running for sheriff was last minute.

Every urban area had political bosses who delivered services in return for votes. Tammany Hall of New York is by far the most famous. Among political historians, however, Pennsylvania earns a special place. In the space of 30 years, it managed to have two political bosses, Matthew Quay of Pittsburgh and William Vare of Philadelphia, refused seating by the United States Senate because of corruption.[11]

In the first decades of the twentieth century, Pennsylvania was the most dependable large state for Republicans in a presidential contest. This resulted in immense power and influence among Republicans. Pennsylvania was controlled by three interests: Pittsburgh bosses, Philadelphia bosses, and the state business group dominated by business interests in both cities (often centered in Harrisburg, the state capital). Woodrow Wilson said that the Vare machine in Philly (three brothers, with William the head) was worth an extra 200,000 votes to Republicans in Pennsylvania. ("Extra" was a euphemism for illegal.) Over 90 percent of Italian Catholics in South Philly, the Vare political base, voted Republican. African Americans remembered which party favored emancipation and also voted over 90 percent Republican.

The Vare brothers controlled garbage, taxing powers, construction, and transportation. They also rotated as city, state, and federal legislators. Thus, all three brothers soon were very, very rich as well.

Andrew Mellon had different personal goals from Pittsburgh Republicans who were focused on local patronage and contracts. In return for his having helped get them elected, he demanded that Pennsylvania's two United States senators, David Reed and

Wagner was not known as a public speaker, but he was a popular Pittsburgh sports hero.

George Pepper, back him in the Senate by supporting the tax cut that Mellon, as treasury secretary, had developed for President Coolidge. It was the number one issue for Coolidge and Mellon.[12]

Coolidge's personal view was clearly stated in his Inaugural Address of 1925: "The collection of any taxes which are not absolutely required, which do not beyond reasonable doubt contribute to the public welfare, is only a species of legalized larceny."[13] Coolidge was frustrated with earlier defeats of his tax bill, but 1926 would be the final showdown. To pass, Republicans had to control Pennsylvania in 1925. In return, the bosses could do their grubby work in Pittsburgh and Philadelphia. Senators from Pittsburgh included Mellon's former partner and Mellon's personal attorney, which is one way to assure loyalty. The Philadelphia bosses also gave Mellon full support.[14]

However, as 1925 dawned, Pittsburgh was at war. Two factions had turned on each other in a fight over division of patronage and spoils, which endangered GOP control of the entire state. On top of that, Pennsylvania governor Gifford Pinchot—famous environmentalist friend of Roosevelt's and a pain-in-the-neck progressive reformer as far as the bosses were concerned— was still carrying the progressive torch that had split the party the previous decade and resulted in the election of the Democrat Wilson to the White House. Mellon decided that if the Coolidge plan was to get needed support from Pennsylvania, he needed to knock some heads together in Pittsburgh. So Mellon met with both factions, and they developed a "unity" ticket of political bosses. Everything seemingly was back to normal. The deal was made. Then in walked Honus Wagner with some troublemaking friends in Pittsburgh calling themselves a "non-partisan ticket" and attacking the "compromise" ticket as a front for corrupt bossism.[15]

It's naive to think that a candidate runs for office all by himself, that the people carefully choose a candidate they like, and that if that candidate, especially if famous, had just worked harder, victory should have been easy. Politics are fluid and you must always adapt. One of the factions in Pittsburgh, and it appears it may have been the dominant coalition in 1917, had wanted Wagner to run for sheriff to help the entire ticket corral votes. Wagner didn't run. In 1925 they faced a new crisis and formed a new coalition. It didn't include Wagner.

Instead, Wagner was aligned with a man named William L. Smith, who was running for mayor of Pittsburgh. One of the newspapers friendly to Honus Wagner and company reported nearly verbatim speeches from a "non-partisan" slate event, and they should have screamed "You're in political trouble" to Wagner. The *Pittsburgh Press* quoted Smith calling all Republican city and county elected officials—and the "unscrupulous" machine that controlled them—corrupt.[16]

"Attacking" the now unified GOP leaders—who happened to include all the local elected officials, state legislators, congressman, both of Pennsylvania's United States senators, Treasury Secretary Mellon, and almost every top businessman in Pittsburgh—is not a path to victory.[17]

The machine also included Gus Greenlee, who helped deliver African American voters critical to establishment control. He was the owner of several establishments that anchored the Hill Street district. Greenlee—Republican treasurer in the predominantly black Third Ward for Judge Charles Kline's machine organization—began running a "numbers" operation the year after the election.[18] His earnings led to his purchase of a local black baseball team and building it into one of baseball's all-time great teams, the Pittsburgh Crawfords.

Machine opponent and Wagner political teammate Smith explained their goals to a small gathering of non-partisans: "Our quarrel is not with the Republican Party itself, but with the unscrupulous political machine that has been operating in the city and in the county for years under the cloak of that party. What right have those machine candidates, these political harmony tools, to ask for the support of the good people of this city?" He then proceeded to rip his mayoral opponent, Kline.[19]

The speech by Wagner was much shorter than the others made that evening but his opening says every-thing one needs to know about his campaign, his goals, and why he lost: "I am a candidate on the Non-Partisan ticket for the office of sheriff of Allegheny County to aid in the fight against corrupt machine politics now rampant in the administration of city and county offices." He went on with somewhat less of a fiery challenge: "I believe that we need strict enforcement of all laws because they are laws, regardless of politics or party, and to this purpose I pledge myself and influence if I am elected."[20]

I don't think it is accurate to say that Honus Wagner lost because he didn't campaign. Smith lost to Kline 70,680 to 19,838 in the Republican primary and then, running on the Labor ticket in the fall, lost again, 69,831 to 15,210. The Democrat candidate had 5,342 votes. (The Democrats weren't very relevant at the time in Pennsylvania.) Wagner lost primarily because he was part of a political slate that took on the entire power structure of Pittsburgh. And was crushed. Twice in one year.[21]

Pittsburgh Mayor Kline ran for reelection in 1929 and won, this time with Wagner pulling out of the race after again filing for sheriff. Somebody must have warned him not to get pounded again, or more simply: "We have a slate of candidates. You are not on it." But corruption usually catches up with politicians. Mayor Kline was arrested and convicted, resigned, and appeared to be headed to jail, but he died first. History did prove that Wagner was right about the corruption. Winning isn't everything.[22]

It is also worth noting that the politicians who had been convinced of his easy victory early on (and the newspaper writers) seemed little concerned as to whether Wagner was qualified to be sheriff. The bosses figured they would choose his deputy and have someone else run the office, with Wagner as the "front man." Wagner biographer Arthur Hittner writes that Wagner had been approached "by William H. Coleman, later a congressman, to run for sheriff of Allegheny County but Wagner had (originally) declined." Wagner later quipped that he had told Coleman that "I knew more about hanging up base hits than murderers."[23] When Wagner finally did run, apparently his interest in being sheriff, and in listening to the pipe dreams of politicians who hoped to utilize his fame for their own purposes, overwhelmed his own honesty.

At the state and national level, the tax deal played out this way: The Coolidge-Mellon tax bill passed but, while Philly boss Vare defeated Governor Pinchot and the incumbent senator in the May 1926 primary, the Senate refused to seat Vare because of his corrupt practices in Philadelphia. The incumbent senator thus retained the seat. That incumbent was Senator George Wharton Pepper, who had been baseball's counsel in the antitrust lawsuit of the Federal League in 1915, which resulted in the so-called antitrust exemption that still provides a protective shield to Major League Baseball today.[24] ∎

Notes

1. Arthur D. Hittner, *Honus Wagner: Life of Baseball's Flying Dutchman* (Jefferson, NC: McFarland, 2003). 244.

2. "Wagner Files His Papers for Nomination as Sheriff of Allegheny County," *Miami* (FL) *News*, August 20, 1925.

3. "Honus Wagner for Sheriff: Famous Pirate Is Logical Candidate of Pittsburg Republicans," *New York Sun*, March 25, 1917. Pittsburgh had lost its final "h" in an 1891 ruling by the US Board on Geographic Names but voted to restore it in 1911. Publications around the country were slow to adapt to the change.

4. "Groom Honus Wagner for Job as Sheriff of Allegheny County," *Binghamton* (NY) *Press*, March 31, 1917.

5. Robert S. McElvaine, "I'm a Depression historian. The GOP tax bill is straight out of 1929," *Washington Post*, November 30, 2017.

6. "County W.C.T.C. Selects Ticket," *Pittsburgh Gazette Times*, September 10, 1925.

7. Jan Finkel, "Honus Wagner," SABR.org, https://sabr.org/bioproj/person/30b27632.

8. Hittner, *Honus Wagner*; Dennis DeValeria and Jeanne Burke DeValeria, *Honus Wagner: A Biography*, (New York: Henry Holt and Company, 1995); William R. Cobb, ed., *Honus Wagner: On His Life & Baseball* (Ann Arbor: Sports Media Group, 2006). These three biographies of Wagner served as background sources. Most key facts are repeated in all of them, and this section incorporates them into the flow of the narrative.

9. Robert Peyton Wiggins, *The Deacon and the Schoolmaster: Phillippe and Leever, Pittsburgh's Great Turn-of-the-Century Pitchers* (Jefferson, NC: McFarland, 2011). 253.

10. Hittner, *Honus Wagner*, 213.

11. Samuel J. Astorino, "The Contested Senate Election of William Scott Vare," *Pennsylvania History*, 28, no. 2 (April 1961): 187–201, https://journals.psu.edu/phj/article/view/22800.

12. David Cannadine, *Mellon: An American Life* (New York: Alfred A. Knopf, 2006), 294–95.

13. "U.S. Cherishes No Purpose Save to Merit Favor of God—Coolidge," *Sioux Falls Argus-Leader*, March 3, 1925.

14. Astorino, "Contested Senate Election"; John B. Townley, "Pittsburgh Has Had Three Democratic Mayors in 50 Years, Success is Story of Deals Within G.O.P., Ranks of 'Machine' Domination and of Political Giants Who Ruled from Behind the Scenes," *Pittsburgh Press*, June 23, 1934.

15. Townley, "Pittsburgh Has Had Three Democratic Mayors"; Bruce M. Stave, *The New Deal and the Last Hurrah: Pittsburgh Machine Politics* (Pittsburgh: University of Pittsburgh Press, 1970), 28.

16. "Smith Assails Lawlessness and High Taxes," *Pittsburgh Press*, October 20, 1925.

17. "Wagner Speaks," *Pittsburgh Press*, October 20, 1925.

18. "Kline Forces," *Pittsburgh Courier*, August 31, 1929.

19. "Wagner Speaks."

20. "Wagner Speaks."

21. "Election in Pennsylvania," *Lebanon Semi-Weekly News*, September 17, 1925.

22. Stave, "The New Deal," 30.

23. Hittner, *Honus Wagner*, 244.

24. "Chronology of the Year—1926," Edw. Webster, *Trenton* (IL) *Sun*, December 30, 1926.

Moses YellowHorse, Pittsburgh Pirate

George Skornickel

Moses YellowHorse was 23 years old when he made his major league debut in 1921 with the Pittsburgh Pirates. Said to have been the first full-blooded Native American to play in the majors, the Pawnee may also have been the darkest-skinned major leaguer since the color line was drawn in the late nineteenth century. Certainly no big-leaguer before him had a name that sounded more Native American than Moses YellowHorse. From Jim Thorpe and Chief Bender to Louis Sockalexis, who helped put the "Indian" in the Cleveland Indians, indigenous people had been sporadically represented on the rosters of major league teams since before World War I.

Moses attended the Federal Indian School at Chilocco, Oklahoma, where he honed his baseball skills by throwing stones at rabbits and squirrels for the cook pot. At the age of 19, in 1917, he was playing both varsity and semipro ball. By 1920, he helped pitch the Little Rock Travelers to the Southern Association championship with a record of 21 wins and 7 losses.

On September 16, YellowHorse's contract was purchased by the Pittsburgh Pirates. *The Sporting News* reported: "The sale of Moses Yellowhorse was rather un-expected, not that the Indian is not worthy of advancement, but it was generally expected that the young Pawnee would be allowed to spend another season here."[1] *The Pawnee Chief*'s writer wrote, "YellowHorse is sure to make good. He is a close student and soaks up every ounce of information that is given in a wise manner. The Indian will keep National League batters swinging with one foot free when he is on the mound. He has terrific speed, but wonderful control of it. He also has a good curve ball and controls it equally as well as his fast one."[2]

Later it was revealed that the purchase of YellowHorse by the Pirates was a ruse to prevent his being drafted from Little Rock. The Pirates were to return him to the Travelers for the 1921 season, but YellowHorse pitched so well in spring training that manager George Gibson insisted on keeping him for the season, whatever the price that might be asked for his release. Gibson's judgment seemed justified. YellowHorse demonstrated in his brief trials that he was worth it to a club that needed just one more winning pitcher to make it a pennant favorite.

Although Native people were not formally banned from baseball, Pirates owner Barney Dreyfuss's signing of YellowHorse flew in the face of tradition. From time to time a few Native people—like Thorpe, Bender, and Chief Meyers—had made it to the majors, but because of their mixed ancestry, the color line had not been invoked.[3] So how did Moses YellowHorse, "as dark as the previous night's lunar eclipse," gain entry in the league?[4]

For one thing, Dreyfuss was a powerful force, and Commissioner Kenesaw Mountain Landis was intrigued by YellowHorse's American Indian heritage.[5] Landis's fascination with YellowHorse was so great that in the spring of YellowHorse's first season with the Pirates, the commissioner summoned manager Gibson and YellowHorse to his chambers. After their meeting,

Moses YellowHorse.

COURTESY OF THE PITTSBURGH PIRATES

highlighted by a question and answer session, Landis was impressed by the Pirates' latest addition.[6] Many newspapermen were impressed by him too. *The Sporting News* reported, "Fandom here has gone wild with Moses YellowHorse, the young Indian slabman, who has been used to date only as a relief artist. They like the young Indian's actions, and are convinced he is going to shine when given the right opportunity."[7]

Other writers were mixed in their reviews. One anonymous scribe in the March 19 *Sporting News* wrote, "Pirates are comparing Moses YellowHorse, the Indian pitcher Barney Dreyfuss brought from Little Rock, to Chief Bender. All he lacks is Bender's size, stuff and disposition. He's an Indian, with two legs and two arms, not a bad pitching prospect at that, however, but hardly a Bender."[8]

A Pittsburgh tradition was born with YellowHorse's penchant for successful relief pitching appearances. It wasn't long before fans began to chant, "Put in YellowHorse" whenever the starting pitcher faltered. The chant became so ingrained during his short career with Pittsburgh that it survived him by many years. Jim Nasium, a *Sporting News* writer, related in a 1926 column that during a lecture at the nearby University of Pittsburgh, a professor became lost in his notes, confused, and tongue-tied, and that his stammering was interrupted by a student who yelled, "Put in YellowHorse."[9]

In a July 5 game against the Cardinals, the 5-foot-10, 180-pound reliever suffered an arm injury that required surgery and shelved him for two months. His 5-3 record helped the Pirates finish in second place, four games behind the New York Giants. Had he been healthy, he might have significantly altered their finish, but he was sorely missed by the Pirates and the fans.

Because of his long layoff, YellowHorse's teammates voted him only a ⅖ share of their second-place money. Commissioner Landis overruled the decision and decreed him a full share.

Much blame for the failure to win the pennant was placed upon manager Gibson, who was accused of being unable to discipline his team. The press was rife with charges of heavy drinking against unnamed players. Bill McKechnie replaced Gibson as manager and Gibson warned McKechnie that he would have to keep an eye on roommates YellowHorse and Rabbit Maranville. Maranville gave YellowHorse the nickname Chief, and his first drink of whiskey.

YellowHorse had insomnia and couldn't sleep in hotel rooms. McKechnie, in a stroke of genius, decided the best way to keep an eye on his two problem children was to have them room with him. McKechnie would rent hotel suites with three beds, taking the third himself.

As Pat Harmon reported in the *Cincinnati Post and Times Star*:

The first night on the road, McKechnie entered the suite about 9 PM only to discover YellowHorse and Maranville playing a game. They were standing on the window ledge, 16 stories above the ground, catching pigeons by scooping them off the ledge.

Maranville had made a bet with YellowHorse that he could get more pigeons in fifteen minutes than YellowHorse. Rabbit won 8–5. But the fun wasn't over. McKechnie then opened a closet door. Out flew several pigeons. McKechnie immediately retreated and went to another closet to hang up his coat. "Don't open the door," Maranville warned. "The chief has his pigeons in there." Following that incident, McKechnie got a room by himself.[10]

Dissatisfaction with YellowHorse began to surface among Pirates fans after he was injured and had surgery. His drinking problem had also become well known. An October newspaper account predicted that "as a pitcher and player his days are few." Sadly, this was the same paper that earlier in the year had touted him the "best all-round player."[11] YellowHorse was not meeting the expectations of the owners, either. He did little to dispel stereotypes about Native Americans with his drinking and disruptive behavior

Years later, tribal leader Earl Chapman told of YellowHorse drinking during the Pirates' 1922 games. Not in the bullpen, but while he was pitching. According to Chapman's tale, YellowHorse would signal the Pittsburgh groundskeeper that the mound needed more dirt. The groundskeeper would then come out and put shots of whiskey all around the mound. YellowHorse would then sneak shots without anybody noticing and—if you believe Chapman's tale—he never got caught.[12]

YellowHorse's effectiveness both as a pitcher and a crowd pleaser waned as the 1922 season wore on. Alcohol had a definite deleterious effect on his performance. Both Dreyfuss and McKechnie were disheartened. Healthy except for a bout with tonsillitis that cost him a few weeks in early August, YellowHorse appeared in 28 games for Pittsburgh in 1922, all but four of them in relief. He compiled a 3–1 record and a 4.52 ERA.

In December, YellowHorse was traded along with three other players and $7,500 to the Sacramento Senators of the Pacific Coast League for pitching phenom Earl Kuns. The trade to Sacramento meant the end of YellowHorse's career in the major leagues.

He played sporadically in the minors over the next two years. In 1923, as the ace of the pitching staff, he helped the Senators to a second-place finish. He ended the season with a 22–13 record and an ERA of 3.68.

YellowHorse injured his arm midway through the 1924 season. Other than a few games in 1926, that was the end of his time in Organized Baseball. At the age of 28, he returned home to Pawnee, Oklahoma.

YellowHorse was a barely functional alcoholic until 1945. He then spent time and energy with tribal concerns. He helped establish and coached in youth baseball, umpired for semipro games, and pitched from time to time. Much of his time was spent teaching Pawnee traditions, ceremonies, and language, which were disappearing. YellowHorse never abandoned his Pawnee heritage.[13]

In 1935, a character based on YellowHorse appeared in the comic strip *Dick Tracy*. Cartoonist Chester Gould, who also grew up in Pawnee, always included aspects of his hometown in the comic. Yellow Pony was a hero who helped capture Boris and Zora Arson, two escaped convicts. His character, however, was portrayed in a racist manner, speaking in guttural, grunting, English. Initially introduced as a naive character, Yellow Pony developed into an ardent crime fighter, shooting villains and helping Tracy plot the capture of various criminals.

Moses YellowHorse "thought Yellow Pony was funny" and the portrayal, he said, "wasn't a big deal."[14] ∎

Notes

1. *The Sporting News*, September 16, 1921.
2. "Pirates Pawnee pitcher went 'way of all bad Injuns," *Sports Collectors Digest*, March 4, 1994:60.
3. William Jakub, "Moses YellowHorse: The Tragic Career of a Pittsburgh Pirate," *Pittsburgh History*, Winter, 1995/96.
4. Todd Fuller, *60 Feet Six Inches And Other Distances from Home*, (Saint Paul: Holy Cow! Press, 2002), 142.
5. "Mose J. Yellowhorse, Pawnee baseball player," AAA Native Arts, https://www.aaanativearts.com/mose-j-yellowhorse-pawnee-baseball-player.
6. *Pittsburgh Gazette*, April 21, 1921.
7. *Pittsburgh Gazette*, April 21, 1921.
8. *The Sporting News*, March 19, 1921.
9. *The Sporting News*, March 19, 1921.
10. Pat Harmon, "Chief Yellowhorse and the Rabbit," *Cincinnati Post & Times-Star*, April 24, 1964.
11. Jim Nasium, *The Sporting News*, 1926.
12. Harmon, "Chief Yellowhorse and the Rabbit."
13. Fuller, *60 Feet Six Inches*, 54.
14. Jakub, "Moses YellowHorse."

A Dark, Rainy Game Seven

The Pirates Defeat the Big Train in the 1925 World Series

Gary Sarnoff

"It was a great day for water polo," quipped *New York Times* sportswriter James R. Harrison.[1] On Thursday, October 15, the Pittsburgh Pirates and Washington Nationals met in horrific weather conditions to play Game Seven of the 1925 World Series. And when Game Seven had concluded, it was considered "the wettest, weirdest and wildest game ever seen."[2] It was also described as one of the most exciting games ever witnessed. "No World Series has ever come to the sensational climax which marked the feverish finish of today's game," wrote sportswriter Harry Cross, also of the *Times*.[3]

During a rainy, foggy, and dark morning on game day, doubt was cast over the seventh game. The decision to play or not fell to the Judge and only he. "From his first World Series in 1921, Landis took complete charge of the annual baseball classic," wrote *Sporting News* editor Taylor Spink.[4] Shortly after noon, as Landis walked along the waterlogged Forbes Field surface, he noted the mud puddles in the outfield and the quagmire that comprised the infield and pitcher's mound. Landis admitted that the conditions were poor, but declared that the show would go on. Word spread quickly throughout Pittsburgh, and by game time, over 42,000 packed Forbes Field.

Could the Pirates win? If they did, they would make history, for no team in a best-of-seven World Series had ever come back from a 3–1 deficit in games to win. And winning would not be easy since the Pirates would have to face the Big Train, Walter Johnson, who had already defeated the National League champs twice in this series. Pirates manager Bill McKechnie believed his team could do it, especially because his Game Seven starting pitcher, Vic Aldridge, had two wins over Washington. "The Senators fear Aldridge as much as we fear Johnson," said the Pirates manager.[5]

The Forbes Field crowd gave Aldridge an ovation when he took the mound. One local writer insisted that he had "plenty of stuff" during his warm-up session, but it was a different story at game time.[6] After giving up a leadoff single and recording one out, Aldridge walked three in a row to force home a run.

An additional single led to his departure, and two Pittsburgh miscues resulted in a 4–0 Washington lead. The crowd, doubting a four-run lead could be overcome against Johnson, began to call upon Jupiter Pluvius to act. A postponement seemed to be their only hope.

Johnson struck out two while retiring the Pirates in order in the bottom of the first. The Pirates also failed to score in their second at-bat, but in the third inning, they finally broke through. "After the Pirates scored their first run, the crowd began to howl," wrote Cross. "They howled and screamed and forgot about the darkness and rain. They were cold and damp, but it was all forgotten in the raucous paeans of joy which echoed over the rolling hills of Oakland."[7] Two more runs were added in the inning to cut the Washington lead to 4–3.

The rain fell harder, the skies grew darker, and the ball became more difficult to see in the top of the fourth, causing a buzz among the crowd that the game would be called, but one writer noted, "The darkness didn't seem to worry [Goose] Goslin or Joe ['Moon'] Harris, for Goose singled and 'Moon' brought Goose home with a [two-run] double" to extend the Washington lead to 6–3.[8] In the bottom of the fifth, Max Carey and Kiki Cuyler hit back-to-back doubles to score one for the Pirates and cut the lead to 6-4. Then Johnson "tightened up like a vise" and retired the next three batters to end the inning.[9] With five innings now in the books, Landis, seated next to the Washington dugout, decided that this was an official game. He turned to Nationals owner Clark Griffith and told him, "You're the world champions. I'm calling this game."

"Once you started in the rain you've got to finish it," replied Griffith, and the game continued.[10]

By the seventh inning, the steady rain became a downpour. The skies grew even darker and visibility became worse. With the Pirates still trailing 6–4, the fans stood and cheered during the seventh-inning stretch and remained standing when Eddie Moore came to the plate to lead off the Pirates' seventh. The second baseman hit a routine pop fly that Senators shortstop Roger Peckinpaugh camped under. "It was the kind of ball Peckinpaugh had caught 999 out of

1,000 times," wrote Hugh Fullerton. "This time he let it slip through his fingers."[11] Moore made it all the way to second base on the misplay. Carey followed with a fly ball down the left field line. Washington left fielder Goslin drifted far to his right. He got his hands on the ball but was unable to hold it. Moore scored and Carey went all the way to second base. The Nats immediately protested, claiming the drive to be foul. Bucky Harris, the Washington manager and second baseman, raced from his position to third-base umpire Brick Owens.

Harris: Mr. Owens, what did you call that ball?

Owens: What did [home plate umpire] McCormick say?

Harris: He said it was a fair ball.

Owens: Then that's what I saw.

A voice was then heard from left field: "Come on down, one of you umpires, and see where this ball was hit."[12] The umpires declined the invitation, the call stood and the game continued. Johnson retired the next two, but then Pirates third baseman Pie Traynor got hold of one. "The ball jarred off his bat so fast that nobody saw it," wrote Cross. The drive sailed to right-center field, then disappeared. Carey easily scored to tie the game 7–7. Washington outfielders Sam Rice and Moon Harris, running in pursuit of the hit, vanished in the darkness.

"The expectant crowd was on its feet cheering every stride Pie took in his mud circuit," was how Cross described the action. "The mud splashed from his spiked shoes as he rounded second and tore toward third."[13] Bucky Harris, taking Moon Harris's throw, wheeled and threw home in plenty of time to head off Traynor, who didn't even slide on the play.

The water dripped from the bill of Peckinpaugh's cap as he came to the plate with one out and nobody on base in the top of the eighth. "Peckinpaugh was shaking with emotion," wrote Fullerton.[14] Poor Peckinpaugh, who had been selected by the sportswriters as the 1925 American League MVP a month earlier, was struggling in this World Series. His error that helped the Pirates tie the game in the prior inning was his seventh, tying the World Series record. "If there ever was a stage set for a hero, that scene grabbed Peckinpaugh as he came up in the eighth," wrote Pittsburgh sportswriter Regis M. Welsh. Pirates pitcher Ray Kremer made his pitch; Peckinpaugh gritted his teeth and grunted when he swung, and he connected. The fans watched the ball fly into the outfield and followed

it until it disappeared in the dark. Left fielder Clyde Barnhart turned and ran toward the fence. Nobody knew what had happened until a fan's loud voice rang out for all to hear: "It's a home run."[15] Washington was now back in the lead, 8–7.

The Washington bench went wild. From World Series goat to World Series hero, Peckinpaugh wept tears of joy as he made the

Vic Aldridge.

circuit. Several Pittsburgh fans, stunned by what they just saw, stared into space with an expression of disbelief across their features. Others headed to the exits. "None would now question Peckinpaugh's right to the valuable player prize. He proved it," wrote Welsh.[16] Washington's shortstop was welcomed in opened arms when he reached the dugout. His teammates patted him on the back. Some hugged him. A few kissed him. "The run scored loomed as the last defense against a game club," Welsh noted.[17] With six outs to go and Walter Johnson pitching, the lead seemed safe.

"There's only two out," Pirates catcher Earl Smith said to himself as he strode to the plate in the bottom of the eighth.[18] Johnson had retired the inning's first two batters and appeared confident of victory. He threw with confidence to Smith, but the Pirates catcher connected on one and drove it into right-center field for a double.

Two outs, a runner on second and the pitcher due up. McKechnie responded by sending a pinch-hitter to the plate. His choice, Carson Bigbee, whose regular season batting average was .238, was a disappointment to the hometown fans. "Everybody started to groan and question the judgment of the Pirates boss," wrote the legendary Honus Wagner, who was covering the series for a Pittsburgh newspaper.[19] "Carson hasn't hit the size of his hat. No one had faith in him but McKechnie."[20]

Bigbee came through with a solid hit over Goslin to score Smith with the tying run. Certain that Johnson was wearing down, the small gathering of Senators fans behind the Washington dugout began to call on Bucky Harris to replace Johnson, but the Washington manager was determined to stick with his best pitcher. The Washington fans made more noise when Moore, who had hit the wayward popup in the seventh, walked to put runners on first and second. "Johnson

COURTESY OF THE PITTSBURGH PIRATES

Pennsylvania Governor Gifford Pinchot tosses the ceremonial first ball prior to a World Series game in 1925.

was tired," a writer insisted. "He tried to put the ball over for Eddie Moore, but couldn't make it."[21]

The next batter, Carey, grounded directly to Peckinpaugh, who was unable to handle the wet ball. He then reached for the ball, but it slipped out of his hands. Now too late to get the speedy Carey heading to first, the Washington shortstop threw to second base but his throw was too high. Bucky Harris, covering second on the play, leaped into the air and came down too late to force the runner. Peckinpaugh was charged with another error, his eighth of the World Series, to set a record.

Up came Kiki Cuyler with the bases loaded and two outs. Johnson got ahead in the count with a ball and two strikes. The great hurler then went into a long windup. Thinking he was about to see Johnson's fastest pitch, Cuyler inched to his right. Johnson made his delivery, a curveball that fooled Cuyler to the point where he took the pitch. The crowd let out a loud groan when the ball split the heart of the plate. Ruel took off his mask and Johnson walked off the mound, thinking the inning was over. Then the crowd's groans turned to cheers when home-plate umpire Barry McCormick called ball two.

Cuyler stepped back into the box. Johnson pitched, Cuyler swung, and—"Whack," wrote the *Pittsburgh Press*—drove the ball down the right-field line.[22] The ball fell into fair territory, then rolled into foul territory, into the bullpen, and under the tarp. All three runners scored and Cuyler rounded the bases. The umpires, however, ruled the hit a ground-rule double, meaning that Cuyler would have to return to second and Carey was sent back to third base. Two runs did count to give the Pirates a 9–7 lead.

The Nats had one last chance in the top of the ninth. McKechnie, with one more trick up his sleeve, sent in Red Oldham, a former American League pitcher who had been signed by the Pirates in midseason. Oldham's best value was that he had defeated the Nationals seven times in 1922, and he came through by retiring the Senators in order. The Pirates had done it. They were world champions. ∎

Notes

1. James R. Harrison, "Pirates Victory Caps Weirdest of Games," *The New York Times*, October 16, 1925.
2. Harrison.
3. Harrison.
4. J.G. Taylor Spink, *Judge Landis and Twenty-Five Years of Baseball* (New York: Thomas Y. Crowell, 1947), 101.
5. Denman Thompson, "Drizzle May Stop Final Game Again; Field a Quagmire," *Washington Star*, October 16, 1925.
6. Regis M. Welsh, "Greatest Drama in History of Sport Enacted as Bucs Rout Senators From Throne," *Pittsburgh Post*, October 16, 1925.
7. Harry Cross, "Pirates Are Now World Champions; Win Last Game, 9–7," *The New York Times*, October 16, 1925.
8. Frank H. Young, "Nationals Drop Deciding Game to Pirates," *Washington Post*, October 16, 1925.
9. Cross, "Pirates Are Now World Champions."
10. Hank W. Thomas, Walter Johnson: Baseball's Big Train, (Lincoln: University of Nebraska Press, 1995), 282.
11. Hugh Fullerton, "Pirates Batter Lame Johnson to Cop, 9–7," *Chicago Tribune*, October 16, 1925.
12. Frank T. Sullivan, "Series Umpiring Was Nothing to Sing Songs About," *Washington Herald*, October 17, 1925.
13. Cross, "Pirates Are Now World Champions."
14. Fullerton, "Pirates Batter Lame Johnson."
15. Welsh, "Greatest Drama in History of Sport."
16. Welsh.
17. Welsh.
18. Welsh.
19. Honus Wagner, "Pittsburgh Speed Was Too Much for Senators," *Pittsburgh Press*, October 16, 1925.
20. Welsh, "Greatest Drama in History of Sport."
21. Ralph Davis, "Sports Chat," *Pittsburgh Press*, October 16, 1925.
22. Davis.

The 1927 Pittsburgh Pirates

More Than the Murderers' Row Opponent

Gordon J. Gattie

The 1927 Pittsburgh Pirates are generally remembered for losing the World Series to the New York Yankees' Murderers' Row, a juggernaut highlighted by Babe Ruth and Lou Gehrig at their offensive peak. Although the Yankees did sweep the Pirates in four straight games, two of them—games one and four—were decided by a lone run, and the clinching game was won in walk-off fashion. The Pirates were a good ballclub. They'd won the World Series two years earlier against the Washington Nationals and benefitted from five future Hall-of-Famers on their roster: outfielders Paul Waner, Lloyd Waner, and Kiki Cuyler; third baseman Pie Traynor; and infielder Joe Cronin, who wasn't even a regular position player yet.

In 1926 the Pirates finished third in the National League, 4½ games behind the St. Louis Cardinals and 2½ games behind the Cincinnati Reds. Although they started slow, ending April in seventh place, a strong May and July propelled them into first place from July 24 through August 21. During these weeks, rising clubhouse tensions caused by front-office interference noticeably divided the clubhouse. The episode, later known as the ABC Affair, led to several dismissals.[1]

Pittsburgh temporarily relinquished the NL lead to St. Louis on August 23, the day longtime Pirates center fielder Max Carey played his first game for Brooklyn—which happened to be in Pittsburgh.[2] Carey, the Pirates' captain that season, had been waived along with pitcher Babe Adams and outfielder Carson Bigbee, bringing the ABC Affair, named for the trio's initials, to a close. The players had led a "mutiny" against former player and manager Fred Clarke, who'd led the Pirates to four pennants and a World Series championship between 1901 and '09. Now a vice president and bench coach for manager Bill McKechnie, he often clashed with players. Adams, Bigbee, and Carey conducted a secret ballot among the team, asking if Clarke should be removed from the dugout. The players voted 18–6 for Clarke to stay, and within days it was Adams, Bigbee, and Clarke who were gone.[3]

The fallout led to veteran manager McKechnie's departure and helped define individual roles and responsibilities within the modern baseball front office, as the idea of a coach/vice president was now outdated.[4] The Pirates regained the league lead the following night, but then lost four games during a key six-game matchup against surging St. Louis during the final week in August. Following a doubleheader loss to the Cardinals, Pittsburgh dropped to third place and remained there for the season.[5] The Pirates featured two 20-game winners in Ray Kremer and Lee Meadows. Paul Waner finished with the most Wins Above Replacement among position players with 5.3 and Cuyler led the NL in games played (157), runs scored (113), and stolen bases (35). Although disappointed with their finish, most stars were eager about returning to the Pirates in 1927.

Pittsburgh owner Barney Dreyfuss switched managers, hiring Donie Bush from Indianapolis and signing him to a one-year contract.[6] Bush had some experience guiding competitive ballclubs. His only major-league managerial experience had occurred in 1923, in his last year as an active player, when he'd skippered the Washington Nationals to a 75–78 record. That was good for fourth-place with a team that was fourth in runs scored and near the bottom of the league in Defensive Efficiency. Following his year with Washington, he'd guided the American Association's Indianapolis Indians to three consecutive second-place finishes. Bush had appeared in 1,945 games covering 16 seasons during his major-league career, most notably with the Detroit Tigers as a shortstop, where he led the American League in assists five times and putouts three times.[7] He also finished in the top 20 in Most Valuable Player voting three times and led the junior circuit in plate appearances and walks five times each. A lifelong baseball man, Bush later served as owner of the Indianapolis Indians and president of the Indians 1953–69.[8]

Heading into the 1927 season, Bush was cautiously optimistic about his ballclub: "I am not a prophet. I feel sure that my boys will give a good account of themselves, but I am not going to say where they'll finish. That's too far ahead."[9] Interestingly, both New York

Kiki Cuyler played his final year with Pittsburgh in 1927. He was traded to the Cubs during the offseason.

Giants manager John McGraw and Cincinnati's Jack Hendricks touted Pittsburgh as the team to beat for the upcoming season.

Pittsburgh started the season with a three-game sweep of the Reds at Redland Field in Cincinnati.[10] Star pitcher Kremer, who'd finished third in NL MVP voting the prior year, fired a six-hitter to help Pittsburgh win the opener. Paul Waner delivered a two-run single during the first inning to provide Kremer with all the needed offense; the Reds did strand the tying run at second base.[11] Two days later, Meadows followed with a complete game, and then the Pirates exploded for 10 runs during the final game of that initial series. After losing for the first time the following day against the Chicago Cubs, the Pirates reeled off a four-game winning streak to start the season 7–1. However, the Boston Braves were close behind with a 7–4 record.

The team struggled with a late April swoon, losing eight of 11 games between April 23 and May 7. Of those eight losses, four were by one run, including a tough loss on May 7 against Philadelphia. Pittsburgh scored two runs in the top of the ninth to take a 5–3 lead, only to lose in a dramatic fashion on a Cy Williams two-run clout with two outs in the bottom of the frame.[12] That loss dropped their record to 10–9, the nearest to .500 the Pirates fell for the rest of the season. The following day, the Pirates made their first in-season transaction, selling pitcher Don Songer to the Giants. Songer had compiled a 7–8 record with 3.13 ERA over 126 innings the previous season, but only saw 4⅔ innings with Bush's club.[13]

The Pittsburgh offense found its stride in mid-May, leading the Pirates on an 11-game winning streak May 18–29, when they scored an average of 7.4 runs per game. Following their 8–5 win over the Cubs on May 29, the Pirates were 24-11 with a 3½-game lead over Chicago. In that game, five different Pirate hitters had multiple hits, with Paul Waner hitting a two-run triple in the fourth inning that gave Pittsburgh the lead.[14] The Pirates now had three players among NL batting average leaders: Traynor (.377), Paul Waner (.350), and shortstop Glenn Wright (.347). Unfortunately, Cuyler injured his ankle during the streak, leaving him out of the lineup for two weeks.[15] Replacement Clyde Barnhart performed admirably in his absence, though.

The Pirates spent all of June in first place but watched their four-game lead over St. Louis reduced to a half-game as the Cardinals assembled a 17–9 record that month. Led by future Hall-of-Famers Frankie Frisch and Pete Alexander, the Cardinals were hungry to repeat as World Series Champions. The Pirates responded to the Cardinals' threat by sweeping them in a Fourth of July doubleheader.[16] Traynor starred in the opener with three hits and a strong defensive game while Carmen Hill pitched a complete game in the nightcap. The following afternoon, Pittsburgh trounced St. Louis, 14–2, extending the Cardinals' losing streak to six games. Bush keenly changed his lineup to include mostly right-handers against St. Louis left-handed starter Art Reinhart. His choices paid dividends when Pittsburgh scored 12 runs in the fourth and fifth innings.[17]

With St. Louis struggling in third place, Pittsburgh's threat now came from Chicago. The Cubs also gained ground in June; their 12-game winning streak June 5–16 bolted Chicago from fourth place, 6 games out, to second place, one game behind Pittsburgh. The Cubs wrestled first place from the Pirates with a 2–1 victory on July 7 at Forbes Field. The game ended with Pittsburgh threatening to tie the game, but a steady 30-minute downpour halted the Pirates' ninth-inning rally and eliminated the frame from the books. Tough-luck Pittsburgh starting pitcher Joe Dawson, who was winless through early July, suffered the loss despite allowing only three hits and one earned run.[18] As the season's midpoint approached, Bush's concerns rested more with his pitching staff than his offense; he had four reliable pitchers—mostly starters—but he needed his entire staff to be more consistent.[19] Hill and Meadows had combined for 23 of the Pirates' 43 wins, with Vic Aldridge also pitching well but Kremer struggling with shoulder issues and the relievers ineffective. Pittsburgh continued leading the NL in hitting and often needed big leads to win ballgames.[20] Kremer compiled an 8–2 record and 2.77 ERA over 74 innings through June 18 but made only four short relief appearances from June 22 through July 16.[21] Through the next two weeks, Chicago and Pittsburgh frequently mirrored each other's results, with the Pirates never falling more than 1½ games behind the Cubs. The Pirates briefly regained sole possession of first place from July 27 through July 30, but a three-game sweep by Boston—including two extra-inning games—dropped Pittsburgh to second place.

The Pirates had a 14–12 record in August, while the Cubs went 16–11 to remain in first place all month. The Cardinals won 14 and lost nine to pull within two games by August 31. The surging Giants, mired in fourth place when August started, 6 games behind Pittsburgh, won their last seven games in August to pull within 2½ games and make the NL pennant race a four-team contest in September. During this stretch, tensions between Bush and Cuyler, which had been brewing since early July, reached new heights when Bush questioned Cuyler's commitment and judgment, fining and benching him for "indifferent play" after the August 6 matchup with New York.[22] Cuyler was out of the lineup until August 16 and didn't start another game until the nightcap of a doubleheader against Cincinnati on September 5, and then was benched for the remainder of the season and the World Series. The full explanation for that benching remains a mystery.[23]

Pittsburgh returned to sole possession of first place on September 2 following a 5–3 victory over St. Louis. Kramer outpitched Alexander for his 12th win while Paul Waner delivered his 200th hit in just his second season.[24] The Pirates extended their lead to 4½ games after their second 11-game winning streak. A three-game sweep of the Philadelphia Phillies, a six-game sweep of Boston, including back-to-back doubleheaders, and a doubleheader win against Brooklyn helped the Pirates distance themselves from the other contenders. The Cubs tumbled to fourth place with a 12–17 September while New York couldn't overcome its slow start despite a 20–10 record in the same month. St. Louis threatened during the stretch with three winning streaks of five or more games, but the Cardinals couldn't match Pittsburgh's 22–9 September pace. Kramer led Pittsburgh hurlers with an 8–0 record and 1.39 ERA over his final 10 games and 71⅓ innings from September 2 to October 1. His strongest performance came during the second game of a doubleheader with Brooklyn when, on two days' rest, he fired a three-hitter, striking out three and walking two.[25] After a prolonged battle for first place, the Pirates finally captured the NL crown during the season's last weekend with a 9–6 victory over Cincinnati.[26] Pittsburgh's 94–60 record topped St. Louis (92–61, 1½ games behind) and New York (92–62, two games out), and their 46–29 road record further illustrated their resiliency.

The battle-tested Pirates headed into the World Series against the Yankees, whose 110–44 record bested the second-place Philadelphia Athletics by 19 games. The Yankees led the AL in most team batting and fielding categories, but the Pirates were still confident of their chances; the Pirates were neither overconfident nor awestruck by the Yankees, though many writers back then considered the 1927 Yankees among the greatest teams of all time.[27] Bush said, "Our pitchers have shown wonderful form for a month," noting his pitching staff noticeably improved during the second half. Expectations were high for a close series that would generate new attendance and revenue records.[28] Bush's plans included reliance on four pitchers: Kremer, Meadows, Hill, and Aldridge, with an outfield of the Waner brothers and Barnhart; Cuyler would remain on the bench.[29]

The Yankees won Game One at Forbes Field, 5–4; Gehrig tripled home Ruth for the game's first run. The Pirates responded with a Wright sacrifice fly, and then New York captured the lead when two errors led to a three-run third inning. Both Ruth and Paul Waner paced their teams with three hits. New York won Game Two, 6–2, behind three-run rallies in the third and eighth innings. Yankees shortstop Mark Koenig

Pie Traynor finished 7th in National League MVP voting and led the league in sacrifice hits.

banged out three hits while George Pipgras pitched the complete game win. Game Three shifted the Series to Yankee Stadium, where Herb Pennock fired a three-hitter for New York. Gehrig's first-inning triple plated two runs, then both teams remained scoreless until the seventh inning, when the Yankees erupted for six runs, highlighted by Ruth's three-run homer. Pittsburgh scored a lone run in the eighth to avoid the shutout but lost, 8–1. In Game Four, the Pirates scored first on a Wright single, but the Yankees responded when Ruth drove in Earle Combs. New York jumped ahead in the fifth inning on a two-run homer by Ruth, but Pittsburgh rallied with two runs in the seventh. Both teams squandered scoring chances in the eighth inning. In the bottom of the ninth, with the score tied, 3–3, a walk, single, and intentional walk loaded the bases with no outs. Pittsburgh reliever Johnny Miljus struck out Gehrig and Bob Meusel. With Tony Lazzeri batting, a wild pitch allowed Combs to score the winning run and give New York the championship.[30] As sportswriter Ralph S. Davis noted, "They won the honors today in one of the most thrilling contests in all world series history. And yet the finish came in one of the most disappointing anti-climaxes the fans have ever seen."[31]

The Bush-Cuyler feud carried into the offseason. In November, the Pirates traded Cuyler to the Cubs for infielder Sparky Adams and outfielder Pete Scott.[32] Both newcomers left Pittsburgh within two years while Cuyler played eight seasons with the Cubs and led the NL in stolen bases during his first three Chicago campaigns.

Some team achievements included: Paul Waner winning the NL MVP and leading the NL in batting average (.380), RBIs (131), and triples (18) while finishing second in on-base percentage (.437) and doubles (42); Ray Kremer pacing NL pitchers with a 2.47 ERA; and Lee Meadows pitching a league-high 25 complete games. In the NL batting average race, Lloyd Waner finished third (.355) and Traynor finished fifth (.342), among seven Pirates topping .300, to help Pittsburgh lead the NL in team batting average (.305), although the Giants ended with slightly more runs per game (5.27) than Pittsburgh (5.24).

Unfortunately, the Pirates wouldn't return to the World Series until 1960, when they upset the Yankees. Pirates fans endured many challenging years during the 1940s and '50s, although Pittsburgh did reach second place in three of the next six seasons after 1927. The Pirates may have lost to the Yankees during that Series, but the team overcame a slow start and managerial misgivings and delivered a strong September to close out the season. This team should be remembered primarily for their offensive strength, solid pitching, and resiliency. ■

Paul Waner was the 1927 NL MVP, leading the senior circuit in batting average, runs batted in, and plate appearances.

COURTESY OF THE PITTSBURGH PIRATES

Notes

1. Angelo J. Louisa, *The Pirates Unraveled: Pittsburgh's 1926 Season* (Jefferson, NC: McFarland, 2015).
2. Charles J. Doyle, "Bucs Divide, Lose Lead to Idle Cards," *Pittsburgh Gazette Times*, August 24, 1926.
3. Stephen V. Rice, "August 11, 1926: Mutinous Pirates ousted after loss to Brooklyn," SABR.org, https://sabr.org/gamesproj/game/august-11-1926-mutinous-pirates-ousted-after-loss-brooklyn; John Bennett, "Max Carey," SABR Biography Project, https://sabr.org/bioproj/person/e3347ea3.
4. Bill James, *The Bill James Guide to Baseball Managers from 1870 to Today* (New York: Scribner, 1997), 83–84.
5. "Pirates, Beaten Twice, Drop to Third Place in Hectic Flag Race," *Pittsburgh Post*, September 1, 1926.
6. "Bush is Named New Pirate Manager," *Pittsburgh Gazette Times*, October 26, 1926.
7. Jim Moyes, "Donie Bush," SABR Biography Project, https://sabr.org/bioproj/person/20beccce.
8. Bill Felber, "Donie Bush and Kiki Cuyler," The National Pastime Museum, March 7, 2016, https://www.thenationalpastimemuseum.com/article/donie-bush-and-kiki-cuyler.
9. Ralph S. Davis, "Cautious Pittsburg Will Wait and See," *The Sporting News*, April 14, 1927.
10. "Buccaneers Win, Sweep Series With Reds," *Pittsburgh Gazette Times*, April 16, 1927.
11. Doyle, "Kremer Pitches Team to Brilliant Victory Over Cincinnati Reds," *Pittsburgh Gazette Times*, April 13, 1927.
12. Doyle, "Phils Top Bucs in Series Opener, 6–5," *Pittsburgh Gazette Times*, May 8, 1927.

13. "Pirates Ship Songer to Giants by Waiver Route," *Pittsburgh Gazette Times*, May 9, 1927.

14. "Bucs Score 11th Straight Win, 8 to 5," *Pittsburgh Gazette Times*, May 30, 1927.

15. "Ki Cuyler's Ankle Not Fractured, X-Ray Shows; To Be Out Two Weeks," *Pittsburgh Gazette Times*, May 30, 1927.

16. Doyle, "Bucs Score Double Victory Over Cards," *Pittsburgh Gazette Times*, July 5, 1927.

17. Doyle, "Buccaneers Hammer Out 14-2 Triumph," *Pittsburgh Gazette Times*, July 6, 1927.

18. Doyle, "Bucs Surrender League Lead to Bruins," *Pittsburgh Gazette Times*, July 8, 1927.

19. Davis, "Bucs Take Things Just As They Come," *The Sporting News*, July 7, 1927.

20. Davis, "Every Day Is Test For Pirate Pitchers," *The Sporting News*, July 14, 1927.

21. Gregory H. Wolf, "Ray Kremer," SABR Biography Project, https://sabr.org/bioproj/person/139cb5e0.

22. Felber, "Donie Bush and Kiki Cuyler."

23. Wolf, "Kiki Cuyler," SABR Biography Project, https://sabr.org/bioproj/person/7107706b.

24. Edward F. Balinger, "Pirates Defeat Cards, 5-3; Increase Lead," *Pittsburgh Post-Gazette*, September 3, 1927.

25. Lou Wollen, "Pirates Defeat Dodgers Twice, 2-1; 6-0," *Pittsburgh Press*, September 18, 1927.

26. "Pirates Clinch 1927 Flag By Trimming Reds," *Pittsburgh Press*, October 2, 1927.

27. Alan J. Gould, "Believes Buc Hurling Staff Will Stop Yankee Sluggers," *Pittsburgh Press*, October 3, 1927.

28. "Coming Series Is Expected To Set Gate Mark," *Pittsburgh Press*, October 3, 1927.

29. Davis, "Bush Puts Job Up To Four Twirlers," *The Sporting News*, October 6, 1927.

30. John Thorn, Pete Palmer, Michael Gershman, and David Pietrusza, *Total Baseball: The Official Encyclopedia of Major League Baseball* (New York: Viking Press, 2004): 2,708.

31. Davis, "Yanks Win Baseball Championship," *Pittsburgh Press*, October 9, 1927.

32. Balinger, "Cuyler is Traded to Chicago Cubs for Adams, Scott," *Pittsburgh Post-Gazette*, November 29, 1927.

Guy Bush

That Guy From Pittsburgh

Matthew M. Clifford

During a professional baseball career of 18 seasons spread out over a span of 23 years, Guy Terrell Bush only spent one full season and part of another in Pittsburgh. But with bloody fists and a heart filled with frustration, he left a few marks in the baseball history books while wearing Pirates flannel. In the span of a few weeks in 1935, he was a key figure in two of the most memorable moments of the decade for the Bucs.

Old-time fans recall Bush's nickname as "The Mississippi Mudcat," after a breed of catfish that occupies the murky waters of the Mississippi Delta. Bush's Chicago Cubs teammates gave it to him when they learned he was born in Aberdeen, Mississippi, and had pitched for the Tupelo Military Institute. The 22-year-old made his debut for the Cubbies on September 17, 1923.

Between 1924 and 1933, Bush was regarded as one of the team's most reliable hurlers. He appeared in two World Series as a Chicago employee, in 1929 and 1932. In 1934, though, he butted heads with Cubs manager Charlie "Jolly Cholly" Grimm, who became frustrated with Bush as he struggled through June and July with a strained muscle in his left side and then an ear infection.

The bad blood between Grimm and Bush became clear during one weekend in August when most of the Chicago team gathered for Grimm's birthday celebration. Bush chose to skip the party due to personal commitments involving his gas station businesses. He sarcastically requested his teammates to advise Grimm that he was unable to attend as he needed to supervise the gasoline pumps "to make sure his customers' tanks were filled properly." The business relationship between Bush and Grimm became more and more difficult as the '34 season scraped to an end with the Cubs finishing third, eight games out.

Bush finished with an 18–10 record with the Cubs. He was involved in a car accident in Chicago during the late weeks of October and suffered a few minor cuts and bruises. While he was healing at home, he received news that he had been traded to the Pirates.

The details of the big deal made the sports papers in late November: Grimm agreed to part with pitchers Bush and "Big" Jim Weaver and outfielder Babe Herman in exchange for stellar southpaw Larry French and veteran outfielder Freddy Lindstrom.

After the dismal 1934 season he'd shared with Grimm and the Cubs, Bush was excited to bid farewell to the Wrigley Field mound. Fueled with resentment, Bush told the press, "You don't know how tickled I am to join the Pirates, whom I consider the greatest club in the world. I can hardly wait for the season to start and I will be rarin' to go when it does."[1] A few months later, Bush packed his bags in Chicago and headed for spring training in California to meet with his new boss, Pie Traynor, and the rest of his Buccaneer teammates.

Bush befriended rookie pitcher Cy Blanton during spring training and the two became travelling roommates throughout the 1935 season. Bush was ready to give the Pirates everything he had, especially when the NL schedule led the Pirates to meet up for a duel with his old boss, Charlie Grimm, and his Chicago Cubs. The meeting took place at Wrigley on April 29, and the brutal incident would forever be remembered as "The Battle of Chicago."

The game became interesting in the fifth inning after Pirates infielder Harry "Cookie" Lavagetto hit a double to score player/manager Traynor from second to give the Pirates a 6–2 lead. As Lavagetto was sliding into second, he felt the spikes of shortstop Billy Jurges. The Pirates' dugout cleared out, led by Bush. The Chicago bench cleared too and the brawl began.

Bush swung at Cubs pitcher Roy Joiner. His punches led to bloody injuries to Joiner's nose and jaw. Three Pittsburgh teammates held Bush back while the rest of the team fought with the Chicago boys. One of the men holding Bush in place was pitcher Hal Smith, who cut a finger on his right hand in the process. Blanton also sustained a spike injury to his foot, but he was unable to determine if his offender was a Cub or a Pirate. Jurges and Lavagetto exchanged punches as the Wrigley crowd went wild. Joiner was dragged back to the dugout and Grimm assessed his injuries. Noticing

Guy Bush on his 1933 Goudey baseball card

a deep gash in Joiner's jaw line, Grimm insisted that the ghastly slice had come from a blade held by his ruthless ex-employee, Guy Bush.

The umpires went over to Bush, who was being calmed by the warm dirt of the Wrigley infield on his back and three of his Pittsburgh cohorts sitting on top of him. It was quickly determined that the Mississippi Mudcat wasn't in possession of a knife. The six-inch cut to Joiner's jaw was possibly made by a sharp ring on Bush's right hand. The exciting event was frowned upon by Commissioner Kenesaw Mountain Landis, who witnessed it from his box. Umpires Bill Klem, George Magerkurth, and George Barr eventually calmed the brawl and ordered all players back to their dugouts. Some profanity continued and all were threatened with ejections if their foul mouths continued. Lavagetto and Bush were ejected, along with their Chicago opponents, Joiner and Jurges. National League President Ford Frick suspended the quartet for several games and fined them all.

The game continued, but Traynor was in a predicament. Two of his pitchers were injured, another was ejected, and his starter, Waite Hoyt, was getting tired in the seventh inning. Traynor put in Jack Salveson to relieve Hoyt and four Chicagoans ran the four corners around Salveson. The battle ended with a score of 12–11 in favor of Grimm's determined Cubbies. Bush left Wrigley Field with more hard feelings—and proof of his bad blood with Chicago stained on his Pittsburgh flannel.

The sportswriters scribbled about the Battle of Chicago throughout the 1935 season and Bush was inevitably noted as the villain. "The affair between the Pirates and the Cubs here at Wrigley Field may have started because there was a jam around second base between Bill Jurges and Harry Lavagetto," read one

report in *The Sporting News*. "But it reached full bloom because only a spark had been needed to touch off the pile of resentment that Guy Bush had been accumulating toward Manager Charlie Grimm."[2]

After completing his suspension, Bush returned to the Pirates' lineup in early May. A few weeks later, he made the headlines again when another old rival came to Forbes Field: Babe Ruth.

The last time Bush had seen Ruth, Bush was wearing his Chicago garb in the 1932 World Series against the New York Yankees. Bush had been one of Ruth's most vicious bench jockeys. After Game Three, which would come to be known as the game of Ruth's "called shot," Bush happily admitted that Ruth was yelling back at him moments before the Bambino pointed to Wrigley's center field. Decades after the called shot, Bush hand-wrote his recollection of the historic event to an autograph seeker: "Ruth was talking to me. At the time when he raised his right hand it is of my belief he pointed to center field. The only thing I am sure of he hit the next pitch in center field stands."[3]

Guy's written statement was corroborated by a letter handwritten by Ruth's New York teammate, Joe Sewell, who was also present to witness the called shot. Sewell wrote, "Babe Ruth never said a word to Charlie Root the pitcher, but he was cussing Burley [sic] Grimes Bob Smith and Guy Bush who was on their bench cussing Ruth. When he got two strikes on him he got out of the box with two fingers on his right hand he pointed to the centerfield, and on the next pitch he hit the homerun."[4]

The day after Ruth's called shot, Bush's personal frustration against the Babe was still scalding. During the fourth and last game of the series, he intentionally hit the Babe with a wild pitch. Regardless, the Yankees swept the Cubs to claim the 1932 championship. Three years later, Bush and Ruth would meet again.

The Sultan of Swat had switched leagues and uniforms in late 1934, hoping to gain a management position with the Boston Braves of the National League.

Bush was more than ready to take the mound and put the Bambino to bed. Traynor put Charles "Red" Lucas on the hill to start the game and the Babe's first plate appearance resulted in a home run, the 712th of his career. The fanatics at Forbes Field went wild. Bush got his wish to take the hill after that. Traynor pulled Lucas and sent in the Mississippi Mudcat. Bush kept the Braves quiet for the remainder of the first inning. The atmosphere changed when Ruth stepped up to swing against Bush in the third inning. Guy threw as fast as his right arm would allow and Ruth smashed a home run with Braves second baseman Les Mallon on base. The Braves were ahead of Pittsburgh, 4–0. Furious that his name had been added to the long line of Ruth's pitching victims, Bush growled as he closed the third inning.

The Pirates shared Bush's determination in the bottom of the fourth. Braves hurler Huck Betts couldn't stop the Pittsburgh boys and the score was tied, 4–4. Bush met with Ruth again in the fifth inning and the Babe hit a single to score Mallon from second for a 5–4 lead. The Pirates pushed back and ended the fifth inning ahead, 7–5. The teams stayed blank in the sixth. The golden ink of the history books began to glow in the top of the seventh when the Babe stepped in the box and stared at Bush perched on the Forbes mound. Bush tossed Ruth a strike, followed by a screaming fastball to the outside corner. His second twirl couldn't escape a kiss from Ruth's legendary bat. The ball shot high above Bush's head and disappeared over the right-field wall. No player in the history of Forbes Field had ever hit the ball that far out of the park. The Sultan of Swat had hit his 714th career home run. It was the last one that George Herman "Babe" Ruth would hit. Bush recalled the details of Ruth's home run finale in a 1985 interview. "As he went around third, Ruth gave me the hand sign meaning 'to hell with you.' He was better than me. He was the best that ever lived."[5] Traynor pulled Bush off the mound after he let two more Braves on base. Despite the fever and excitement Ruth brought to Pittsburgh, the Pirates won the game, 11–7.

Five days after the hurrah at Forbes Field, the Babe appeared in his last major-league game. At Baker Bowl in Philadelphia on May 29, he struck out twice off Syl Johnson of the Phillies. The following day, Ruth stepped to the plate one last time in Philly to face "Gentleman" Jim Bivin. The Bambino grounded out. He trotted off the field to the clubhouse and never appeared in another major-league game. Ruth announced his retirement to the press on June 2. Johnson later confessed that he tried to hand Ruth "easy ones" on May 29. He'd hoped to gain the same notoriety Bush had earned a few days before. It seemed that everyone (with the exception of Bush) wanted to witness Ruth collect another home run. Four years later, on June 12, 1939, Johnson got another chance to repeat his offering to Ruth at the first Hall of Fame game at Doubleday Field in Cooperstown. The Babe swung at Johnson's pitch and popped it up high for the fans, but it was caught by catcher Arndt Jorgens.

Without the sensational exceptions of being Ruth's last victim and the only Pirate accused of bringing a knife on the diamond, Bush's 1935 highlights with Pittsburgh lacked the luster of his years with the Cubs. The Mississippi Mudcat's 1935 record of 11–11 and ERA of 4.32 were disappointing. His rookie roommate, Blanton, received accolades from the press for his 1935 season and the young hurler credited the tips Bush had passed down to him. Blanton told the press, "Whatever I've accomplished this year has been through the efforts of Guy Bush."[6]

Bush kept his Pittsburgh flannel for four more months in 1936. He appeared in 16 games and posted a 1–3 record before playing his last game with the Pirates on July 15. Five days later, the Pittsburgh club released the Mudcat to the wild, and the Brooklyn Dodgers had their baited poles in the waters. But Bob Quinn, boss of the Boston Bees, as the Braves were now called, snatched the pitcher before Brooklyn's hook could intervene. Bush signed with Boston on July 23 and took his place on the mound soon after the contracts were completed. But his once reliable right arm was not so reliable. He went 4–5 in 16 games. Bees skipper Bill McKechnie kept Bush on the 1937 roster, hoping his arm would return to its old Chicago form. It did not. In February 1938, the Bees told Bush to buzz off and the Mudcat was picked up by the St. Louis Cardinals. But on May 7, 1938, less than a month into the season, the 36-year-old Mudcat was thrown into the murky waters of the minor leagues after six appearances and an 0–1 record.

The Cubss' Pacific Coast League affiliate, the Los Angeles Angels, took Bush to finish their 1938 season. He left baseball in 1939 to focus on his ownership of gasoline stations in Chicago, which would soon suffer the effects of World War II fuel rationing. In 1944, the baseball itch came back and the hurler was picked up by the Chattanooga Lookouts, a minor-league club owned by the Washington Nationals. At 42, Bush was the oldest member of the team. The Mississippi Mudcat got one more chance in the majors in 1945, when he was signed by his old boss McKechnie for a spot on the Cincinnati Reds' roster. Bush stayed with the team briefly, hanging up his glove after four appearances.

Guy Bush threw his last major-league pitch on May 26, 1945. He returned to Chicago and ran a sporting

Cy Blanton.

goods supply business in addition to managing his gas stations. In 1973, sportswriter Bob Broeg interviewed Bush, who complained that current major-league pitchers were feeding easy tosses to Hank Aaron, then getting close to breaking Ruth's home run record. Broeg teased Bush about his historical link to Ruth. "With piercing black eyes, shallow complexion, long sideburns, plastered black hair, sporty clothes and a racy car, Guy Bush looked like a Mississippi card shark transplanted in the 20th century," Broeg wrote. "But he was a good pitcher and a great competitor. He was a good, hard-working and, yes, a colorful righthander who won 176 games, 40 more than he lost in 13 full major league seasons and parts of three more seasons."[7]

The old Mudcat retired from his gas station and sporting goods careers and eventually made his way back to Mississippi, where he settled in the town of Shannon. While he was tending his backyard garden on July 2, 1985, Bush suffered cardiac arrest and died. He was 83 years old.

In 2001 the Donruss Trading Card Company released the "Timeless Treasures" collection, which included a card that commemorated Babe Ruth's final magnificent moments at Forbes Field. The card, recognized as number 2 in the series, featured a black-and-white photo of the Bambino on the right half. Though Ruth was playing for the Braves on that day in Pittsburgh, the card bears a Yankees logo and he wears his Yankees uniform in the photo. On the left side of the card is a tiny wooden piece of a seat that had been in Forbes Field in 1935. The back of the card includes this description: "The enclosed piece of stadium seat was cut from an Authentic Stadium Seat used in an official Major League Baseball Game at Forbes Field on May 25, 1935 in which Babe Ruth collected his final home run."[8] The card continues to hold value: It was being offered on eBay at $73 and up in April 2018.[9] The card's worth almost certainly stems from Ruth's name and photograph. But it might not even exist if it hadn't been for a skinny, hot-headed Mississippi pitcher and his stubborn animosity against a baseball Sultan who had swatted his final home run deep into the Pittsburgh skies in 1935. ■

Acknowledgments
Special thanks to fellow SABR biographer Gregory H. Wolf for his detailed literary BioProject contributions of Guy Bush and Cy Blanton. Personal thanks to my son Thomas D. Clifford for fact checking. Thanks to Retrosheet, Paper of Record, Cooperstownexpert.com, Old Fulton Postcards, and Baseball-Reference.com, and to Cecilia Tan for the opportunity and her painstaking efforts organizing and editing.

Notes
1. "Buc Fans Put Okay On Deal With Cubs," *The Sporting News*, November 29, 1934, 2.
2. "Scribbled By Scribes," *The Sporting News*, May 30, 1935, 4.
3. "Guy Bush," Big Six Sports, http://www.cooperstownexpert.com/player/guy-bush. Grammatical and punctuation errors in handwritten note sic.
4. "Guy Bush," Big Six Sports, errors sic.
5. "Guy T. Bush," *The Sporting News*, 15 Jul 1985, 57.
6. "Blanton Credits Guy Bush, Pal And Roomie, For Success," *The Sporting News*, 16 May 1935, 3.
7. "Bush's Not-So-Fond Memories," *The Sporting News*, July 21, 1973, 4.
8. "Final Home Run, Forbes Field, Babe Ruth," Timeless Treasures Card TT-2, Donruss Trading Card Co., 2001.
9. Search result, eBay, April 22, 2018. https://goo.gl/eJBcYy.

The 1931 Homestead Grays

The Greatest Baseball Team of All Time

Charlie Fouché

Major league baseball has been a fixture in Pittsburgh since 1882.[1] Alongside that well-known history, there's a rich heritage of another brand of baseball in Pittsburgh. The Negro Leagues had a strong presence in Western Pennsylvania from the 1920s through the 1940s. In 1932, numbers king Gus Greenlee put together the finest black baseball team money could buy. Led by future Hall of Famers Josh Gibson, Satchel Paige, Oscar Charleston, and Cool Papa Bell, the Pittsburgh Crawfords won three Negro National League championships in a four-year span beginning in 1933.[2]

As great as the Crawfords of the 1930s were, there was a greater Negro League team in Pittsburgh: the Homestead Grays, led by Gibson, a larger-than-life figure. The Grays set a record that has never been equaled by any professional team in any sport by winning nine consecutive league titles from 1937 through 1945.[3] But the greatest Homestead Grays team wasn't one of those nine.

Most historians of an earlier generation would nominate the 1927 New York Yankees as the greatest team of all time. Later generations might favor the 1975 Cincinnati Reds. Among Negro League historians, one of the favorites (among many) is the 1931 Homestead Grays. In 2009, Kansas City baseball historian Phil S. Dixon published a work in which he painstakingly researched, collected, and collated every box score available for the 1931 Grays. According to Dixon's research, they finished with a 143–29–2 record for an .828 winning average. Gibson batted an estimated .390 with a team-leading 40 home runs.

Charleston batted an estimated .346 with 58 doubles, 19 home runs, and an estimated 26 triples. Third-baseman Jud Wilson batted an estimated .486 and outfielder (and later manager) Vic Harris batted an estimated .403. Lefty Williams won 23 games and was joined in the 20-win club by George "Chippy" Britt (21), Willie Foster (20), and Smokey Joe Williams (20).[4]

With the individual statistics Dixon compiled in hand, we can go through a process that can tell us if the 1931 Homestead Grays should be considered among the greatest baseball teams of all time. Using the popular APBA tabletop baseball game, I had the 1931 Homestead Grays play a dream schedule against the greatest major league and Negro League teams of all time, as chosen by APBA. (See Table 1.)

Tabletop (as well as computer) baseball games are a fun way of playing teams from different eras to see how they might compete. They're also a way to educate fans who might not have seen the greats of years gone by and to see how these players might perform against contemporary players and teams. Baseball is a remarkable institution in that it spans generations. Using that as a background, we can approach a schedule that would give an across-the-board platform to discover some of the greatest teams in baseball history. Since we cannot pit these teams against one another on a real-life baseball diamond, using a simulated schedule based on real-life stats will give an accounting of how these great teams might have fared against one another.

The truth is that before 1947, baseball was a segregated institution. Black baseball teams had to play any team that offered a sure payday. They played a

Table 1. Championship Series Schedule: The Homestead Grays versus the APBA all-time great teams

1902 Pittsburgh Pirates	1930 St. Louis Stars	1961 New York Yankees	1975 Cincinnati Reds
1906 Chicago Cubs	1939 New York Yankees	1962 Los Angeles Dodgers	1980 Kansas City Royals
1910 Chi. Leland Giants	1942 St. Louis Cardinals	1967 St. Louis Cardinals	1982 Milwaukee Brewers
1924 K.C. Monarchs	1946 Newark Eagles	1968 Detroit Tigers	1984 Detroit Tigers
1925 Hilldale Daisies	1953 Brooklyn Dodgers	1969 New York Mets	1986 New York Mets
1925 Washington Nationals	1954 Cleveland Indians	1970 Baltimore Orioles	1998 Atlanta Braves
1927 New York Yankees	1954 New York Giants	1971 Oakland A's	1998 New York Yankees
1929 Philadelphia Athletics	1957 Milwaukee Braves	1971 Pittsburgh Pirates	2001 Seattle Mariners

league schedule during the years when there were Negro Leagues, but even then they barnstormed against local semipro and amateur teams in order to make ends meet. The Negro National League crumbled soon after Rube Foster's demise in December 1930. Cumberland Posey would not found the East-West League until 1932. All games in 1931 were essentially non-league games. (There was a voluntarily organized group of eastern teams that competed, but with no league schedule nor championship.) It was no fault of their own that Negro League teams could not play a major-league schedule.

It could also be argued that because of segregation, the major-league teams didn't play against the best competition of their times, either. Granted, not all of the Negro League players would have been great major-league players, but some would have been. Not all major-league players were stars either.

Also, we must remember that this type of research is subjective. It may be that 100 different people playing the same schedule with the same teams using the same tabletop or computer game would come out with 100 different outcomes. But the object of this research is to see if the 1931 Grays could be considered among the great teams of all time. We just want enough data to see if that is a plausible hypothesis.

Another concern would be that this team was created in the APBA as a stronger club than they were in

real life. I have testimony from a longtime APBA card creator that the 1931 Homestead Grays cards that were used in this simulation were accurate to the statistics that Phil Dixon provided through his research.[5]

With this background in mind, a 162-game season was played between the 1931 Homestead Grays and the group of APBA's company-produced greatest teams of all time. Each series was a five-game set with a modern five-man pitching rotation. This would guarantee that each team's top starting pitcher would face the opponent's top starting pitcher. That would avoid the overuse of a higher-rated pitcher. Players were used according to actual lineups and regularity. One huge difference was the type of strategy employed. The Negro Leagues played a much faster style of baseball than their major-league counterparts. Stolen bases and hit-and-run plays were used at a higher rate in the Negro Leagues than in the majors. This manifested itself on the cardboard playing diamond. Also, no designated hitter was used. This was not a comment on the validity of the rule, just a manifestation of historical baseball.

The Grays went 5–0 or 4–1 against almost every opponent. The only teams that managed to beat the Grays twice in their five-game series were the 1927 Yankees, the 1930 Stars, the 1953 Dodgers, the 1975 Reds, and the 1984 Tigers. To account for the full season of 162 games, the '27 Yankees and '75 Reds were given a sixth game and the chance to even up

The Greatest Baseball Team of All-Time. Standing (L–R): Cum Posey, owner; Bill Evans, SS-OF; Jasper Washington, 1B-3B; Ambrose Reid, OF-INF; Smokey Joe Williams, P; Josh Gibson, C; George Scales, 2B; Oscar Charleston, 1B; Charlie Williams, office. Kneeling (L–R): George Britt, P-C-OF-INF; Lefty Williams, P; Jud Wilson, 3B; Vic Harris, OF; Ted Radcliffe, P-C; Tex Burnett, C; Ted Page, OF.

the season series, which they both did to become the only teams to earn even a split.

The 1931 Homestead Grays boasted six Hall-of-Fame players and a Hall-of-Fame owner. The players were catcher Gibson, first baseman Charleston, third baseman Wilson, and pitchers Smokey Joe Williams, Willie Foster, and Paige (although he only appeared in one game). The Hall-of-Fame owner was Cum Posey. Also on this team were several other star players, including outfielder Harris, infielder George "Tubby" Scales, and pitcher/catcher Ted "Double Duty" Radcliffe. On talent alone, this team should receive credible consideration as one of the greatest teams of all time.

Scales, Wilson, Gibson and Charleston contributed highlights of the 1931 Homestead Grays dream season against the great teams of all time. Scales hit for the cycle against the 1946 Newark Eagles. Gibson led the team in home runs (67) and RBIs (267). Gibson also hit three home runs in a game at Yankee Stadium. Two of those went into the upper decks in left and right field. In the series against the 1942 St. Louis Cardinals, Gibson hit seven home runs, including five in the final two games—three in the last game at Sportsman's Park. Wilson led the team with a .470 batting average. Charleston led in at-bats (685) from the leadoff spot. The 35-year-old also led the team with 31 triples and 45 stolen bases. Three batters—Wilson, Gibson, and Harris—batted better than .400 on the season.

On the mound, the 1931 Grays had five 20-game winners. These were Smokey Joe Williams (26–6), Willie Foster (27–4), Radcliffe (23–6), Lefty Williams (26–4), and Britt (22–3). Foster led the team in shutouts with five. Smokey Joe Williams led the team with 282 strikeouts in 294⅓ innings. He also led the staff with a 2.35 ERA. Oscar Owens, who also played the outfield, led the team with 15 saves. Smokey Joe Williams threw a one-hit shutout against the 1939 New York Yankees in Yankee Stadium.

In the field, several Grays players showed their versatility by playing different positions. This was not out of the ordinary for Negro League teams, which rarely carried more than 16 players due to finances. Britt played all nine positions over the season. Radcliffe pitched in 32 games and caught in 31. Ambrose Reid played seven different positions. Owens played six.

The 1931 Grays outscored their opponents 1,251–514. That results in an average game score of 7.7–3.2. There is no doubt that the 1931 Grays were the original Pittsburgh Lumber Company, the nickname given to the World Series-winning 1971 Pirates. As a team, they batted .346 against the greatest competition, while holding their opponents to a .207 batting average. The pitching for the Grays was a pleasant surprise. The Grays had 774 extra-base hits to their opponents' 438.

The 1931 Grays shut out their opponents 15 times. Their opponents shut out the Grays twice. The first pitcher to shut out the Grays was Tom Phoebus of the 1970 Baltimore Orioles. The second was Gary Nolan of the 1975 Cincinnati Reds in the next-to-last game of the season. The 1931 Grays recorded a team ERA of 2.95 as opposed to a 7.53 ERA of their opponents.

The data show the 1931 Grays had the best success against American League teams, going 62–9 (.873 winning average). They were 55–11 (.833) against National League teams. The teams that gave the 1931 Grays the most competition were the Negro League teams, who managed to win five out of 25 games, so even against them, the 1931 Grays recorded an .800 winning average.

Overall, the 1931 Grays won at an .846 clip over the greatest teams of all time. This is enough to enter the 1931 Homestead Grays into the discussion of the greatest teams in history. Would the real 1931 Homestead Grays have won 137 out of 162 games against the real greatest teams ever? Probably not, but these kinds of projects are what makes baseball fun to people across generational lines.

It is impossible for these teams to play one another in real life, but the APBA tabletop baseball game, and others like it, give us the ability to size up opponents from different ages. These games also perform a great deal of education. We have all heard of the great players like Babe Ruth and Lou Gehrig, but simulation games bring these black-and-white images to life in front of our eyes. We can manage these great players, get familiar with their playing styles, their averages, their abilities against others. In short, the games educate and entertain. These are the kinds of experiences that fans across the decades are able to share. Isn't that what baseball is all about? ∎

Notes

1. 1882 AA Team Statistics, Baseball-Reference.com, https://www.baseball-reference.com/leagues/AA/1882.shtml.

2. Pittsburgh Crawfords, Seamheads, http://www.seamheads.com/NegroLgs/organization.php?franchID=PC, accessed April 20, 2018.

3. Brady Smith, "Let's learn from the past: Homestead Grays and Pittsburgh Crawfords," Pittsburgh Post-Gazette, February 22, 2017, http://www.post-gazette.com/life/my-generation/2017/02/23/Let-s-learn-from-thepast-Homestead-Grays-Pittsburgh-Crawfords/stories/201702230042, accessed April 20, 2018.

4. Phil S. Dixon, Phil Dixon's American Baseball Chronicles Great Teams: The 1931 Homestead Grays, Volume I (Bloomington, IN: Xlibris Corporation, 2009). Some statistics are "estimated" because some categories were not tracked in all box scores. In those cases, the figures were arrived at by using 1931 American League averages.

5. Email message, January 29, 2018. The card-creator's name is being withheld out of respect for his privacy. He cautioned that the Grays players likely wouldn't have accumulated such gaudy stats against major-league competition.

The Greatest Outfield?

Ted Knorr

On July 12, 1966, National League All-Star manager Walter Alston wrote out a lineup card with arguably the greatest outfield ever to appear in a baseball game—on any team, in any league, in any era. Leading off was center fielder Willie Mays, batting second was right fielder Roberto Clemente, and hitting third was left fielder Hank Aaron.[1] This trio were teammates for just 15 games, all Midsummer Classics, over a 13-year period and they played only 23 innings together as an outfield unit.

It seems reasonable to require greater longevity than 23 innings when trying to identify the greatest outfield in major-league history. Bill James, in his 2001 *New Historical Baseball Abstract*, offers a list of the 34 greatest single-season outfield units ranked by his then-newly announced statistical tool, Win Shares.[2] He concluded that the Detroit Tigers outfield of 1915 was the greatest as their single-season Win Share total was the highest ever. A glance at his top 10 below (Table 1) indicates that James's methodology had zeroed in on some of the great outfields of all time.

The full list includes 24 teams (71 percent) from the Segregated Era, 1876–1946 and 10 (29 percent) are from the Integrated Era since 1947. James refers to this "bias," concluding that baseball was less competitive during earlier eras and player performance of the greats was further removed from average than they are now. Between a third and a half of qualified players were not permitted in the major leagues because of segregation, lowering overall quality and expanding the difference between great and average. Despite this qualifier, James notes that the list indeed does identify many of the expected outfields. This is underscored when one notes that 13 of his 34 are anchored by one of the first three outfielders elected to the Hall of Fame in 1936 and '37: There are seven outfields with Ty Cobb, four with Babe Ruth, and two with Tris Speaker. An additional three outfields include Ed Delahanty from a late nineteenth century Philadelphia Phillies outfield.

In ranking outfields, once a single-season best is determined, the next question is how many seasons should be required by an intact outfield to be considered the best of all-time. Before answering that question, using the James list, I calculated the best two- and three-year outfields using the same Win Shares system. In addition, my prior research had found only 17 four-year intact outfields, 10 that lasted five years, and two six-year outfields to which it was easy to apply the same Win Share methodology. Shockingly, all six

Table 1. Greatest Major-League Single-Season Outfields by Win Shares per 154 Games

Rank	Year	Team	Outfield	WS per 154
1	1915	Detroit Tigers	Veach-**Cobb**-**Crawford**	106.0
2	1902	Pittsburgh Pirates	**Clarke**-Beaumont-**Wagner**	105.3
3	1895	Philadelphia Phillies	**Delahanty**-**Hamilton**-**Thompson**	104.6
4	1907	Detroit Tigers	Jones-**Crawford**-**Cobb**	103.7
5	1908	Detroit Tigers	McIntyre-**Crawford**-**Cobb**	101.7
6	1941	New York Yankees	Keller-**DiMaggio**-Henrich	99.0
7	1927	New York Yankees	Meusel-**Combs**-**Ruth**	97.0
8	1901	Philadelphia Phillies	**Delahanty**-Thomas-**Flick**	95.7
9	1917	Detroit Tigers	Veach-**Cobb**-**Heilman**	95.6
10	1899	Philadelphia Phillies	**Delahanty**-Thomas-**Flick**	95.2

NOTES: Hall of Famers in bold. This list is different from the original in The New Bill James Baseball Abstract in two ways:
1) Updated Win Share data from James' successor book, Win Shares, replaces earlier work; and
2) Win Shares have been prorated to 154 games since not all teams listed played the same number of games.
The best one-year outfield of all-time remains the 1915 Detroit Tigers.[3]

categories—outfields that stayed together for one, two, three, four, five, and six years—are led by trios anchored by Cobb, Ruth, Speaker, or Delahanty (Table 2).

I think it is fair to require an outfield to remain intact for four years and contain at least one Hall of Famer to be considered the best. I have been able to identify 17 outfields intact for a four-year period, of which 10 included at least one Hall of Famer.[5] The below list then may not be the 10 best but it is my strong feeling that the best outfield in major-league history is surely on the list. The table includes: franchise; tenure; number of Hall of Famers, Bill James average rank of the outfielders (e.g. in the case of the Phillies, James, in his *New Historical Abstract*, offers Delahanty as the 12th-best left fielder, Hamilton the ninth-best center fielder, and Thompson the 37th-best right fielder for an average of 19.3); Gross Production Average Plus (a refinement of OPS+ where on base percentage is weighted at 1.8 times slugging percentage); average Win Shares per 154 games over the outfield's best four-year run; and the team's winning average over the duration of that run.[6] The list is in composite order weighing the six factors equally (Table 3).

I have no problem declaring any of the top four outfields listed above as the greatest major-league outfield

Fats Jenkins and Oscar Charleston.

of all-time. But the title of this article is "The Greatest Outfield" not the greatest major-league outfield. I truly feel the best baseball ever played is being played today, in 2018, and, if not today, definitely since the integration of MLB began on April 15, 1947. However, in addition to the statistical bias James points out, other factors, such as expansion, platooning, free agency, higher salaries, designated hitters, and disabled lists,

Table 2. Greatest Major-League Outfields in Consecutive Seasons by Win Shares

Seasons	Span	Team (Outfield)	Total WS
One	1915	Detroit Tigers (Veach-Cobb-Crawford)	106
Two	1927–28	New York Yankees (Meusel-Combs-Ruth)	188*
Three	1926–28	New York Yankees (Meusel-Combs-Ruth)	265*
Four	1913–16	Detroit Tigers (Veach-Cobb-Crawford)	332*
Five	1911–15	Boston Red Sox (Lewis-Speaker-Hooper)	387*
Six	1910–15	Boston Red Sox (Lewis-Speaker-Hooper)	459

Table 2 simply adds Win Shares for each season.[4] However, the Phillies of 1891–95 only played an average of 135 games per season. Extrapolated to 154-game seasons, the Phillies' outfield (Delahanty-Hamilton-Thompson) of that span had more Win Shares per 154 games for two, three, four, and five consecutive seasons (all ending in 1895) than any other team in baseball history.

Table 3. 10 Greatest Major-League Outfields in the Opinion of the Author

Team	Tenure	Hall of Famers	James Average	GPA+	Top 4-year Avg. WS	Win Avg.
Philadelphia Phillies	1891–95	3	19.3	128	84.5	.557
Detroit Tigers	1913–16	2	15.3	129	85.4	.542
New York Yankees	1925–29	2	38.0	123	87.2	.596
Boston Red Sox	1910–15	2	44.0	119	84.9	.587
Pittsburgh Pirates	1966–70	2	28.3	122	70.8	.531
Boston Red Sox	1954–58	1	50.0	126	66.8	.517
Pittsburgh Pirates	1929–32	2	61.7	111	66.1	.535
Pittsburgh Pirates	1957–62	1	68.3	116	51.3	.523
Brooklyn Dodgers	1919–22	1	88.3	108	71.1	.525
Chicago White Sox	1922–25	1	77.7	108	49.6	.473

make it difficult for an outfield to remain intact for four years. Not to mention the influx of talent due to the integration of the game, which had the opposite effect of the bias James noted in that the abundance of talent increases competition and narrows the gap between the greats and the average. Consider that of the 41 major-league Hall of Fame outfielders beginning their major-league careers during segregation, *zero* are black or Latino (with the unrecognized, at the time, exception of Ted Williams), while 18 of the 23 major-league Hall of Fame outfielders beginning careers since integration would not have been permitted to play in the earlier era. I think before pronouncing those Phillies, Tigers, Yankees, or Red Sox outfields as the best, we must examine the Negro Leagues.

Fortunately, the Baseball Hall of Fame has done the heavy lifting. There are seven Negro League outfielders in the Hall and five more who were on the final 2006 ballot; meaning that the dozen best Negro League outfielders in the opinion of the National Baseball Hall of Fame have been identified.[7] There is only one outfield that includes three of the dozen as regulars during their primes: the Harrisburg Giants, featuring Fats Jenkins, Hall of Famer Oscar Charleston, and Rap Dixon. Further, the outfield was intact for four years, except when right fielder Dixon was in Japan for the beginning of the fourth season.

Table 4 shows what the Harrisburg Giants' line would have looked like placed in Table 3:[8]

In the Historical Abstract James ranks Negro League outfielders by position, with left fielder Jenkins eighth and Charleston first among center fielders and Dixon ninth among right fielders. This outfield thus averages 6.0 per position and is the best among all Negro League outfields. In Table 4 I refer to this as NA until I adjust this number to, in my opinion, an average ranking among the 10 best four-year outfields in major-league history.

The line shown in Table 4 would place them sixth in Table 3. However, when you consider the achievement of outfielders since integration by players who would not have been permitted to play during the Segregated Era, I think one could read the 6.0 James average as at least equal to the average such rank among the 10 outfields in Table 3. Further, given that 78 percent of Hall of Fame outfielders who began their careers during the Integrated Era would have been Negro Leaguers prior to integration, and that only 15 percent of pre-integration outfielders in the Hall of Fame are from the Negro Leagues, it is reasonable to see the five Negro League outfielders who were left out in the 2006 Hall of Fame balloting are deserving Hall of Famers. Those two adjustments bring the rank of the Harrisburg Giants to second, behind the Phillies. If one uses a timeline adjustment in calculating Win Shares, the Harrisburg outfield moves to the top of the list. I do not presume to think that I have objectively proven my case, but I do feel that I have demonstrated sound logic for my opinion.

Table 5 shows that Harrisburg Giants' line again, adjusted for the assumptions in the previous paragraph.

To close, I want to briefly introduce my choice for the Greatest Outfield of all-time, the 1924–27 Harrisburg Giants.

In left field, **Fats Jenkins**: Buck Leonard includes Jenkins as left fielder on his all-time nine and ranks him as the most deserving of induction into the Hall of Fame among the five outfielders remaining on the 2006 ballot.[9] Jenkins was named to the 1952 *Pittsburgh Courier* Poll Honor Roll.[10] Only Jackie Robinson was inducted into any of the four North American professional team sport Halls of Fame prior to Jenkins, who went into the Naismith Memorial Basketball Hall of Fame in 1963 with his teammates from the 1939 New York Renaissance. Jenkins was captain of the team that won the first professional basketball world championship.

Seamheads Statistics: .328/.399/.417, 118 OPS+.[12]
Hall of Fame ballot, 2006.

In center field is the incomparable **Oscar Charleston**: He was ranked by Bill James as the greatest of the Negro League players behind only Ruth, Wagner, and Mays among 20,000 major-league-equivalent baseball

Table 4. Harrisburg Giants Outfield with Same Criteria as Table Three

Team	Tenure	Hall of Famers	James Average	GPA+	Top 4-year Avg. WS	Win Avg.
Harrisburg Giants	1924–27	1	NA	131	83.3	.576

Table 5. Harrisburg Giants Outfield After Adjustments Described Above

Team	Tenure	Hall of Famers	James Average	GPA+	Top 4-year Avg. WS	Win Avg.
Harrisburg Giants	1924–27	3	49.1	131	83.3	.576

players.[13] Charleston was second to Josh Gibson in the 1952 *Pittsburgh Courier* poll and the second deceased Negro Leaguer, behind Gibson, inducted into the National Baseball Hall of Fame.[14] He led all Negro Leaguers in singles, doubles, triples, home runs, runs, RBIs, steals, and walks, and was in the top six in on-base percentage, OPS, and OPS+.[15]

Seamheads Statistics: .350/.428/.571, 179 OPS+.[16]
Hall of Fame, 1976.

Last, my favorite, the right fielder, **Rap Dixon**: He was listed on the all-time Negro Leagues team by Hall of Famers Cool Papa Bell and Leon Day; player Jake Stephens; executives Lloyd Thompson and Bill Powell; writers Al Moses and Claude Carmichael; and researchers Lou Hunsinger and me.[17] In addition, Larry Doby and Monte Irvin both rank Dixon as the most deserving of induction into the Hall of Fame among the five outfielders who were left out from the 2006 ballot.[18] Charleston told the *Philadelphia Evening Bulletin* in 1949 that Dixon was the greatest African-American outfielder he ever saw.[19] Dixon still holds the major-league-equivalent record for consecutive base hits with 14 in 1929; hit the first home run by a Negro Leaguer in Yankee Stadium in 1930; along with Gibson replaced Johnny Mize on the 1934 Concordia Eagles Winter League team, sparking them to the Caribbean title; and managed an integrated minor Negro League team in 1942.[20] I know of no Negro Leagues player who isn't in the Hall of Fame who had more Hall of Fame teammates than Dixon.

Seamheads Statistics: .322/.400/.531, 146 OPS+.[21]
Hall of Fame ballot, 2006.

I consider this Harrisburg Giants outfield, the best in Negro Leagues history, the best outfield to ever play the game of baseball on any team, in any league or era. I appreciate the opportunity to present my feeling to you and I hope that you will give some consideration to my point of view and look at this great outfield anchored by Oscar Charleston as comparable to those led by Ty Cobb, Babe Ruth, Tris Speaker, and that marvelous three-Hall of Famer outfield from Philadelphia in the 1890s. ∎

Notes

1. "1966 All-Star Game Box Score," Baseball-Reference.com, https://www.baseball-reference.com/allstar/1966-allstar-game.shtml.
2. Bill James, *The New Bill James Historical Baseball Abstract* (New York: The Free Press, 2001), 673–76.
3. Bill James and Jim Henzler, *Win Shares* (Chicago: Stats Publishing, 2002).
4. James and Henzler.
5. I've been collecting four-year outfields for the past 20 years and have been influenced/assisted by the work of Bill Gilbert, Jerrold Casway, and Robert Tracy, who was particularly helpful in confirming the 17 that I count as being the only major-league outfields intact four or more years.
6. James, *New Historical Abstract*; James and Henzler, *Win Shares*; Lee Sinins, *Complete Baseball Encyclopedia*, http://www.baseball-encyclopedia.com.
7. 2006 Special Committee on the Negro Leagues Election, Baseball-Reference.com, https://www.baseball-reference.com/bullpen/2006_Special_ Committee_on_the_Negro_Leagues_Election. The seven Negro Leagues outfielders in the Hall of Fame are Monte Irvin, Cool Papa Bell, Oscar Charleston, Turkey Stearnes, Pete Hill, Cristobal Torriente, and Willard Brown. The five who were on the 2006 ballot who didn't make it in, logically the eighth- through 12th-best outfielders in Negro Leagues history in the Hall of Fame's view, are Rap Dixon, Fats Jenkins, Spottswood Poles, Alejandro Oms, and Roy Parnell.
8. James, *The New Bill James Historical Abstract*, 187–92; Robert Peterson, *Only the Ball Was White* (Old Tappan, NJ: Prentice-Hall, 1970); "Negro Leagues Database," Seamheads, http://www.seamheads.com/NegroLgs/; Harrisburg Giants GPA+ was calculated by the author using statistics found at Seamheads.com, supplemented for 1927 with statistics developed by the Negro Leagues/Researchers & Authors Group, 2001–06, and contained in the February 27, 2006, Hall of Fame press release. GPA is a refinement of OPS, where OBP is weighted 1.8 times SLG. GPA+ is GPA/league GPA. Win Shares for the Harrisburg outfield are from Seamheads.com except for 1927, which do not yet exist and have been conservatively estimated by the author. The WS for the '24–27 period is prorated to 154 games for each of the four consecutive years. Harrisburg seasonal won-loss record is taken from Seamheads.com for 1924–26 and for 1927 from Peterson, *Only the Ball Was White*.
9. William F. McNeil, *Cool Papas and Double Duties* (Jefferson, NC: McFarland, 2001), 157.
10. "Courier Experts' Roll of Honor," *Pittsburgh Courier*, April 19, 1952.
11. "New York Renaissance," Naismith Memorial Basketball Hall of Fame, http://www.hoophall.com/hall-of-famers/new-york-renaissance.
12. "Fats Jenkins," Seamheads Negro Leagues Database, http://seamheads.com/NegroLgs/player.php?playerID=jenki01fat.
13. James, *New Historical Abstract*, 358. James ranks Cobb fifth, behind Charleston.
14. "Courier Experts' Roll of Honor."
15. "Batting," Seamheads Negro Leagues Database, http://seamheads.com/NegroLgs/history.php?tab=bat_basic_at.
16. "Oscar Charleston," Seamheads Negro Leagues Database, http://seamheads.com/NegroLgs/player.php?playerID=charl01osc.
17. Larry Lester, Black Baseball's National Showcase (Lincoln: University of Nebraska, 2001); NcNeil, *Cool Papas and Double Duties*; Chester Washington, "Sez Ches: The Scintillating Stevens Selects An All-Time All-Star Team," *Pittsburgh Courier*, January 30, 1943; "Courier Experts' Roll of Honor," *Pittsburgh Courier*, April 19, 1952; *Negro Baseball Pictorial Year Book* (Washington, DC: Sepia Sports, 1945).
18. NcNeil, *Cool Papas and Double Duties*.
19. Dick Clark & Larry Lester, eds., *The Negro Leagues Book* (Cooperstown, NY: SABR, 1994), 37.
20. *Baltimore Afro American*, August 3, 1929; William G. Nunn, "Diamond Stars Rise to Miracle Heights in Big Game at Yankee Bowl," *Pittsburgh Courier*, July 12, 1930; Concordia Golden Eagles 1934 Team Photo, https://www.hakes.com/Auction/ItemDetail/72452/CONCORDIA-EAGLES-1934-TEAM-PHOTO-WMARTIN-DIHIGO-JOSH-GIBSON, featuring Hall of Famers Martin Dihigo and Josh Gibson and greats like Tetelo Vargas, Luis Aparicio Sr, and Rap Dixon, who is by himself in the middle; "Daisies Play Harrisburg Giants 2 Games," *Philadelphia Tribune*, August 22, 1942.
21. "Rap Dixon," Seamheads Negro Leagues Database, http://seamheads.com/NegroLgs/player.php?playerID=dixon01rap.

From Bat to Baton

Josh Gibson, the Pittsburgh Opera, and The Summer King

David Krell

Josh Gibson was the best player never to play in the major leagues. Perhaps. Such is fodder for debate among baseball historians, scholars, and armchair managers. At 35 years old, Gibson passed away from a brain tumor three months before Jackie Robinson broke the color line with the Brooklyn Dodgers. But Gibson's life was more than bashing nearly 800 home runs, a statistic celebrated on his plaque at the Baseball Hall of Fame; nobody really knows for sure how many round-trippers the slugger hit because there are no complete accounts of games in the Negro Leagues.

While his off-the-field behavior, at times, appeared to be caused by drunkenness, the tumor is the culprit, a fact that went largely unnoticed, as did Gibson's career, until Negro Leagues scholarship exploded in the 1990s. A member of the Pittsburgh Crawfords and the Homestead Grays, Gibson has enjoyed a renaissance, of sorts. In the 1996 HBO movie *Soul of the Game*, the icon known as "the black Babe Ruth" gets a just treatment from his portrayer, Mykelti Williamson. Without any gloss, Williamson showcases Gibson's erratic decorum.

"The Unnatural," an episode of *The X-Files* set in 1947, honors Gibson in the final scene. Alien conspiracy investigator Fox Mulder—played by David Duchovny,

who also wrote and directed the flashback episode—wears a Grays jersey bearing Gibson's name while he hits baseballs off a pitching machine at night in the final scene. After leaving a message for his partner, Dana Scully—played by Gillian Anderson and named by the show's creator, Chris Carter, after Dodgers announcer Vin Scully—to meet "Fox Mantle" at the baseball diamond, Mulder teaches her how to hit a baseball by getting behind her, gripping the bat, and swinging in tandem. Flirtation is evident.

Duchovny, a baseball fan, paid homage to alien and baseball lore by placing the episode in the year of an alleged UFO landing in Roswell, New Mexico. Mulder and Scully learn of a slugger named Josh Exley, who played for the fictional Roswell Grays. Exley is discovered to be an alien by the original X Files investigator, Arthur Dales, whose brother, also named Arthur, tells the tale to his brother's successors.

There is also a 2009 documentary highlighting Gibson's life, *The Legend Behind the Plate: The Josh Gibson Story*, produced by a dozen Duquesne University students, journalism professor Dennis Woytek, and Pittsburgh television news anchor Mike Clark. While Gibson's life is celebrated and his death mourned

In this scene from *The Summer King*, Josh Gibson (played by Alfred Walker) hallucinates seeing Joe DiMaggio, and is agitated when DiMaggio doesn't answer him.

by these two productions, there has been a dearth of Gibson stories. That paradigm changed in 2017 with the opera *The Summer King*.

Not since Martina Arroyo entertained Howard Cosell on an episode of the 1970s sitcom *The Odd Couple* have the worlds of opera and sports blended to great appeal. "What? An opera about Josh Gibson?"[1] recalls Christopher Hahn about the initial reaction to the idea. Hahn has been with the Pittsburgh Opera since 2000, serving as artistic director until 2008 and general director since then.

"Opera is about compelling stories of myths and legends told through music and action. What's happening across America is a trend of opera companies exposing their audiences to a different range of subject matters in an attempt to engage audiences and communities in ways beyond *Madame Butterfly* and *La Bohème*," Hahn says.

"People in this region are extraordinarily proud and very interested in all things Pittsburgh. It's very different from other big metropolitan areas in that you're living in a city with a small-town feel. Sports is one of the big fascinations and obsessions, but it is not so well-known that the theatrical community contributes to the life and pulse of the city."[2]

Pittsburgh Opera is the seventh oldest opera company in the United States, but *The Summer King* was its first world premiere. It bridges the gap of knowledge for an arts culture that tends to think of sports as a diversion that neither informs nor elevates society. Sports fans got exposed to a subcategory of the performing arts that they tend not to be interested in. Forty percent of the single-ticket buyers for *The Summer*

King had never bought a ticket to a Pittsburgh Opera performance before.[3]

Composed by Dan Sonenberg and directed by Sam Helfrich, *The Summer King* also benefits from contributions by Daniel Nester and Mark Campbell; Maine's Portland Ovations launched the project with a trial concert reading in 2014.[4] *Pittsburgh Post-Gazette* reviewer Robert Croan lauded the performance, highlighting Alfred Walker in the title role: "He can be tender in a love duet with his young wife Helen (bright and edgy coloratura Jacqueline Echols), heartbreaking in an aria describing her death during childbirth, and yet, in the second act, elicit the viewer's admonition for the character's dissolution and self-destructive behavior."[5]

Additionally, 53-year-old Denyce Graves got high praise as Gibson's girlfriend, Grace. "When this woman is on the stage, everything around her disappears into her own luminosity."[6]

The Summer King came to Hahn's attention through the trade organization Opera America, which provides workshops for new productions. "When I started to say the name Josh Gibson around Pittsburgh, it got instantaneous recognition," Hahn says. "In addition to the sporting community, there's also a really powerful story of integration and social justice. It's happening in the 1930s and 1940s with those aspirations.

"Gibson is a tragic character whose story is palpable. His wife died giving birth to twins. Though he was bereft, he had to raise them, which was a challenge when he was on the road playing baseball to earn a living. It's a compelling story that he missed out on playing in the major leagues."[7]

The opera also highlights Wendell Smith, the *Pittsburgh Courier* scribe later selected by Branch Rickey to be Jackie Robinson's road companion and press conduit during Robinson's rookie year of 1947; he wrote a column under Robinson's name. In addition to baseball and the *Courier*, Pittsburgh's black community had a prosperous cultural world that included the Crawford Grill, a cornerstone of black nightlife and a central location in *The Summer King*; when famous jazz artists came through the city, they often played there.

"There was a real sense of identity that was connected to the world of Negro League baseball. And what was really important to me was to address some of the complexity of the story because I think the most well-known narrative is

DAVID BACHMAN PHOTOGRAPHY FOR PITTSBURGH OPERA

Sam Bankhead (Kenneth Kellogg) mourns the death of his best friend Josh Gibson (Alfred Walker), who died at the age of 35.

the narrative of Jackie Robinson, how Jackie Robinson came along in baseball and integrated baseball and everything was sort of great after that," says composer Sonenberg.

"What I wanted to convey here is that there was also something lost. There was this sense of community and identity that a lot of people had who belonged to the world of Negro League baseball and its surrounding cultural life in one way or another. And when baseball integrated which, of course, was a great thing that it happened, but a lot of these cultural institutions then began to fade away. Ultimately, the Negro Leagues themselves kind of completely disbanded by the end of the '50s. They were no more."[8]

There's a scarcity of documented information about Gibson's insights regarding baseball, racism, and the Negro Leagues. This presented both a challenge and an opportunity for Sonenberg to fill in gaps in public knowledge through research, lore, and creative license. In turn, he got a sense of the slugger's persona. "Research was a long process. It was an on again, off again journey, but the more I worked on it, the more I gained a deeper understanding of the context of the Negro Leagues in the 1930s and 1940s," he says. "Then, it became more and more clear to me how perfect a medium opera is to tell the scope of his story and the tragic component of it. From the start, I had an innate connection to the material.

"Josh Gibson still has not received his just acclaim. One of the real joys has been the response in Pittsburgh, where he's celebrated as a hometown hero. It was my dream to have the opera premiere in Pittsburgh, so I think the idea that I was introducing this historical figure to opera fans not likely to know about him is to say that Josh Gibson is important to the city and important to all of us."[9]

To ensure the accuracy of family information in the opera, Sonenberg worked with the Gibson family. "When I heard about the idea, the first thing that I said was, 'How is this going to work?'" says Sean Gibson, the slugger's great-grandson, who leads the Josh Gibson Foundation. "So Dan came down to Pittsburgh and explained how he wanted to do the story. Ten years later, we had the world premiere."

Sean Gibson says a lot of parents approached him in the lobby after performances to ask him about his great-grandfather. "I hope that when people leave the theater, they get a better sense of Josh's life," he says. "We helped Dan with some of the facts because we want people to know the family side of Josh. The opera tapped into groups that you usually don't see at operas. African Americans. Teenagers. Children."[10]

Born on December 21, 1911, in Buena Vista, Georgia, the future Hall of Famer—the second Negro Leaguer inducted after Satchel Paige—had a ninth-grade education. When he was 16, he began playing semipro baseball. A few years later, in 1930, according to legend, he came out of the stands at an exhibition game to replace Homestead Grays catcher Buck Ewing, who'd injured his hand. He was on his way to becoming the Steel City's prince of power.[11] When Gibson died on January 20, 1947, Smith wrote the obituary for the *Courier*, highlighting Gibson's $6,000 salary being the second highest in the Negro Leagues, next to Paige's. "There is no doubt that he would have been in the big leagues had it not been for the long and unjust ban against Negroes in organized baseball,"[12] wrote Smith.

And the rest is history, revived in an art form that, at first, seemed questionable for its pursuit and now presents answers to dispel myths, enhance knowledge, and shed light on a corner of baseball history long since cloaked.

Bravo! ∎

Notes

1. Christopher Hahn, telephone interview, January 17, 2018.
2. Hahn.
3. Hahn.
4. Robert Croan, "Review: Pittsburgh Opera's 'The Summer King' makes for thoughtprovoking performance," *Pittsburgh Post-Gazette*, April 30, 2017. http://www.post-gazette.com/ae/music/2017/04/30/Pittsburgh-Opera-review-The-Summer-King-Benedum-Center/stories/201704300302.
5. Croan.
6. Croan.
7. Hahn, telephone interview.
8. "Daniel Sonenberg and Sam Helfrich," Voice of the Arts, WQED Radio, April 28, 2017. https://wqed.org/fm/podcasts/voice-arts/daniel-sonenberg-and-sam-helfrich.
9. Daniel Sonenberg, telephone interview, February 9, 2018.
10. Sean Gibson, telephone interview, January 22, 2018.
11. "Josh Gibson," National Baseball Hall of fame and Museum, https://baseballhall.org/hallof-famers/gibson-josh; Gibson's SABR bio has Joe Williams as the injured catcher. Bill Johnson, "Josh Gibson," SABR Biography Project, https://sabr.org/bioproj/person/df02083c.
12. Wendell Smith, "Grays' Home-Run King Dies at 36," *Pittsburgh Courier*, January 25, 1947.

Why Isn't Sam Bankhead in the Baseball Hall of Fame?

Richard "Pete" Peterson

In 1971, Satchel Paige became the first Negro Leagues player to be elected to the Baseball Hall of Fame. It was the same year the Pirates fielded the first all-black lineup in major-league history on their way to a World Series title.

Since 1971, over 30 Negro Leagues players and executives have been elected to the National Baseball Hall of Fame based primarily on their careers in the Negro Leagues. Those honored include Josh Gibson, Cool Papa Bell, Oscar Charleston, and Judy Johnson, Paige's teammates on the 1936 Pittsburgh Crawfords—arguably, with its five future Hall-of-Famers, the greatest team in Negro Leagues history. Also in the Hall of Fame are Buck Leonard, Raymond Brown, and Jud Wilson, who, along with Gibson, were part of the dominant Homestead Grays' team that won nine consecutive Negro National League pennants 1937–45 and three Negro World Series titles.

One of the most important members of the great Pittsburgh Crawfords and Homestead Grays teams, however, is not in the Hall of Fame. Sam Bankhead was one of the most accomplished and versatile players in Negro Leagues history. An eight-time selection to the East-West All-Star Game, he was a clutch hitter, an excellent baserunner, and, possessed with a powerful throwing arm, such a skilled infielder and

Sam Bankhead with Santa Clara in 1939

outfielder that he was named the top utility player on the all-time Negro Leagues team selected in a 1952 poll by the *Pittsburgh Courier*.[1]

Born on September 18, 1910, in Sulligent, Alabama, Sam Bankhead played his way into professional baseball on sandlots while working in coal mines. He began his Negro Leagues career with the Birmingham Black Barons in 1930. He played with the Nashville Elite Giants in 1930, the Black Barons in 1931, and the Louisville Caps in 1932 before returning to the Elite Giants, where he began to establish his reputation as a star. Bankhead was selected to the first East-West All-Star team in 1933 and played right field for the West. In 1934, he made the West squad in the All-Star Game as a right fielder again. In his eight appearances in All-Star games, he would start at five different positions (second base, shortstop, and all three outfield positions).

In 1935, Bankhead signed a contract with Gus Greenlee to play for the Pittsburgh Crawfords and quickly became a friend to Gibson. In his biography of Gibson, Mark Ribowsky wrote that "Bankhead served as a father confessor, a baseball coach, and a drinking crony."[2] Ribowsky wrote that Gibson's son, Josh Jr., said that "Sammy was a constant. I'd see a lotta guys come by our house…Satchel, Cool Papa, Buck Leonard. All of them great players. But the only guy whose face I got to know was Sammy's."[3]

With Sam Bankhead having his best season, the 1935 Crawfords won the Negro National League pennant. In 1936, while there were no playoffs, they had the best record in the Negro National League. In the 1936 All-Star Game, several Crawfords were in the East starting lineup, including Bankhead, who played left field and had two hits. The Crawfords' domination of Negro Leagues baseball ended in 1937, however, when Paige convinced several of the team's best players, including Gibson and Bankhead, to join him with the Dragones de Ciudad Trujillo in the Dominican Republic.

After spending most of the 1937 season with Ciudad Trujillo and playing winter ball in Cuba, Bankhead returned to the Pittsburgh Crawfords in 1938. While the Crawfords were failing financially and soon to leave Pittsburgh, Bankhead made the starting lineup in the East-West All-Star Game, this time as the East's center fielder, and, at the end of the regular season, he was picked up by the Birmingham Black Barons for the Negro American League playoffs.

In 1939, Cum Posey moved his Crawfords to Toledo. Bankhead began the season with the Crawfords, but ended up with the Homestead Grays and helped the Grays to their third straight Negro National League pennant. In 1940, Bankhead joined a wave of Negro Leagues players, including Gibson, who jumped to the Mexican League, run by the wealthy Jorge Pasquel and his brothers.

After two years playing with the Monterrey Industriales, Bankhead returned to the United States to play for the Homestead Grays, where he had his best years. In 1942 he played in his fifth East-West All-Star Game, this time as the starting second baseman for the East. The Grays won their sixth consecutive Negro National League pennant that year but lost the World Series to Paige and the Kansas City Monarchs.

In 1943, Bankhead was once again the starting second baseman in the East-West All-Star Game and helped the Grays to their seventh consecutive pennant and a World Series victory over the Black Barons. In 1944 he started and played second base and shortstop in the East-West All-Star Game. The Grays went on to win their eighth pennant in a row and, once again, defeated the Black Barons in the World Series.

While he appeared in only 35 games in 1945, Bankhead hit well enough in his limited play to help the Grays win their ninth consecutive pennant, though they were swept by the Cleveland Buckeyes in the World Series. In 1946 the Grays failed to win the Negro National League pennant for the first time in a decade, but Bankhead, at the age of 35, had an outstanding season. He was the East's starting shortstop in the first of two East-West All-Star games played that year. His younger brother Dan pitched for the West in both All-Star games. The following season Dan became the first black player to pitch in the major leagues since the nineteenth century when he took the mound at Ebbets Field in Brooklyn on August 26 against the Pittsburgh Pirates.

In that year, 1947, when Jackie Robinson crossed baseball's color line, the Homestead Grays again fell short of winning the Negro National League pennant, but they bounced back to win it in 1948 and defeat the Black Barons in the World Series. It turned out to be the last Negro National League championship for the

Grays. With the Negro National League's star players signing with major-league teams, the circuit folded after the 1948 season.

The Homestead Grays managed to operate for two more years, but one of the most fabled teams in Negro Leagues history played its last games in 1950. During those two years, Sam Bankhead became the team's player/manager and used his influence to convince the Grays to sign 18-year-old Josh Gibson Jr. to a contract. Since Josh Gibson's death in January 1947, just months before Jackie Robinson played his first game with the Brooklyn Dodgers, Bankhead and his wife, Helen, had taken responsibility for the care of Josh Jr.[4]

In 1951, Bankhead made history when he became the player/manager of the minor-league Farnham Pirates in Canada's Class C Provincial League. He was the first black manager of a minor-league team in organized baseball. While the Pirates finished in seventh place with a 52–71 record, Bankhead, at the age of 40, played in all but one of his team's 123 games and batted a respectable .274. Bankhead also brought Gibson with him to Farnham, but the teenager batted only .230 in 68 games before breaking his ankle sliding into second base. The injury ended his baseball career.

When Bankhead returned to Pittsburgh, he was out of options in baseball, so he took a job with the city's sanitation department. When he was joined by Gibson, the two worked together on the same truck, collecting the city's garbage. Bankhead eventually took a job as a porter in the William Penn Hotel in downtown Pittsburgh. On the night of July 24, 1976, Bankhead got into an altercation at the hotel's bar that led to someone pulling out a gun and shooting Bankhead to death. The All-Star, the greatest utility player in Negro Leagues history, was dead at the age of 65.

While Sam Bankhead has been passed over year after year by the Baseball Hall of Fame, he was not forgotten by August Wilson, a Pittsburgh native and one of the most important dramatists of the twentieth century. Wilson's plays have received numerous honors, including Pulitzer Prizes and Tony Awards. His greatest achievement was a cycle of 10 plays, one for each decade of the 20th century, that dramatized the long and continuing struggle of African Americans against racial hatred and injustice.

Fences, often acclaimed as Wilson's best play and his first to win a Pulitzer Prize, is set in Pittsburgh's Hill District and takes place in the 1950s, the pivotal decade for the civil rights movement. Rather than a landmark decision or a history-changing moment, Wilson decided to use baseball as the backdrop for his play about the lives of mid-century African Americans.

It's easy to assume that Wilson based his main character, Troy Maxson, on Josh Gibson, but the likely model was Gibson's teammate and close friend, Bankhead. Like Bankhead, Maxson, after starring in the Negro Leagues, is working on a garbage truck for the city's sanitation department. A hard drinker, Maxson is so bitter about never having had a chance to play in the major leagues that he's building a fence around his Hill District house in a futile attempt to protect his family from the racism that destroyed his dream. He never finishes his fence and dies of a heart attack in his backyard while swinging his bat at a ball made of rags: "Troy assumes a batting posture and begins to taunt Death, the fastball in the outside corner," Wilson writes. Then Troy says: "Come on! It's between you and me now!"[5]

Bankhead made another appearance in the arts when Daniel Sonenberg, resident composer at the University of Southern Maine, decided that opera, with its emotional power, was the perfect medium for the story of a larger-than-life baseball player who was tormented by the forces that denied his greatness and eventually destroyed him. Sonenberg found his story in the tragic life of Josh Gibson, transformed Gibson's life into an opera, and called it *The Summer King*.

The Summer King had its world premiere in Pittsburgh on April 29, 2017. While Judy Johnson, Cool Papa Bell, and Double Duty Radcliffe appear in the opera, Sam Bankhead is a lead character. In the final scenes of the opera, he becomes the chronicler of Gibson's life. At one point, Bankhead intervenes when a group of younger Homestead Grays mock a fading Gibson. He asks them to respect Gibson because of his past greatness.

As he's dying, Gibson reminds Bankhead about Gibson's fabled Yankee Stadium home run: "It went a long way. I hope you'll remember that."[6] At the moment of Gibson's death, Bankhead steps forward to deliver a powerful aria in memory of the fallen Summer King. In the aria, Bankhead portrays Gibson as baseball's Moses, who led black players to "the promised land" but never had the opportunity to play there. At the end of the aria, Bankhead laments his own fate now that his king is gone. He asks the question that would haunt Sam Bankhead after his baseball career was over: "What will become of me?"[7]

Sam Bankhead, like his friend Josh Gibson, never made it to the promised land, never lived the dream of playing in the major leagues. Even with all his flaws, including his struggles with alcohol and drugs, Gibson, in 1972, became the second Negro Leagues player to be elected to the Hall of Fame. Since that time, other Negro Leagues legends, like Cool Papa Bell and Buck Leonard, have entered the Hall of Fame. Bankhead, their teammate and one of the greatest stars in Negro Leagues history, is still waiting to cross over. ∎

Sources

In addition to the sources cited in NOTES, the author consulted the following:
Baseball-Reference.com.
Robert Peterson, *Only the Ball Was White* (New York: Oxford University Press), 1970.
James A. Riley, *The Biographical Encyclopedia of the Negro Baseball Leagues* (New York: Carroll and Graf), 1994.
Fred C. Bush and Bill Nowlin, eds., *Bittersweet Goodbye: The Black Barons, the Grays, and the 1948 Negro League World Series* (Phoenix: Society for American Baseball Research), 2017.

Notes

1. James A. Riley, *The Biographical Encyclopedia of the Negro Baseball Leagues* (New York: Carroll & Graff, 1994), 52.
2. Mark Ribowsky, *The Power and the Darkness* (New York: Simon and Shuster, 1996), 164.
3. Ribowsky, 164.
4. Ribowsky, 303.
5. August Wilson, *Fences* (New York: Plume, 1986), 89.
6. *The Summer King*, music by Daniel Sonenberg, libretto by Sonenberg and Daniel Nester, with additional lyrics by Mark Campbell, Pittsburgh Opera, Benedum Center in Pittsburgh on May 7, 2017.
7. *The Summer King*.

A View from the Bench
Baseball Litigation and the Steel City

John Racanelli

"Hardly anything in America symbolizes a large city more than its National or American League baseball team. To take the Pittsburgh baseball team out of Pittsburgh would be to deprive its people of the opportunity for a spontaneous outburst of civic pride, for which there is no substitute. In fact, it is practically impossible to visualize Pittsburgh without its Pirates. To take the Pirates out of Pittsburgh would be like taking them out of the history of the Spanish Main, it would be like diverting the course of the Allegheny and Monongahela River so that they would not form the Ohio at the immortally historical Fort Pitt, it would be like turning the Golden Triangle into a Tin Pin Alley, it would be like transforming the 42-story Cathedral of Learning into a one-room country schoolhouse."[1] So rhapsodized Pennsylvania Supreme Court Justice Michael Musmanno in 1966 when the court was tasked with deciding whether the city of Pittsburgh overstepped its authority in securing $28 million to finance the construction of Three Rivers Stadium. Long before this decision paved the way for the construction of the ballpark that would replace venerable Forbes Field, however, the courts played a vital role in shaping Pittsburgh's baseball history.

Here are some stories of Pittsburgh baseball in the courts.

MARK BALDWIN, CHRIS VON DER AHE, AND THE BIRTH OF THE PIRATES

In 1890, Pittsburgh native Mark Baldwin pitched for the Chicago Pirates in the Players' League's only year of existence. When the league folded at the end of the season, the rights of all players reverted to the National League or American Association teams they had played for in 1889.[2] Accordingly, Baldwin was to report back to the AA Columbus Solons for the 1891 season; however, he and several other players, including pitcher Silver King and infielder Charlie Reilly, refused to report to their former clubs, signing instead with Pittsburgh.[3] The Philadelphia AA team owners felt Pittsburgh had acted "piratical" in their signing of the players, and thus the nickname "Pirates" was born. The team didn't formally adopt the name until 1931, but the nickname appeared on their uniforms as early as 1912.[4]

King's refusal to return to the St. Louis club incensed hot-blooded Browns owner Chris Von der Ahe, who was convinced that Baldwin had made a trip to Missouri specifically to persuade King to sign with Pittsburgh.[5] Seeking his pound of flesh, Von der Ahe swore out a complaint against Baldwin on charges of felony conspiracy and had him arrested on March 5, 1891.[6]

Naturally, Baldwin denied the charges and King averred via affidavit that Baldwin had not swayed him to sign with Pittsburgh. Baldwin prevailed and was cleared of all charges at his trial in St. Louis on April 3. The victory was short-lived, however, as Von der Ahe had Baldwin rearrested as he left the courthouse, claiming that the conspiracy was perfected when King failed to report to the Browns on April 1.[7]

Soon after Baldwin was acquitted of the second set of conspiracy charges, he sued Von der Ahe in Philadelphia for malicious prosecution.[8] Due to continuous deliberate delays on the part of Von der Ahe, however, Baldwin eventually dismissed the Philadelphia case and brought the same allegations against Von der Ahe in Pittsburgh in May 1894, seeking $10,000 in damages.[9]

Cleverly timed by Baldwin, this warrant was served on Von der Ahe right as he arrived at Pittsburgh's Exposition Park on May 3 for the first of a three-game set between the Browns and Pirates. After being advised by the police officer that he was to post bail or stay in jail until the hearing, Von der Ahe sought refuge in the office of Pirates team president William Kerr, where Kerr posted the $1,000 bond for Von der Ahe.[10]

When the malicious prosecution case was tried in May 1895, Baldwin triumphed and was awarded $2,500; however, a new trial was granted due to alleged jury tampering.[11] The case was retried in January 1897 and Baldwin prevailed again with a similar award of $2,525 (approximately $75,000 today).[12] Von der Ahe promptly skipped town without paying Baldwin the verdict amount or repaying the $1,000 bond.

True to form, Von der Ahe appealed the case to the Supreme Court of Pennsylvania. But the court agreed

Pirates owner William Benswanger vehemently opposed broadcasting home games from Forbes Field.

with the jury and affirmed the verdict in favor of Baldwin on January 3, 1898.[13] On the heels of the ruling, Baldwin sued the bondsman (now former Pittsburgh club president William Nimick) to recover the verdict amount.[14] Nimick, in turn, wrote several times to Von der Ahe demanding repayment of the bond but received no response.[15] Undeterred, Nimick hatched a devious plan to return Von der Ahe to Pittsburgh.

Nimick hired a private detective, Nicholas Bendel, who was to trick Von der Ahe into meeting for dinner at a St. Louis hotel on February 7, 1898. When Von der Ahe arrived, Bendel handcuffed him and forced him into a carriage, whose driver was instructed to drive around aimlessly until Von der Ahe could board the train to Pittsburgh.[16] When Von der Ahe arrived in Pittsburgh, he was taken directly to the federal courthouse, where Judge Marcus Acheson released him on $2,500 bail.[17]

At the hearing held on February 8, Von der Ahe argued that his arrest and forcible return to Pittsburgh was tantamount to imprisonment for debt, which had been abolished in 1842.[18] Judge Joseph Buffington, however, held that Nimick had the right to pursue Von der Ahe "into another state; may arrest him on the Sabbath; and, if necessary, may break and enter his house" to apprehend him, subject to the properly entered bail piece.[19]

Accordingly, Von der Ahe's arrest in St. Louis and return to Pittsburgh was found perfectly legal in light of his failure to repay the bond.[20] Von der Ahe finally settled with Baldwin in September 1898, bringing closure to this strange and protracted legal battle.[21]

OH, THE IRONY! THE PIRATES ARE PIRATED!

Up until 1938, Pirates games at Forbes Field were not broadcast to local fans at the behest of club president William Benswanger, "long considered one of the arch-enemies of broadcasting home games," as the *Pittsburgh*

Press called him.[22] General Mills and the Socony-Vacuum Oil Company had purchased, for the princely sum of $17,500, exclusive rights to broadcast Pirates road games and held an option to broadcast home games if Benswanger ever lifted the ban.[23]

But Pittsburgh radio station KQV's enterprising young broadcaster, Paul Miller, devised an ingenious method to transmit Pirates home games with just "a few minutes delay" during the 1938 season.[24] KQV leased third-floor space in a house on Boquet Street adjacent to Forbes Field and, using field glasses, Miller was able to quickly re-create the game for his radio listeners.[25]

Not surprisingly, KQV's actions riled team ownership, who, along with General Mills and Socony-Vacuum, sued KQV asking the court to stop the unauthorized broadcasts and for damages of $100,000.[26] Not coincidentally, KQV's request to carry the broadcast of the 1938 All-Star Game from Cincinnati was denied as a reprisal for its pirated Pirates broadcasts.[27]

Initially, the Pirates could not determine how KQV was getting the game information so quickly. Staffers carefully watched for fans dropping written accounts from the stands, signaling to nearby rooftops, or talking over vest-pocket radios.[28] The staff "detectives" finally located KQV's base of operations by erecting a large sheet of canvas in such a way as to individually block each of the houses on Boquet Street while they listened to the ongoing broadcast. When the sheet was placed in front of Miller's vantage point—"gadzooks!"—KQV went silent.

Undaunted, KQV fought back, contending that the ballgames were "news" and vowing to continue broadcasting the "doings of Paul Waner, Johnny Rizzo and all the lads."[29] KQV's attorney, former Judge Elder Marshall, argued that the core of the matter was "whether a person shall be restrained from seeing things on his own property and not be permitted to tell about the things he witnesses."[30] KQV's position was based in part on a 1936 case in which telegraph accounts of New York Giants games were being distributed without the team's consent.[31] The New York court ruled against the Giants, deciding that the game ticket gave each fan a complete license to give an account of the game when and in whatever form he or she chose.[32] Marshall maintained that KQV's position was even stronger in that they were observing the ballgames from a vantage point in which they held a leasehold interest.[33]

In the KQV case, however, Judge Frederic Schoonmaker disagreed with the reasoning in the Giants case and granted a preliminary injunction, holding that the Pirates most certainly had a property right in the news of the games "for a reasonable time following the games" and that KQV's nearly contemporaneous broadcasts amounted to unfair competition.[34] The Pittsburgh club, "at great expense, acquired and maintains a baseball park, pays the players who participate in the game, and have, as we view it, a legitimate right to capitalize on the news value of their games by selling exclusive broadcasting rights."[35]

KQV was given leave to appeal but the station ultimately settled the lawsuit, consenting to a permanent injunction and dropping its appeal in exchange for plaintiffs waiving their right to monetary damages.[36] This ruling turned out to be a monumental win for local Pirates fans as Benswanger acquiesced and finally granted permission to KDKA and WWSW to broadcast home games, with the exception of Sunday and holiday contests.[37] Broadcasts of Sunday and holiday games at Forbes Field were finally added in 1947.[38]

THE TRAGIC DEATH OF A PIRATE LEGEND AND GENUINE FOLK HERO

Pirates right fielder Roberto Clemente laced a double off Mets pitcher Jon Matlack to reach the 3,000-hit milestone in his final regular-season at-bat on September 30, 1972. After closing out the season with a playoff series loss to the Cincinnati Reds, Clemente traveled to Nicaragua in November and managed the Puerto Rican All-Stars to a third-place finish in the Amateur Baseball World Series.[39]

A 6.25-magnitude earthquake rocked Managua, Nicaragua, on December 23, 1972, causing widespread tragedy. An estimated 10,000 people died, another 40,000 were injured, and over 200,000 were displaced from their homes.[40] In response, Clemente coordinated a momentous effort to provide emergency supplies to the victims, accumulating donations totaling $150,000, along with tons of food, clothing, and medicine.[41]

KQV argued that Pirates game action, including that of rookie sensation Johnny Rizzo, was "news" they had the right to broadcast.

On December 30, 1972, Clemente went to see off what should have been the last of three relief supply flights. But the donations were so bountiful that Clemente had to arrange for yet another airplane to transport the remaining supplies to Managua. At the airport just outside San Juan, Puerto Rico, Arthur Rivera approached Clemente and offered him the use of his DC-7 cargo plane to airlift the remaining relief provisions.[42] Clemente inspected the plane and agreed to pay Rivera $4,000 (approximately $24,000 today) upon his return to Puerto Rico.[43] Fatefully, Clemente decided to personally accompany this final delivery, believing that earlier shipments had fallen into the hands of profiteers.[44]

By law, Rivera was required to provide a pilot, co-pilot, and flight engineer for the flight. Rivera hired a pilot but appointed himself as co-pilot, despite his lack of certification to fly the DC-7. Rivera also neglected to hire a flight engineer.[45]

Unbeknownst to Clemente, Rivera's DC-7 had been involved in an accident on December 2, when a hydraulic power loss caused the aircraft to leave the taxiway and crash into a water-filled concrete ditch.[46] After the incident, the Federal Aviation Administration was advised and an inspector confirmed with Rivera that he intended to repair the plane. Thereafter, the damaged propellers were replaced and the engines were run for three hours, showing no signs of malfunction.[47] The airplane was returned to service by the repairmen and no further inspection was conducted by the FAA prior to the ill-fated flight.[48] In fact, the plane had not even been flown since its arrival from Miami in September 1972.

Rivera's aircraft, fully loaded with cargo, crew, and Roberto Clemente aboard, was cleared for takeoff at 9:20 p.m. on December 31 with favorable weather and visibility at 10 miles. Upon takeoff, the plane gained very little altitude and at 9:23, the tower received a message that they were turning back. Unfortunately, the aircraft did not make it back, crashing into the Atlantic Ocean about a mile and a half from shore.[49] Everyone on aboard perished in the crash, including Clemente, just 38 years old.

Clemente's wife, Vera Zabala Clemente, and the next of kin of the other passengers filed a lawsuit against the United States alleging that FAA employees were responsible for the fatal crash.[50] Specifically, the plaintiffs claimed that the FAA breached its duty to promote flight safety by failing to revoke the airworthiness certificate of the DC-7 after the December 2 accident; monitor the repair process; discover that the plane was not airworthy; inspect for proper weight and balance; and screen for a qualified crew. It was the plaintiffs' contention that if the FAA had acted in accordance with its own internal procedures—an order known as "Continuous Surveillance of Large and Turbined Powered Aircraft"—the plane would have been denied flight clearance, Clemente would have been advised of the deficiencies, and the tragic crash would never have happened.[51]

The United States countered that the FAA did not have any legal duty to "discover or anticipate acts which might result in a violation of Federal Regulations" and that there was no causal connection between the FAA's inspection procedures and the fatal crash. Federal attorneys argued that the FAA's conduct could be a legal cause of the accident only if it constituted a substantial factor in the crash and not mere speculation.[52]

The court scrutinized the FAA's investigative report, which revealed that the fatal crash was caused by an engine failure exacerbated by the plane having been nearly 4,200 pounds over the maximum allowable gross weight at takeoff.[53] The court held that the FAA had failed to exercise due care and violated its own rules.[54] Because the flight crew was inadequate, the situation was such that "for all practical purposes the Captain was flying solo in emergency conditions."[55] Accordingly, the FAA's failure to inspect and ground the plane "contributed to the death of the…decedents."[56]

If the required ramp inspection had been completed by the FAA, the lack of a proper crew and overloading would have been discovered, Clemente would have been notified, and he would not have agreed to board the plane, thereby avoiding his untimely death.[57] Under these circumstances, the court found in favor of Vera Zabala Clemente and the other plaintiffs on the issue of negligence.

The United States appealed the decision, claiming that the trial court erred in the finding of a duty on the part of the FAA.[58] The critical question the appellate court was asked to address was whether the FAA staff in Puerto Rico had a duty to inspect the DC-7 and warn the decedents of "irregularities."

The appellate court acknowledged that the Federal Aviation Act's purpose is to promote air safety; however, this "hardly creates a legal duty to provide a particular class of passengers particular protective measures." Further, the issuance of the "Continuous Surveillance of Large and Turbined Powered Aircraft" order was done gratuitously and did not create a duty to the decedents or any other passengers.

The appellate court ultimately held that the order created a duty of the local inspectors to "perform their jobs in a certain way as directed by their superiors." The failure to comply with this order, however, did not create a cause of action based on negligent conduct against the FAA. Ultimately, the pilot-in-command has the responsibility to determine that an airplane is safe for flight and nothing in the FAA directives shifted the burden onto the federal government.[59]

Finally, the court found that there was no evidence that any of the deceased had relied on the FAA to inspect the aircraft prior to takeoff. Accordingly, the finding of negligence on the part of the FAA was reversed.[60]

The appellate court concluded, "The passengers on this ill-fated flight were acting for the highest of humanitarian motives at the time of the tragic crash. It would certainly be appropriate for a society to honor such conduct by taking those measures necessary to see to it that the families of the victims are adequately provided for in the future. However, making those kinds of decisions is beyond the scope of judicial power and authority. We are bound to apply the law and that duty requires the reversal of the district court's judgment in favor of the plaintiffs."[61]

The plaintiffs' request that the case be heard by the United States Supreme Court was denied.[62]

CONCLUSION

Baseball is, as Justice Musmanno wrote in 1966, "an indispensably integral part of our municipal American way of life."[63] While baseball and American courtrooms have been inexorably linked since the earliest days of the game, these particular cases illustrate the lasting impact each has on us as fans. The Pittsburgh club is still called the Pirates, we are still prohibited from broadcasting accounts of games without the express written consent of Major League Baseball, and Roberto Clemente is fondly remembered both for his baseball prowess and his off-field compassion. ∎

Notes

1. *Conrad v. City of Pittsburgh*, 421 Pa. 492, 508–9, 218 A.2d 906 (Pa., 1966).
2. "Baseball Notes," *Pittsburgh Daily Post*, February 5, 1891.
3. Silver King was to report back to the St. Louis Browns, Charlie Reilly to the Columbus Solons, both of the American Association.
4. Dressed to the Nines: A History of the Baseball Uniform, an online exhibit produced by the National Baseball Hall of Fame and Library, Cooperstown, NY; Pittsburgh Pirates 1912 page.http://exhibits.baseball-halloffame.org/dressed_to_the_nines/detail_page.asp?fileName=nl_1912_pittsburgh.gif&Entryid=197.
5. *Allegheny Base-Ball Club v. Bennett*, 14 Fed. 257 (W.D. Pa., 1882).
6. "Von Der Ahe Swears Out a Warrant Charging Mark With Conspiracy," *Pittsburgh Dispatch*, March 4, 1981.
7. "Baldwin's Troubles," *St. Louis Post-Dispatch*, April 4, 1891.
8. "Von Der Ahe Sued," *Times-Picayune* (New Orleans), April 12, 1891.

9. "Tough on Chris," *Pittsburgh Post-Gazette*, May 4, 1894; $10,000 in 1894 would be equivalent to about $287,500 in 2017. Inflation Calculator, https://westegg.com/inflation.

10. "Tough on Chris."

11. "Ball Tosser in Court," *Pittsburgh Daily Post*, May 21, 1895; "Chris Makes an Appeal," *Pittsburgh Press*, July 1, 1897.

12. "Von Der Ahe Wants a New Trial," *Chicago Tribune*, January 22, 1897.

13. *Baldwin v. Von der Ahe*, 39 A. 7, 184, Pa.St. 116 (Pa., 1898).

14. "W.A. Nimick Sued," *Pittsburgh Press*, August 2, 1897.

15. "Abducted by Force," *Sporting Life*, February 12, 1898.

16 "Von Der Ahe is Kidnaped," *Topeka State Journal*, February 8, 1898; "Abducted by Force," *Sporting Life*.

17. "Abducted by Force."

18. "In re Petition of Chris Von Der Ahe," *Pittsburgh Legal Journal*, February 11, 1898, 269.

19. "In re Petition of Chris Von Der Ahe," 270.

20. "In re Petition of Chris Von Der Ahe," 267–70.

21. "The Baldwin Case," *Sporting Life*, September 10, 1898.

22. "Pirates Finally Smoke Out Broadcast Secret of KQV," *Pittsburgh Press*, July 14, 1938.

23. "Radio Suit Is Opened By Pirates," *Pittsburgh Post-Gazette*, July 7, 1938. Additionally, Pirates road games against the Brooklyn Dodgers and New York Giants were not authorized for broadcast; $17,500 in 1938 would be equivalent to about $310,000 in 2017. Inflation Calculator, https://westegg.com/inflation.

24. "Pirates Finally Smoke Out," *Pittsburgh Press*; "Pioneering Radio Men Broadcast Pirate Game 'Over the Fence,'" *Pittsburgh Press*, April 27, 1947.

25. "Judge Gets 'Knot Hole' Radio Suit," *Pittsburgh Post-Gazette*, July 27, 1938; "Court Bars 'Knot Hole' Broadcasts," *Pittsburgh Post-Gazette*, August 9, 1938.

26. "Pirates Seek Ban on KQV as Baseball Broadcasters," *Pittsburgh Press*, July 6, 1938; $100,000 in 1938 would be equivalent to about $1.77 million in 2017. Inflation Calculator, https://westegg.com/inflation.

27. "Radio Suit Is Opened By Pirates," *Pittsburgh Post-Gazette*, July 7, 1938.

28. "Pirates Seek Ban," *Pittsburgh Press*.

29. "Pirates Finally Smoke Out," *Pittsburgh Press*.

30. "Judge Gets 'Knot Hole,'" *Pittsburgh Post-Gazette*.

31. *National Exhibition Co. v. Teleflash, Inc.*, 24 F.Supp. 488 (SDNY, 1936). National Exhibition Co. was the legal name for the New York Giants.

32. *National Exhibition Co. v. Teleflash*, 489.

33. *Pittsburgh Athletic Co., et al., v. KQV Broadcasting Co.*, 24 F.Supp. 490, 493 (W.D. Pa., 1938).

34. *Pittsburgh Athletic Co.*, et al. 490, 492.

35. *Pittsburgh Athletic Co.*, et al. 492.

36. "Pact Ends Pirate Suit Against KQV," *Akron Beacon Journal*, October 5, 1938.

37. "Pirates Finally Smoke Out," *Pittsburgh Press*.

38. "Pioneering Radio Men," *Pittsburgh Press*.

39. "Veteran Cuban Team Captures Amateur Title; U. S. Runner-Up," *The Sporting News*, December 30, 1972.

40. "Quakes Kill Thousands in Nicaragua," *Pittsburgh Press*, December 24, 1972.

41. "Clemente Dies in Plane Crash," *Pittsburgh Post-Gazette*, January 2, 1973; $150,000 in 1972 would be equivalent to about $890,000 in 2017. Inflation Calculator, https://westegg.com/inflation.

42. *Clemente v. United States*, 422 F.Supp. 564, 566 (D.P.R., 1976).

43. *Clemente v. United States*, 422 F.Supp. 564, 567 (D.P.R., 1976).

44. "Clemente, Pirates Star, Dies in Crash of Plane Carrying Aid to Nicaragua," *The New York Times*, January 2, 1973.

45. *Clemente v. United States*, 422 F.Supp. 564, 567 (D.P.R., 1976).

46. *Clemente v. United States*, 422 F.Supp. 564, 565 (D.P.R., 1976).

47. *Clemente v. United States*, 422 F.Supp. 564, 566 (D.P.R., 1976).

48. *Clemente v. United States*, 422 F.Supp. 564, 566, fn5 (D.P.R., 1976).

49. *Clemente v. United States*, 422 F.Supp. 564, 567 (D.P.R., 1976).

50. *Clemente v. United States*, 422 F.Supp. 564, 565 (D.P.R., 1976). The Federal Tort Claims Act is a limited waiver of sovereign immunity that authorizes parties to sue the United States for tortious conduct.

51. *Clemente v. United States*, 422 F.Supp. 564, 568, 570-571 (D.P.R., 1976). FAA regulation Order SO8430.20C called for "continuous surveillance of large and turbine powered aircraft to determine noncompliance of Federal Aviation Regulations." Furthermore, a "ramp inspection" was required to determine whether the crew and operator were in compliance with the safety requirements regarding the airworthiness of the aircraft as to the weight, balance and pilot qualifications. Any indication of an "illegal" flight crew was to be made known to the crew and persons chartering the service. Finally, discovery of such noncompliance was to be given the highest priority by the FAA, second only to accident investigation.

52. *Clemente v. United States*, 422 F.Supp. 564, 569 (D.P.R., 1976).

53. *Clemente v. United States*, 422 F.Supp. 564, 567-568 (D.P.R., 1976).

54. *Clemente v. United States*, 422 F.Supp. 564, 575 (D.P.R., 1976).

55. *Clemente v. United States*, 422 F.Supp. 564, 570 (D.P.R., 1976).

56. *Clemente v. United States*, 422 F.Supp. 564, 576 (D.P.R., 1976).

57. *Clemente v. United States*, 422 F.Supp. 564, 571 (D.P.R., 1976).

58. *Clemente v. United States*, 567 F.2d 1140, 1143 (C.A.1 (Puerto Rico), 1977).

59. *Clemente v. United States*, 567 F.2d 1140, 1145, 1149 (C.A.1 (Puerto Rico), 1977).

60. *Clemente v. United States*, 567 F.2d 1140, 1148, 1151 (C.A.1 (Puerto Rico), 1977).

61. *Clemente v. United States*, 567 F.2d 1140, 1145, 1148-1149, 1151 (C.A.1 (Puerto Rico), 1977).

62. *Clemente v. United States*, cert. denied, 435 U.S. 1006, 98 S.Ct. 1876, 56 L.Ed.2d 388 (1978).

63. *Conrad v. City of Pittsburgh*, 421 Pa. 492, 509, 218 A.2d 906 (Pa., 1966).

From Sandlot to Center Stage

Pittsburgh Youth All-Star Games 1944–59

Alan Cohen

Shortly after the invasion of Normandy in 1944, cities throughout the United States selected players to appear in the first *Esquire* All-American Boys Baseball Game in New York. From the time the first Pittsburgh player, Bill Herstek, was selected for the Esquire game in 1944 to the time Glenn Beckert was selected for the Hearst Sandlot Classic in 1959, more than 500 young men played in youth All-Star games in Pittsburgh that served as tryouts for the national games. Some would go on to greatness on the ballfield. For most, a couple of paragraphs in an aged newspaper glued into a scrapbook by a doting mother would be the only lasting tangible evidence of the player's brief encounter with glory.

A blend of altruism, community involvement, and business sense motivated publishing concerns such as *Esquire* magazine and later the Hearst Newspapers to involve themselves in staging youth All-Star games. The *Pittsburgh Post-Gazette* was one of the 29 newspapers around the country that selected youngsters to participate in the first *Esquire* game. Beginning in 1946, the *Pittsburgh Sun-Telegraph* was one of 12 newspapers to sponsor players for the United States All-Stars in the Hearst Sandlot Classic.

Pirates Vice-President Bob Rice scouted boys playing for American Legion teams or attending baseball schools in the Pittsburgh area.[1] The final 32 candidates for the trip to the Polo Grounds had an All-Star game on July 1 at Forbes Field. The players came from four organized youth leagues. One team was managed by John Roehm and Ray Breen, the other by Ottie Cochran and Raymond "Heinie" Boll.

Selected to go to the game in New York was left-handed pitcher William Herstek of Rural Ridge. After observing Herstek in a pregame practice in New York, coach Carl Hubbell said, "The lefthander sure has finesse. He certainly knows what it is all about out there. Look at how easy he works—sure wish I could be out there in his place. Nothing seems to ruffle him—he's been working smooth like that at each practice—he sure is a fine choice for the game."[2] Herstek injured his arm in batting practice and was restricted to one plate appearance as a pinch-hitter. He signed with Detroit in March 1945. He entered the military after the 1945 season and was out of pro ball. Herstek returned for one last try in 1950, going 6–6 with a 5.60 ERA for Class-D Olean. He was out of organized baseball for good at age 23.

Pittsburgh was not represented at the 1945 *Esquire* game, but from 1946 through 1959, the Steel City would be sending youngsters to national contests. There was no absence of support from former Pirates who had been on center stage for decades.

Honus Wagner, then 72 years old, managed the East Squad in the *Esquire* game in 1946, when the event was moved to Wrigley Field in Chicago. "Working with these boys will take me back to my kid days in Carnegie, Pennsylvania," Wagner said. "We'll dig in and learn a lot of baseball while we are together. I can't say that we'll win, but I will say the West will get all the competition they are looking for when the umpire calls, 'Play Ball!'"[3]

Don Ivol from Dormont, who played for the Mt. Lebanon Wildcats in Pittsburgh's City-County League, was selected after an all-star game at Forbes Field on July 13. The game was played under the auspices of a group known as the Dapper Dans. On July 16, Ivol worked out with the Pirates at Forbes Field and got some pointers from first baseman Elbie Fletcher.[4]

Wagner moved Ivol to the pitcher's mound for the *Esquire* game. In practices, Wagner had Ivol throw to White Sox catcher Mike Tresh, who was serving as one of Wagner's coaches. Tresh told the writers covering the game that he thought Ivol had the makings of a fine pitcher.[5] Ivol entered the *Esquire* game in the second inning with one out and the bases loaded. He pitched into the fifth inning, allowing one run while striking out five. Ivol's parents were at the game in Chicago along with 15 residents from Mt. Lebanon, including Wildcats coach Art Long. Local broadcaster Bob Prince, who would become the Pirates announcer in 1948, was also at the game and led the cheering section, exclaiming "That's my boy!" when Ivol was pitching.[6] Ivol did not play professionally.

Later that month, the first Hearst Sandlot Classic was held at the Polo Grounds between the *New York Journal-American* All-Stars and the United States All-Stars. It was the culmination of a summer of activity during which tryouts and all-star games were held in 12 cities from coast to coast to select players for the U.S. All-Stars. In each of these cities, there was a newspaper operated by the Hearst Corporation. In Pittsburgh, the newspaper was the *Pittsburgh Sun-Telegraph*.

For 14 summers, the *Sun-Telegraph* sent two players per year to New York. There were 26 players in all, as two players were selected to go twice. Seven of the players who represented Pittsburgh would make it to the major leagues, and still more who played in the feeder games in Pittsburgh would become big leaguers.

Dick Groat, who appeared in the 1947 and 1948 Hearst Classics, was one of two Hearst alums to play both major league baseball and NBA basketball. He represented Pittsburgh in 1947 after his performance in the Pittsburgh Sun-Telegraph All-Star Game at Forbes Field on August 5. The game had been rained out when originally scheduled and the boys took to the field after a game between the Pirates and the Reds.

In Pittsburgh, they kicked off the selection process with a dinner on July 7. Pie Traynor, Pittsburgh's great third baseman, spoke at the gathering and said, "You kids are the future major leaguers. But you have to work to make it. And in the beginning, you have to forget about the money and love the game. You have to start in at the bottom in the low class minor leagues. If you have the stuff and the will to win, you'll come up and there'll be plenty of money for you then. The only place to play the game is in the big leagues, but you have to earn your way. And you can't do that if you're going to worry about the money in the beginning. Get the experience, learn the game. The rest will come."[7]

"I was fortunate enough to be one of two players picked to represent Pittsburgh both as a junior and a senior in high school in Hearst All-Star games in New York," Groat said long after his playing days ended. "That's how I knew I had special talent. Scouts saw me both years, but I turned them down when they offered me contracts after I graduated. As much as my father wanted me to play major league baseball, he wanted all his kids to get college diplomas before doing anything else."[8]

Groat entered the game in Pittsburgh as a defensive replacement and singled in his first at-bat. Then, with his team trailing by three runs and with runners on first and second in the top of the eighth inning, he tripled to close the gap and scored the tying run. The

game was called after the completion of that half inning due to darkness. Groat was the only player in the game with two hits.[9] He learned of his national selection shortly after the game and he, Bill Hopper (the other player chosen), and Wagner departed by rail to New York on August 7 for the opportunity of a lifetime.

In New York, Groat received a fielding lesson from *Journal-American* team manager Rabbit Maranville. The old shortstop demonstrated a pivot for Groat to save him a fraction of a second on the double play.[10] Groat's one vivid memory of his games in New York is standing outside in the rain, across from St. Patrick's Cathedral, during Babe Ruth's funeral on August 19, 1948.

In 1950, the managers at Pittsburgh's *Sun-Telegraph* Classic were Hall-of-Famer Pie Traynor and Lee Handley, who had played 10 seasons in the majors. Selected to go to New York were Tony Bartirome and Sylvan Lucas, who had also participated in the 1949 game. Bartirome had grown up on Bedford Avenue on Pittsburgh's Lower Hill. One of his fellow players in his youth was Bobby Del Greco, who, like Bartirome, went on to the big leagues. Del Greco, a lifelong friend of Bartirome, had high praise for Traynor: "He was a patient teacher and a great guy. He took us down to Deland, Florida (the spring training facility of the Pirates), for a tryout in 1950."[11] Del Greco was nominated for the 1948 game in Pittsburgh, but not selected to play.

In 1951, Traynor signed Bartirome to a Pittsburgh contract and he made his big-league debut a few days shy of his 20th birthday in 1952. He played in 124 games for the last-place Bucs. "I was thrilled to be signed by the Pirates. I thought I was in heaven. I got a bonus of $3,000, which was big back then," he said in 1998. "I couldn't believe that they were going to pay me to play professional baseball. When I started to play for the Pirates, it was a dream come true."[12]

That was Bartirome's only major-league season. He was then drafted and spent two years in the Army. After leaving the service, he injured himself in spring training prior to the 1955 season, could not return to the Pirates, and spent the remainder of his playing career in the minors. In 1963, he attended the minor-league meetings in San Diego, and his encounter there with Harold Cooper, general manager of the Pirates' Triple-A affiliate in Columbus, Ohio, would change his life. Cooper suggested he pursue a career as a trainer and offered the inexperienced Bartirome a position. Bartirome chose to accept Cooper's offer.[13] He was head trainer for the Pirates from 1967 through 1985, and he collected World Series rings in 1971 and 1979.

L–R: Gino Cimoli, Tony Bartitrome, Fred Patek.

Gino Cimoli represented San Francisco in 1947, and played with the 1960 World Championship Pirates.

Tony Bartirome represented Pittsburgh at the 1950 Hearst Classic, played for the Pirates in 1952, and went on to become the Bucs' long-time trainer.

Freddie Patek represented San Antonio in the 1963 Hearst Classic, spent his first three major league season with the Pirates, and was on the 1970 NL East Champion Pirates.

In 1951, Tito Francona represented New Brighton High School and Pittsburgh in the Hearst Classic. He had been selected after his performance in the *Sun-Telegraph* game on July 16 at Munhall's West Field. He signed with Jim Weaver of the St. Louis Browns for a modest bonus of $5,000 in 1952 and went on to play 15 years in the major leagues.

In 1952, Bobby Locke represented the Pittsburgh area. In the game at Pittsburgh on August 4, Locke, whose County team lost, 12–0, struck out six batters in relief.[14] In New York, Locke palled around with Ralph Mauriello, who tells the story about the boys' excursion to *The King and I*: "In the opening scene, the boy playing the son of Anna looks out over the audience and says, 'Mother, there are men coming in boats and they are half naked.' At which point my Pennsylvania friend (Locke) stands up, looks back at the rear of the theater (we were in the fourth or fifth row) and says, 'There ain't no boats back there. That kid is crazy. I'm leaving.' And he walked out."[15] Locke signed with Cleveland in 1953, and as a major leaguer, he had a career record of 16–15.

Claude Agee was one of but a few African Americans to appear in the Hearst Classic over the years. He starred in the *Pittsburgh Sun-Telegraph* Game at Forbes Field in Pittsburgh on July 31, 1953, earning the trip to New York. He went 2-for-4, including a triple that slammed into the outfield wall 375 feet away, driving in two runs for the County All-Stars. Agee was one of two black players in the 1953 game in Pittsburgh, the other being Donald Feabry, who doubled during the game and was robbed of another bid for an extra-base hit when Agee made a sensational catch in right-center.[16] In New York, Agee went 2-for-2 with a walk in three plate appearances.[17] He became the first player of color to be signed by Detroit. He spent two years in the Tigers organization but made it only as far

as Class C Idaho Falls in the Pioneer League. Feabry did not play organized baseball.

Ted Sadowski represented Pittsburgh at the Hearst game in 1954, coming in to pitch the final two innings and getting a save. He signed with Washington in 1955 and made it to the majors in 1960, the team's last season in DC. He accompanied the club to Minnesota in 1961. He played in parts of three seasons with the Senators and Twins, appeared in 43 games, and had a 2–3 record. His brother Ed was one of four players in the *Sun-Telegraph* game in 1949 to play in the majors (Russ Kemmerer, Paul Smith, and Ron Shoop were the others). None was selected to go to New York. The youngest Sadowski brother, Bob, was nominated to play in the 1956 game in Pittsburgh, but was not selected. He played parts of four major-league seasons.

In 1958, West Virginia was represented in the game played in Pittsburgh by "the erstwhile Flemington Flash."[18] Of his performance in the game at Pittsburgh, it was said, "This 170-pounder is a slick fielder and consistent hitter who surprises with a long ball. He collected three hits Wednesday, took part in a double play and easily made the standout play of the day."[19] Paul Popovich went to the Hearst Classic in New York and then on to West Virginia University for two years before signing with the Chicago Cubs in 1960 for a $42,500 bonus. He first appeared in a Cubs uniform in 1964 and played 11 major-league seasons.

Twenty-four players participated in the game in Pittsburgh on August 6, 1958. Mike Ditka was selected as an alternate. He went on to play football at the University of Pittsburgh. As noted in the *Pittsburgh Sun-Telegraph*, he was "easily the biggest man on the field, Wednesday. The 6-foot, 3-inch 215-pounder, who'll probably play an end at Pitt this fall, showed speed and a healthy swing. He couldn't get hold of one in the game but demonstrated his power in batting drills. He sent two over the wall to the right of the scoreboard in left."[20] Ditka went on to a Hall of Fame career in the NFL and, in the 1963 Championship Game, stood across the field from New York Giants end Joe Walton, who had played in the *Sun-Telegraph* game in 1953.

Glenn Beckert was selected for the trip to New York in 1959, his second year in the Pittsburgh game.[21] Beckert was one of 103 candidates nominated by Pittsburgh-area scouts to play in the annual *Sun-Telegraph* All-Star Game at Forbes Field on July 13. Of those nominated, 24 played in Pittsburgh and Beckert was one of two players selected to go to New York. The nominees included Sam McDowell, who would go on to a fine major-league career. But when the six pitchers selected for the game in Pittsburgh were announced, he was not among them.

The 1959 game was the last hurrah for Pittsburgh at the Hearst Classic. Beckert was the seventh player from Pittsburgh to graduate to the Hearst game in New York and go on to the majors.

Over the years, several Hearst alums made their presence felt as the Pirates contended for and won championships. In the 1960 World Series, Groat and Gino Cimoli of the 1947 U.S. All-Stars played for the Pirates. Others on that team were Hal Smith, who participated in the Hearst program in Detroit in 1948, and Vernon Law, who played in a regional *Esquire* game in 1946. In 1970, the Pirates won the National League Eastern Division title and one of their shortstops was Freddie Patek, who had played in the 1963 Hearst game, representing San Antonio.

Adult leaders like Ottie Cochran and writers like Bill Heyman and Andy Dugo left a wonderful legacy, and the young men who played in the games had moments to cherish the rest of their lives.

Austin T. "Ottie" Cochran was born in 1905 and played sandlot ball in the Pittsburgh area for many years. He graduated from Bethany College and became a successful insurance executive. But his contributions to amateur baseball would be his legacy. He was the founder and first president of the Greater Pittsburgh Amateur Baseball Federation and served a term as president of the National Amateur Baseball Federation. From the first *Esquire* game in 1944 through the last Hearst game in Pittsburgh in 1959, Cochran was there in some capacity from manager to coach to judge. He died in 1967 at the age of 62, having seen several of the boys who started on the Pittsburgh sandlots under his tutelage advance to the big leagues; many more were grateful for his continuing guidance through the years. ∎

Sources

In addition to the sources shown in the notes, the author used Baseball-Reference.com and:
Chester L. Smith, "The Village Smitty," *Pittsburgh Press*, July 5, 1944.
"Ottie Cochran Dies at 62 Playing Golf," *Pittsburgh Press*, April 30, 1967.

The author interviewed the following players:
Dick Groat, May 31, 2014.
Ralph Mauriello, January 18, 2015.
Paul Smith, September 15, 2015.

The following authors have contributed stories about the young players in this essay to the SABR Biography Project:
Alan Cohen, "Gino Cimoli"
Paul Geisler, "Bobby Locke"
John F. Green, "Russ Kemmerer"
Mark Sternman, "Glenn Beckert"
Clayton Trutor, "Ed Sadowski"
Joseph Wancho, "Tito Francona" and "Dick Groat"
Greg Zeis, "Bob Sadowski"

Notes

1. "Rice to Name Worthy Boy for All-Star Baseball Game," *Pittsburgh Press*, June 13, 1944.
2. Paul Kurtz, "Boys Set for All-America Contest: Polo Grounds is Scene Tomorrow of Baseball's Junior All-Star Clash," *Pittsburgh Press*, August 6, 1944.
3. "It's Cobb vs. Wagner Once Again," *Pittsburgh Post-Gazette*, May 10, 1946.
4. "Ivol, Esquire Boy, Drills with Pirates," *Pittsburgh Post-Gazette*, July 17, 1946.
5. Al Abrams, "Honus May Shift Ivol to Slab Role," *Pittsburgh Post-Gazette*, August 8, 1946.
6. Abrams, "Sidelights on Sports," *Pittsburgh Post-Gazette*, August 12, 1946.
7. Harry Keck, "Pie Traynor Points Way to Baseball Stardom," *Pittsburgh Sun-Telegraph*, July 9, 1947.
8. Danny Peary, *We Played the Game: 65 Players Remember Baseball's Greatest Era 1947–1964* (New York: Hyperion, 1994), 157.
9. Bill Heyman, "Hopper and Groat Win All-Star Berths: Players Shine as Teams Tie, 7–7," *Pittsburgh Sun-Telegraph*, August 6, 1947.
10. Heyman, "All-Stars See Giants in Action," *Pittsburgh Sun-Telegraph*, August 9, 1947.
11. Jimmy Dunn, "Ex-Pirates Have Been Teammates for Life," *Pittsburgh Post-Gazette*, July 30, 1997.
12. Chuck Greenwood, "A Baseball Career Spanning Five Decades," *Sports Collectors Digest*, July 24, 1998.
13. Charley Feeney. "Bartirome Finds His Niche as a Trainer," *Pittsburgh Post-Gazette*, March 13, 1967.
14. Andrew Dugo, "Neil Stoernell, Bobby Locke Win N. Y. Trip," *Pittsburgh Sun-Telegraph*, August 6, 1952.
15. Ralph Mauriello, *Tales Beyond the Dugout: The Zany Antics of Ballplayers in the Fifties* (Los Angeles: Mauriello Publishing, 2017), 68.
16. "Tan Diamond Star to Perform in N.Y.," *Pittsburgh Courier*, August 1, 1953.
17. Bill Nun Jr., "Are the Bucs Missing a bet in Claude Agee?" *Pittsburgh Courier*, August 29, 1953.
18. Tony Constantine, "Postscripts," *Morgantown Post*, August 19, 1958.
19. Dugo, "Popovich, Kunzler Picked for Hearst All-Star Game," *Pittsburgh Sun-Telegraph*, August 8, 1958, 15.
20. Dugo, "Tele Stars Shining - Even in Daylight," *Pittsburgh Sun-Telegraph*, August 6, 1958.
21. Dugo, "Donaldson, Beckert Get New York Trip," *Pittsburgh Sun-Telegraph*, July 15, 1959, 26.

Turning the Pirates' Ship

Francis Kinlaw

In 1950 the Pittsburgh Pirates resembled too well
The woeful Washington Nats;
With the fans' only reason for interest and hope,
Contained in Ralph Kiner's bats.

The Senators and Pirates were symbols of defeat
On stages and movie screens:
Damn Yankees was based upon Senators losses . . .
In Pittsburgh, Angels (in the Outfield) intervened.

For eight years in the Fifties, the Bucs finished seventh or eighth,
With the cellar five times claimed outright;
In each of those seasons they were so far from first place,
Pennants weren't remotely in sight.

Around the same time, Abbott and Costello drew laughs
With an exchange that left audiences amused;
In "Who's on First?" Bud did his very best to explain
As Lou only grew more confused!

With Pirate rosters filled with few household names,
What would Costello have thought
If instead of "Who," "What," or "Today," he were told
The true names of guys holding a spot?

The real first sacker never was "Who,"
But observers might have said, "Who is he?"
When holding on runners, or awaiting a toss,
A Hopp, Ward, or Fondy they'd see.

Jack Phillips and Bartirome, in those lean early years,
Also donned a first baseman's mitt;
Despite their best efforts, neither performed well enough
To make the organization commit.

In '56, a first sacker did make national news
By homering in eight straight games,
But elation waned as Dale Long's team hit the skids
And resumed its severe growing pains.

Nor did the fictitious fellow named "What"
Appear at the keystone spot;
Instead Merson and Murtaugh, Basgall and O'Brien
Gave second base their best shot.

That O'Brien was Johnny, not his twin brother Eddie—
The pair sometimes took the field together;
In '54 Curt Roberts called second his home,
While hoping each day to play better.

"I-Don't-Know" wasn't found near the hot corner,
In Forbes Field or in games on the road;
Castiglione, Cole, and Freese all did play there
Though their status as stars seldom glowed.

Pittsburgh's shortstops never uttered, "I don't give a darn"
As they tried to improve and excel;
They didn't succeed but they had a fine view
Of Pittsburgh's "basepaths carousel."

Behind the plate there appeared five masked men—
But not the imaginary "Today;"
Joe Garagiola and the others did all that they could
To keep rival basestealers at bay.

The name of "Tomorrow," the hurler on Abbott's team,
Held meaning for young guys on the farm
As they placed trust in the future and blossoming youth,
Along with sound pitching arms.

There were plenty of names, but not many well-known,
Among those who trekked to the mound;
Dickson and Surkont, LaPalme and Lindell
Were a few Branch Rickey had found.

Dick Littlefield was another one of the bunch
Who pitched in a very large yard;
Forbes Field was spacious with very wide gaps
That swallowed sharp liners hit hard.

Marginal players filled out the various rosters
In each of those frustrating years:
Gair Allie, and Atwell, Macdonald and McCullough,
Came with cold Iron City beer.

The O'Briens and O'Connell, Strickland, Shepard, and Sandlock,
And slugging Frank Thomas, of course,
Whose offensive stats, far better than most,
Eased mood swings bent toward remorse.

Howie Pollet, Bob Purkey, a Hogue and a Hetki,
Dick Hall, Woody Main and Red Munger,
A Werle and a Wilks, a Queen and a Chambers…
All afflicted with "pennant-race hunger."

The losses and pain continued until '58
When maturing finally occurred;
Second place lifted spirits, good times lay ahead—
Valid hopes for a flag had been stirred!

Mazeroski, Groat, Clemente, Virdon, and Skinner
All played quite well in that year;
The pitching of Law and Kline and Friend and Face,
Signaled big celebrations were near.

Danny Murtaugh had now returned to the scene
As manager of an expected rebirth;
That new dawn would be realized just two years hence
When his second sacker shook the earth!

Forbes Field, early 1960s.

Ralph Kiner and Branch Rickey

Not a Happy Marriage

John J. Burbridge, Jr.

INTRODUCTION

Branch Rickey assumed the duties of executive vice president and general manager of the Pittsburgh Pirates on November 3, 1950. Given Rickey's accomplishments, there was significant hope that the Pirates would become a force in the National League. Rickey brought to Pittsburgh his philosophy of winning, which was that it couldn't be done unless you built up the minor-league assets of the franchise. Rickey also was partial to athletic players who could run fast and were good fielders. Rickey also felt it more desirable to trade a proven player one year too early than one year too late.

The Pirates had one proven star: home run-hitting Ralph Kiner. Given that Kiner was slow afoot and had starred for the Pirates between 1946 and 1950, many in Pittsburgh believed that Rickey would trade him quickly. Kiner did stay with the Pirates during 1951 and '52, leading the league in home runs both seasons, as he had in the previous five. However, hard feelings developed between Rickey and Kiner, resulting in the slugger being traded to the Chicago Cubs in 1953. This paper explores the relationship between Rickey and Kiner and will conclude with some comments on Rickey's performance in Pittsburgh, his treatment of Kiner and Kiner's thoughts on Rickey's legacy.

KINER IN HIS EARLY YEARS AS A PIRATE

Ralph Kiner joined the Pittsburgh Pirates in 1946. A right-handed hitter, Kiner had a reputation as a slugger in the minor leagues. He fulfilled such promise by leading the NL in home runs every year from his rookie season through 1952. Johnny Mize tied Kiner in 1947 and 1948. In 1947, Kiner teamed up with Hank Greenberg, who had been sold to the Pirates by the Detroit Tigers. To facilitate these two right-handed sluggers, the Pirates reduced Forbes Field's home run distance to the left field foul pole from 365 to 335 feet and dubbed the area beyond the fence Greenberg Gardens. With their slugging duo, the Pirates saw their home attendance increase by 71 percent from the year before. That was Greenberg's only year in Pittsburgh, and in 1948 the area was renamed Kiner's Korner.

Attendance increased another 18 percent in 1948 as the Pirates drew more than 1.5 million fans, the most in the National League.

While Kiner was leading the NL in home runs, the Pirates were mediocre on the field, finishing in the second division in the NL in each of the five postwar years before Rickey's arrival except 1948, when they finished fourth. While 1949 and '50 attendance did not match the 1.5 million in 1948, attendance in both years exceeded 1 million.

Kiner also became a celebrity off the field. In 1946 singer and movie star Bing Crosby became a minority owner of the Pirates. Crosby introduced Kiner to his Hollywood friends while playing tennis and golf in Palm Springs, California. In 1949, Kiner escorted 17-year-old Elizabeth Taylor to the Hollywood premiere of *12 O'Clock High*.[1] Kiner settled in Palm Springs and had Hollywood movie stars as his neighbors and fellow golfers. In 1951 he married tennis star Nancy Chaffee.

RICKEY JOINS THE PIRATES

In 1950, Brooklyn Dodgers President Branch Rickey lost a power struggle for leadership of the team. Rickey was aware that Walter O'Malley, another executive with the club, was eager to take control. As a result, Rickey laid the foundation to assume an executive role with the Pirates.

In the history of the game of baseball, Rickey is a legend, having orchestrated front office dealings that resulted in pennants for both the St. Louis Cardinals and the Dodgers. Rickey also created the concept of the farm system, which revolutionized player development. Of course, Rickey is best known for breaking the color barrier with the signing of Jackie Robinson.

On November 3, 1950, Rickey, no longer affiliated with Brooklyn, agreed to a five-year contract for $100,000 per year—about $1 million a year in 2018 dollars—with the Pirates as executive vice president and general manager.[2] The contract also called for Rickey to have an advisory role for an additional five years. John Galbreath, principal owner of the club, was mainly responsible for the signing. Interestingly, the other Pirates' owners, mainly Tom Johnson, were not aware of Galbreath's dealings with Rickey and his signing.[3] Purchasing castoffs such as Preacher Roe and Billy Cox from the Dodgers, Galbreath had developed a relationship with Rickey.

Rickey had high hopes for the Pirates. He started what he termed a five-year plan and also revamped the player development and scouting functions. He was cautious in his comments about Kiner. Many of the scribes covering the Pirates assumed Rickey would deal Kiner since he was slow afoot and not the most adept left fielder. In one of Rickey's early statements as general manager, he attempted to defuse such views: "We don't have enough Kiners on the Pittsburgh club, so why would I trade the one I have? We don't intend on trading Kiner."[4]

EARLY SIGNS OF DISSATISFACTION

During spring training in 1951, rumors spread that Kiner was going to be tried at first base. Dan Daniel, the legendary baseball writer for the *World Telegram and Sun*, inferred this move was initiated by Rickey. Billy Meyer, whom Rickey had kept on as manager, responded, "Kiner handles the glove pretty well, but I am not kidding myself about his ability to adapt himself to the general defensive scheme of a first sacker."[5]

The Pirates' performance in 1951 was disappointing. They finished in seventh place with a 64–90 record, with Kiner's 42 home runs leading the league. Rickey became aware the Pirates were in significant financial straits because of a decline in attendance and other issues, and called for some moves to lower costs—but no cuts in player salaries. Rickey's dissatisfaction with

Ralph Kiner.

Kiner grew when the star went directly to Galbreath with a request for a salary increase. Galbreath and Kiner finally settled for $90,000 for the 1952 season, a raise of $25,000, while most Pirates received no increase.[6] This salary made Kiner the highest-paid player in the major leagues. This issue further exacerbated Kiner's less than positive relationship with Rickey.

THE RELATIONSHIP BECOMES CAUSTIC

Seven days after receiving Kiner's contract for 1952, Rickey went into attack mode. He wrote a 15-page "Personal and Confidential" memo to Galbreath detailing his negative views concerning Kiner. Included in the memo is a ditty he composed contrasting Kiner to Babe Ruth:

> Babe Ruth could run. Our man cannot.
> Babe Ruth could throw. Our man cannot.
> Babe Ruth could steal a base. Our man cannot.
> Babe Ruth is a good fielder. Our man is not.
> Ruth could hit with power to all fields.
>   Our man cannot.
> Ruth never requested a diminutive field
>   to fit him. Our man does.[7]

In the last sentence, Rickey was referring to Kiner's Korner. The memo also criticized Kiner's love for golf, his sharing an apartment with another person who was known for "promiscuous domestic infidelity," Kiner's role as the player representative, and his habit of requesting special privileges that were beyond what should be expected of a ballplayer. Rickey also pointed out that Kiner's speed and arm strength had deteriorated.[8] There is no doubt that Rickey was laying the groundwork necessary to convince Galbreath that Kiner needed to be traded.

The 1952 season was terrible for the Pirates and not a great year for Kiner, although he did lead the NL once again in home runs. His batting average was .244 and he did not reach 100 RBIs. The Pirates had a woeful record of 42–112, and attendance plummeted to 686,673 fans. It would seem that Rickey's situation in Pittsburgh was becoming somewhat precarious, although Galbreath still seemed confident in Rickey's leadership, and Rickey showed little concern.

1953 SEASON CONTRACT DISPUTE

After receiving Rickey's memo, Galbreath agreed to have Rickey negotiate Kiner's salary for the 1953 season. As a result, Kiner knew that the salary negotiations would be much more difficult. With the poor performance of the Pirates and Kiner's subpar year, it

Branch Rickey.

was leaked to the press that the Pirates were thinking about offering Kiner a 25 percent cut from his 1952 salary.[9] Rickey's son, Branch Jr., and Rickey both ventured westward to meet Kiner in California to try to convince him to accept such a pay cut. Kiner responded with the following: "The ball club has always been very good to me, and I'll go along with a salary cut this year but not 25 percent."[10]

Rickey issued the following memorable statement to Kiner during the negotiations: "We finished in last place with you. We can finish in last place without you."[11] Rickey was not hesitant in making the contract negotiations public, and when he did, his comments tended to degrade Kiner as looking for additional money and perks.

The Pirates arranged for spring training in 1953 to be conducted in Havana, Cuba. The spring training schedule called for 24 night games. Several Pirates players were not happy with that many night games and they complained to Kiner, the players' representative. Kiner took the protest to NL President Warren Giles and Commissioner Ford Frick.[12] While no changes were made, such a protest must have irked Rickey.

At a February 13 meeting, presumably about Kiner's contract, Rickey offered Kiner the inducement to come to spring training on March 15 rather than March 1, the official beginning of camp.[13] Kiner agreed. However, the contract with Cuban officials stipulated that Kiner be on hand at the beginning of spring training, so Rickey asked Kiner to show up on March 1 after all.[14] Since Kiner had not signed by March 1, he did not show up and became an official holdout.

One report states that Kiner wanted to report later than March 1 because his gift shop in Palm Springs demanded his attention, the beginning of March being the busy season.[15] Obviously, such a request would have angered Rickey and other Pirates' officials. That report also said the Pirates were definitely through with Kiner.[16]

On March 11, Kiner received a letter from Rickey, but the proposal was not agreeable to him. He sent a wire back to Rickey saying that he would report provided he receives a salary of $76,500, a 15 percent cut. Interestingly, Rickey had made such an offer in their February 13 meeting. Rickey then sent a telegram to Kiner agreeing to $76,500 but saying Kiner had until midnight on March 15 to agree or he'd have to take a 25 percent cut.[17] Kiner was quoted by a Pittsburgh newspaper replying, "The only delay in my accepting Pirates terms is salary, and I maintain my legal rights to hold out because of salary difference. Other players have done it, but never has any player had his character questioned or taken the verbal beating I've been subjected to."[18] Kiner signed the contract before midnight on the 15th. The holdout was over.

The relationship, not good before, was further damaged by these negotiations. Rickey was now publicly trying to trade Kiner and Kiner was bitter. Years later, Kiner said about Rickey, "He was a hypocrite. He would use any means to sign a ballplayer for as little as he could get him."[19]

PIRATES NO MORE

Finally, on June 4, 1953, it was announced that Kiner and three other players had been traded to the Chicago Cubs for six players and cash. Many Pittsburgh fans reacted angrily to the news of the popular slugger's trade. However, while Kiner performed well in 1953, Rickey was right that Kiner's future was somewhat bleak given advancing age and back problems. The Pirates finished in the cellar, losing over 100 games.

During the 1954 season, it became known that Rickey would step down when his five-year contract ended at the end of the 1955 season.[20] Rickey's support had significantly eroded, so his announced departure was not surprising.

KINER SPEAKS HIS MIND

After his baseball career was over, Kiner began what would be a 52-year career as an announcer for the New York Mets. He also had a television show after games called *Kiner's Korner*. In 1999, Kiner delivered the keynote address to the New York State Bar Association Labor and Employment Law Section's Annual Meeting held in Cooperstown, New York, in which he recalled his experiences dealing with Rickey and as the player representative for the National League. He also addressed the 1946 initiative by Robert Murphy to organize the Pittsburgh Pirates and the Pirates voting not to strike during midseason.

Kiner recounted bargaining with Rickey over his 1953 salary and erroneously stated that he ended up signing the $90,000 contract with the 25 percent cut. He then said: "Branch Rickey's bargaining tactics were actually one of the reasons that led baseball players to unionize in order to gain representation in the contract negotiation process."[21] There is no doubt that Rickey was a hard bargainer, but it was the contract renewal option commonly referred to as the "reserve clause" that gave him the clout he needed.

CONCLUSION

When Branch Rickey joined the Pirates organization, he had some nice words to say about Ralph Kiner. From that point forward, the relationship between the two went downhill. Obviously, Kiner's role as player representative, his celebrity status, his ability to negotiate salary with John Galbreath, and his lifestyle all contributed to Rickey's distaste for the home run hitting star. It is somewhat surprising, given Rickey's stature in the game and his role in breaking the color barrier, that he would resort to the tactics he employed in dealing with Kiner. As Bill James wrote: "Rickey, in one of the oddest moves of his career, [began] systematically destroying Kiner's reputation as a player, so that he could trade him, it's nuts."[22] This was not Branch Rickey's finest hour. ∎

Notes

1. Ralph Kiner with Danny Peary, *Baseball Forever* (Chicago: Triumph Books, 2004) 164–65.
2. Murray Polner, *Branch Rickey: A Biography*, (New York: New American Library, 1982), 223; "CPI Inflation Calculator," U.S. Bureau of Labor Statistics, https://data.bls.gov/cgi-bin/cpicalc.pl?cost1= 100%2C000.00&year1=195011&year2=201803.
3. Andrew O'Toole, *Branch Rickey in Pittsburgh* (Jefferson, NC: McFarland), 15.
4. O'Toole, 18.
5. Dan Daniel, "Kiner Experiment Not Promising," *New York World-Telegram & Sun*, March 20, 1951.
6. Warren Corbett, "Ralph Kiner," SABR Biography Project, http://sabr.org,bioproj/person/b65aaec9; Ralph Kiner, Baseball-Reference.com, https://www.baseball-reference.com/players/k/kinerra01.shtml.
7. Polner, *Branch Rickey*, 230.
8. O'Toole, *Branch Rickey in Pittsburgh*, 183–91.
9. Lester Biederman, "Pirates Prepare to Trim 25 Per Cent from Kiner's 90-G Salary," *Pittsburgh Press*, December 7, 1952.
10. O'Toole, *Branch Rickey in Pittsburgh*, 96.
11. O'Toole, 97.
12. Biederman, "The Scoreboard," *Pittsburgh Press*, December 31, 1952.
13. Associated Press, "Kiner Standing Pat Despite Rickey Offer," *New York World-Telegram & Sun*, March 12, 1953.
14. Associated Press.
15. Joe Williams, "Pirates, Through with Kiner, Face a Cold Market," *New York World-Telegram & Sun*, March 10, 1953.
16. Williams.
17. "Kiner, Though Hurt and Baffled, Stands Pat in Feud with Rickey," *The New York Times*, March 16, 1953.
18. O'Toole, *Branch Rickey in Pittsburgh*, 98.
19. O'Toole, 99.
20. "Rickey to Resign Management of Pirate Club in '55," *Pittsburgh Post-Gazette*, August 14, 1954.
21. Ralph Kiner, "The Role of Unions and Arbitration in Professional Baseball," *Hofstra Labor and Employment Law Journal*, Vol. 17: Iss. 1, Article 8, 3.
22. Corbett, *Ralph Kiner*.

The Pittsburgh Pirates Go to the Movies

Ron Backer

Small-market teams often complain about the unfairness of baseball's financial structure, contending that teams in large markets have disproportionate access to money to spend on players, giving them an unfair competitive advantage. Big-market teams disagree. But when it comes to the movies, there can be no argument. At the cinema, big-city teams such as the New York Yankees, Brooklyn Dodgers, Boston Red Sox, and Chicago Cubs have disproportionately dominated teams from smaller markets, with one important exception: the Pittsburgh Pirates. The Pirates have appeared in so many movies that they actually rival the Yankees in silver-screen dominance. This article will look at the many times the Pittsburgh Pirates have gone to the movies.

ANGELS IN THE OUTFIELD (1951)

The most famous film to feature the Pirates involves an eight-year-old orphan, Bridget White, who has been praying for the hapless Pirates and their unsuccessful manager, Guffy McGovern, resulting in the Archangel Gabriel sending an aide, along with his heavenly choir of former baseball players (the Heavenly Choir Nine), to assist the Pirates during their games, resulting in the Pirates playing for the pennant on the last day of the season. Much of the film was shot in Pittsburgh, particularly in Forbes Field, the home of the Pirates from 1909 until the ballclub moved into Three Rivers Stadium in 1970 and began to share the new multi-sports field with the Pittsburgh Steelers.

Angels in the Outfield is a tribute to the famous ball yard, with its ivy-covered walls (and no advertising on the walls), the scoreboard in left field in which the numbers were inserted by hand, a center field so deep (457 feet) that the batting cage was placed there during the game, the roofs of the Carnegie Library and Carnegie Museum visible from beyond the left-field wall, and the Cathedral of Learning of the University of Pittsburgh seemingly bending over so that it can get a better view of the action from its perch outside the bleachers down the left-field line. The film also contains cameos from famous Pirates players. Pie Traynor, the Hall-of-Fame third baseman and former manager of the Pirates, has a brief moment as a bullpen coach, and then-current outfielder Ralph Kiner hits a home run in the film.

In 1951, when MGM had to decide which major-league team most needed the help of angels to compete, the choice of the Pirates must have been easy. While the team had the presence of Kiner, the National League leader in home runs for seven consecutive seasons starting in 1946, not much else was going well for the team after the end of World War II.[1] In fact, from 1946 to '57, the Pirates finished in the top half of the National League in only one year, and that was a fourth-place finish in 1948. In 1950, the year before *Angels in the Outfield* was released, the Pirates finished in last place, 33½ games out of first. The Pirates would go on to lose over 100 games in 1952, '53, and '54. In two of those years, the team finished more than 50 games out of first place.[2]

Of course, as bad as the '50s Pirates were, they were never as bad as they are characterized in *Angels in the Outfield*. If the film were to be believed, there were occasions when a Pirates player rounded second and then decided to go back to first, causing a head-on

After another Pittsburgh Pirates' loss early in *Angels in the Outfield* (1951), before the angels arrive to help the cellar dwellers, Manager Guffy McGovern (Paul Douglas), second from the left, has an argument with Pitcher Saul Hellman (Bruce Bennett).

collision with another runner; a fielder got hit in the head by a pop-up; three Pirates runners ended up on third base at the same time; and Pittsburgh lost a game to Cincinnati, 21–2. All of those incidents are examples of cinema exaggeration for the sake of comedy. Nevertheless, the travails of the '50s Pirates were so well known at the time that in the classic 1954 film *On the Waterfront*, which involves a New Jersey dock strike and has nothing to do with Pittsburgh or baseball, a character complains that his coat is full of more holes than the Pittsburgh infield.

CHASING 3000 (2007)

It was the last week of September 1972 and the baseball world was excited about the possibility that Roberto Clemente would get his 3,000th hit. Two teenage Pittsburgh natives and huge Roberto Clemente fans, Mickey and Roger, have recently moved to California because of Roger's health problems. When their mother goes out of town on a business trip, Mickey and Roger decide to drive the family car back to Pittsburgh to see, in person, Clemente reach the 3,000-hit plateau.

Chasing 3000 is primarily a road movie about Mickey and Roger's eventful trip back to Pittsburgh, but baseball and Pittsburgh are the themes throughout. Mickey and Roger constantly discuss Clemente as archival footage of Clemente hitting, catching, and throwing is shown to the viewer. There are lots of Pittsburgh references in the film, such as Isaly's chipped ham sandwiches, Clark candy bars, and a hot dog shop known as "The Dirty O."

It is not giving anything away to disclose that despite the travails during their road trip, Mickey and Roger do get to Pittsburgh by the end of the movie, just in time to see The Great One achieve his great accomplishment. The moment occurred on September 30, 1972, at Three Rivers Stadium during a game between the Pirates and the New York Mets. In the bottom of the fourth inning, Clemente, in his second at-bat of the day, smacked a line drive to left-center field. The ball hit off the wall on one bounce. Clemente ended up on second base with a double. It was his 3,000th career hit, and as the scoreboard flashed on that day, "Roberto is now one of 11 players in major league history to get 3000 or more hits."[3] Well-known footage of Clemente reaching the milestone is incorporated into the new footage shot for *Chasing 3000*, making it appear that Mickey and Roger are really in Three Rivers Stadium in 1972, despite the fact that the film was shot many years after Three Rivers Stadium had been demolished.

This statue of Roberto Clemente in Roberto Clemente State Park in the Bronx, New York City, memorializes Clemente's pose on second base in Three Rivers Stadium in Pittsburgh on September 30, 1972, after getting his 3,000th career hit.

The story of the film is told in retrospect by a grown-up Mickey to his two teenage children, while they are on their way to PNC Park for Roberto Clemente Day. Thus, at the end of the film, there are shots of PNC Park from the Clemente Bridge and shots of the Clemente statue situated outside the stadium.

42 (2013)

The second film biography of Jackie Robinson dramatizes three years of Robinson's life, 1945 (when he was playing in the Negro Leagues with the Kansas City Monarchs), 1946 (when he was playing in the International League with the Montreal Royals), and 1947 (when he was playing in the National League with the Brooklyn Dodgers). Through the magic of digital imagery, the major-league games in the film appear to take place in Ebbets Field, Shibe Park, Crosley Field, and Forbes Field, ballparks that had long since been demolished by the time of the movie's release.

There are two scenes at Forbes Field. The first involves a game on May 17, 1947. Fritz Ostermueller, pitching for the Pirates, deliberately throws a beanball at Robinson, hitting him in the head and knocking him down. The result is a bench-clearing argument. The second is a game on September 17, 1947, when, according to the film, the Dodgers won the pennant by winning the game on a late-inning home run by Robinson, coincidentally off Ostermueller. In fact, but less dramatically, Robinson's home run came in the fourth inning on that day, and the game only clinched a tie for the pennant.[4]

While the computer-generated effects work fabulously to make it appear that the games are really being played in the old ball yards, there are numerous inaccuracies when it comes to Forbes Field. For example, despite what is shown in 42, there was never advertising on or above the walls of Forbes Field; the batting cage, which was always placed during a game at the deepest part of center field, is missing in the film; the right-field stands did not wrap around the center-field wall; and the large scoreboard in left field was much closer to the left field line than is shown in the film.

There is also an ironic aspect of 42, at least in retrospect. In the film, it seems that general manager Branch Rickey's punishment for Dodgers players who do not want to play with Robinson is a trade to the lowly Pirates. For example, pitcher Kirby Higbe, who started the 1947 season 2–0 for the Dodgers, is traded by Rickey to the Pirates because of Higbe's unwillingness to play alongside an African American teammate.[5] (Higbe can be seen disgustedly saying "Pittsburgh" as he sits on the Pirates bench watching Robinson's movie-ending home run.) Later, in 1950, Rickey had a dispute with another owner of the Dodgers and left the organization. He then became the general manager of the Pirates, his personal banishment from the top tier of major-league baseball.[6]

BABE RUTH'S LAST GREAT DAY

In 1935, Babe Ruth was released by the Yankees and signed by the Boston Braves, finally providing National League fans with a chance to see the Great Bambino in person on a regular basis. Unfortunately, Ruth was 40 years old that year and in ill health. His season was a personal disaster. In late May, the Braves came to Pittsburgh for a three-game series, oddly, a Thursday-Friday-Saturday series. Ruth's batting average before the Saturday game was just .153 and he had only hit three home runs.[7] And then the spectacular happened.

On Saturday, May 25, 1935, Ruth hit three home runs in one game. To punctuate the event, Ruth's third home run was one of the longest he ever hit. The ball cleared the roof of the 86-foot high, double-decked right-field stands of Forbes Field and purportedly landed across the street from the ballpark. It was the first time anyone had ever hit a ball over the Forbes Field roof.[8] That moment, the greatest home run hitter of his generation accomplishing such a feat so late in his career, is so amazing that both of Ruth's sound film biographies re-create the scene.

William Bendix stars as Ruth in The Babe Ruth Story (1948). In this version of the incident, after being jeered by the crowd and a teammate for his poor play, Ruth hits those three home runs in succession, turning, as the film's narrator says, the jeers of the crowd into cheers. After then hitting a single in his fourth at-bat, Ruth removes himself from the game, permanently retiring from baseball. While that creates an interesting moment for the movie, in fact, Ruth did not quit baseball on that day, although several people, including his wife, Claire, suggested that he should. Ruth continued to play after he left Pittsburgh, appearing in the first game of a Memorial Day doubleheader in Philadelphia on May 30, then retiring a few days later.[9] Oddly, the film does not even mention that Ruth's final home run went over the right-field roof, perhaps because the film was not shot at Forbes Field and therefore there was no roof for the ball to go over. Thus, the film misses one of the most important attributes of Ruth's last great day.

The Babe (1992), starring John Goodman as the title character, cleverly uses that same game for the conclusion of the film, allowing Babe to walk off the field while he is on top, even though that part of the story, as noted above, is fictional. Forbes Field had been torn down by 1992 and the film technology that was used in 42 to re-create the ballpark was not readily available, so again, the spectacular nature of Ruth hitting a ball over the right-field roof could not be shown in the film. Instead, Ruth hits a ball over the low, center-field seats of the playing field used in the movie and the announcer incorrectly states that it was the first ball ever hit out of Forbes Field. In addition, Ruth calls his home run shot on his first home run, something he supposedly did in the 1932 World Series in Chicago and in other games, but not that day in Pittsburgh.

Both films also omit another intriguing fact about Ruth's last great day in Pittsburgh. Despite Ruth's four hits that day, a single plus the three home runs, and his six RBIs, the Braves lost to the Pirates, 11–7.[10]

ROOKIE OF THE YEAR (1993)

This comedy involves a 12-year-old boy, Henry Rowengartner, who, after recovering from an injury to his arm, discovers that he can now throw a baseball at an incredible speed. That leads to a stint as a major-league pitcher for the Chicago Cubs, where Henry's

Barry Bonds, then an outfielder for the Pittsburgh Pirates, strikes out against 12-year-old pitching sensation Harry Rowengartner in *Rookie of the Year* (1993).

throwing skills are so good that perhaps he could win Rookie of the Year honors.

Rookie of the Year contains a nice montage sequence that shows how effective Henry's fastball truly is. In quick succession, Bobby Bonilla, who was playing in his first season for the Mets in 1992 (the year the movie was filmed), after being an All-Star for the Pirates for many years; Pedro Guerrero, who was playing his last season of baseball for St. Louis in 1992 after a long career in the majors; and Barry Bonds, still an outfielder for the Pirates in 1992, each swing and miss one of Henry's pitches. In particular, Bonds, in his Pirates uniform, does a nice acting job after the strikeout, seeming to marvel at how fast Henry's pitches are. Interestingly, by the time the film was released in 1993, Bonds was playing for the San Francisco Giants, so the Pirates uniform he wore in the film was already out of date.

THE ODD COUPLE (1968)

Neil Simon's play opened on Broadway in March 1965, with Art Carney playing neat freak Felix Ungar, and Walter Matthau playing his best friend, the slovenly sportswriter Oscar Madison. When Felix's wife kicks him out of their home, he moves into Oscar's New York apartment, where the entire play takes place.

In the 1968 movie version, Matthau reprises his role as Oscar and Jack Lemmon plays Felix. As was common when stage plays were adapted into films, the action was opened up somewhat for the cinema. Thus, there are scenes on the streets of New York and in a bowling alley and a diner, and because Oscar was

a sportswriter, a new scene was specially written for Shea Stadium, then the home of the Mets. In that scene, Oscar is distracted by a phone call from Felix, causing Oscar to miss a triple play by the Mets.

The scene at Shea Stadium was filmed on June 27, 1967, just prior to an afternoon game between the Mets and the Pirates. Roberto Clemente was supposed to be the batter who hit into the triple play, but after thinking about the scene overnight, he turned down the part. Clemente was unhappy with the paltry sum being paid to each player, only $100, and he did not believe that his fans in Puerto Rico would understand him hitting into a triple play.[11] The task was handed over to the only other Pirate who had some kind of national recognition in those days, Bill Mazeroski, the hero of the 1960 World Series. Mazeroski bats in the fake game with Pirates first baseman Donn Clendenon on first base, outfielder Matty Alou on second base, and pitcher Vernon Law on third base. Mazeroski hits a one-hopper to Yankees third baseman Ken Boyer, who steps on third and throws the ball to Jerry Buchek at second, who tosses the ball to Ed Kranepool at first for a 5–4–3, around-the-horn triple play.[12]

THE PRIDE OF ST. LOUIS (1952)

While much of this biography of Dizzy Dean is fanciful, the film does accurately depict an incident that occurred in the third inning of the 1937 All-Star Game. With Dean on the mound, Earl Averill of the Cleveland Indians hit a sharp line drive back at the pitcher. The ball hit Dizzy in the foot, fracturing Dizzy's big toe. (Dizzy allegedly told the doctor that his toe was not fractured, it was broke.) Dizzy came back to pitching too soon after the accident, changing his throwing motion and hurting his arm. His famous fastball was quickly no more.[13]

That true incident leads to the most ludicrous scene in the film, when Dean is struggling on the mound in his first game back after suffering the injury. The opposing manager from the Pirates calls time and goes out to the mound to give Dizzy some advice about his pitching! For some reason, no one from the St. Louis team complains about the actions of the Pirates manager.

BRIEF MENTIONS

The first time the Pirates made it to the cinema was in 1906, very early in the silent era. The short film was called *How the Office Boy Saw the Ball Game*, a five-minute fragment of which survives to this day. In the movie, the title character deceitfully informs his boss that his grandmother has died, allowing him to leave work in order to see a New York Giants-Pittsburgh Pirates game. Watching from the top of a telephone pole outside the park through a telescope, the office boy has the opportunity to see Christy Mathewson pitching for the Giants and Honus Wagner batting for the Pirates.

In the famous conclusion to *The Natural* (1984), the New York Knights (a team approximating the New York Giants of the National League) is playing a team from Pittsburgh. While they have the word Knights spelled out on the front of their jerseys, the uniforms of the Pittsburgh team only have the word Pittsburgh. However, the radio announcer describing the game sometimes refers to the Pittsburgh team as the Pirates.

City Slickers (1991) involves three New Yorkers vacationing for several weeks on a cattle drive out West. One day at mealtime, two of the guys have an argument as to who is the best right fielder of their generation, Hank Aaron or Roberto Clemente. A woman in the group complains that she does not understand how men can spend so much time discussing the game and memorizing the names of the players, such as who played third base for the Pirates in 1960. The three guys respond, almost simultaneously, "Don Hoak."

Abduction (2011) is a spy movie shot in the Pittsburgh area. The climax of the film occurs inside and just outside of PNC Park, with most of the action filmed during a Mets-Pirates game played on August 22, 2010. (Perhaps the Mets were returning a favor to the Pirates from *The Odd Couple*, over 40 years before.) The teenage hero of the film, Nathan Harper, wears a Clemente jersey during the action sequence, and in the final shots of the movie, Nathan spends time with his girlfriend in the seats of an empty PNC Park.

Million Dollar Arm (2014) is based on the true story of a contest to find two young athletes from India who had never played baseball before but could be trained to become professional ballplayers within one year's time. Just before the closing credits, the film reveals, "Rinku Singh and Dinesh Kumar Patel were both signed by the Pittsburgh Pirates 10 months after the day that they first picked up a baseball. They were the first Indian athletes to be signed by a major American sports league."

CONCLUSION

There are other examples of the Pirates in the movies. The "Pittsburgh Team," never specifically identified as the Pirates, appears in *Hot Curves* (1930) and *It Happens Every Spring* (1949). Characters wear a Pirates hat or jersey in *Grand Canyon* (1991) and *The Next Three Days* (2010). Along with Harmon Killebrew and Bob Feller, Bill Mazeroski attends the funeral of a minor-league pitcher in *Pastime* (1990). Small-market team though it may be, the Pittsburgh Pirates have always been one of the most dominant organizations in baseball, at least when it comes to the movies. ∎

Notes

1. Warner Corbett, "Ralph Kiner," SABR Biography Project, http://sabr.org/bioproj/person/b65aaec9.
2. Pittsburgh Pirates Team History & Encyclopedia, Baseball-Reference.com, https://www.baseball-reference.com/teams/PIT.
3. David Maraniss, *Clemente: The Passion and Grace of Baseball's Last Hero* (New York: Simon & Schuster, 2006), 281–3.
4. Brooklyn Dodgers at Pittsburgh Pirates Box Score, September 17, 1947, Baseball-Reference.com, https://www.baseball-reference.com/boxes/PIT/PIT194709170.shtml.
5. Jules Tygiel, *Baseball's Great Experiment: Jackie Robinson and His Legacy* (New York: Oxford University Press, 1997), 168–72.
6. Lee Lowenfish, *Branch Rickey: Baseball's Ferocious Gentlemen* (Lincoln: University of Nebraska Press, 2007), 488–500.
7. Jack Zerby, "May 25, 1935: Ruth smashes 3 homers in final hurrah," SABR Games Project, https://sabr.org/gamesproj/game/may-25-1935-ruth-smashes-3-homers-final-hurrah.
8. Robert W. Creamer, *Babe: The Legend Comes to Life* (New York: Simon & Schuster, 1974), 397.
9. Creamer, 397–400.
10. Zerby, "May 25, 1935."
11. Steve Wulf, "December 31: ¡Arriba, Roberto!" *Sports Illustrated*, December 28, 1992, https://on.si.com/2HDSSUK; Bruce Markusen, *Roberto Clemente: The Great One* (New York: Sports Publishing, 2013), 166–67.
12. Barry Kremenko, "Maz Raps Into Triple Play, But It's Only for Hollywood," *The Sporting News*, July 15, 1967.
13. Peter Golenbock, *The Spirit of St. Louis* (New York: Avon Books, 2000), 207–9.

Roy Face's Incredible 1959 Season

Ed Edmonds

In 1959, ace Pittsburgh Pirates fireman Roy Face set a major-league record by winning 18 games in relief against one loss. His .947 winning average also established the record for pitchers with at least 15 decisions. Face's incredible numbers far exceeded those of the Pirates, who went 78–76 and finished fourth, nine games behind the National League champion Los Angeles Dodgers. In an era without established closers or setup men who pitched in only one inning, Face threw 93⅓ innings and pitched two or more innings in 24 of his 57 appearances. Face was retroactively awarded 10 saves for his 1959 efforts in 1969, when his performance was analyzed under the new rules established to determine saves. He was also charged with nine blown saves.

How did Face amass these impressive totals? Was it the result of entering numerous tie games and benefitting from Pittsburgh rallies? Did he surrender tying or go-ahead runs only to be bailed out by his team's offense? This article will present a narrative description of Face's season with an analytical breakdown of each of his 19 decisions. The article will also present a brief summary of his 10 saves. The primary source for this analysis comes from game breakdowns on Baseball-Reference.com and Retrosheet.

INTRODUCTION

After four minor-league seasons, Face, a Rule 5 draftee from the Brooklyn Dodgers, made the jump from the Class AA Fort Worth Cats to the Pirates for the beginning of the 1953 season. In his major-league debut against the Philadelphia Phillies on April 16, he retired Stan Lopata before giving up two doubles, a single, a walk, and another single before Johnny Hetki was summoned from the bullpen to replace the 25-year-old hurler. At 5-foot-8, Face was an unlikely candidate for major-league stardom, and he started the 1954 season with the Class AA New Orleans Pelicans, managed by Danny Murtaugh. Needing an off-speed pitch, Face ultimately mastered an uncommon one that would make him successful in a major league career that spanned 16 seasons and 848 appearances. As Jim O'Brien, the

author of numerous books on the Pirates, wrote in 2005: "He didn't invent the fork-ball, but he certainly made it famous. He still likes to show people how he placed the baseball between two of his fingers to throw that pitch. Most people can form a 'V' or victory sign, but Face can form a 'U' with his two fingers."[1]

An analysis of Face's 1959 season reveals two significant statistics. The first is that half of his 18 wins came when he entered a tie game. In three of those, he gave up the go-ahead run, but the Pirates rallied and gave Face the win. The second is that 11 of his wins, including the last eight, were in extra-inning games. There is an overlap of seven games in those two categories (May 3 and 7; June 8, June 18, June 25; August 30; September 19).

TIE GAMES

Face's first victory of the season came at Forbes Field at night on April 22 against the Cincinnati Reds, when he entered the game with the score tied, 7–7. Gus Bell greeted him with a home run to push the Reds ahead, 8–7. But Face retired the next six Reds and the Pirates scored two runs to secure the win.

Face's May 3 effort in the first game of a doubleheader was one of his strongest of the year. The score

Roy Face, the Pirates relief ace and winner of 18 of 19 decisions in 1959.

was tied 3–3, when he entered the game in the eighth inning in relief of Vern Law. He retired all nine Phillies batters that he faced and his teammates rewarded him with an extra-inning victory when Bill Mazeroski singled with the bases loaded and two outs in the 10th.

On May 7, Face relieved Law in the top of the 10th inning of a 4–4 game against the Phillies. Face pitched to four batters, surrendering only a two-out single to Ed Bouchee. Ted Kluszewski slammed a home run leading off the bottom of the inning to provide Face his fourth victory of the season.

Just a bit over one month later on June 8, Face entered a game against San Francisco in the ninth inning with the score 9–9. Although Face gave up three hits in the inning, the Giants could not score a run. Face pitched well in the 10th and 11th innings, retiring all six hitters he faced. The Pirates won the game in the bottom of the 11th when Harry Bright hit a three-run homer off Mike McCormick. The victory advanced Face's record to 8–0.

On June 14, Face was called in from the bullpen in the eighth inning of the first game of a doubleheader against the Dodgers with the score tied, 3–3. The Pirates scored three runs in the eighth inning to take the lead and Face shut down the Dodgers in the top of the ninth to record his 10th win. He struck out four of the eight Dodgers he faced.

He entered the June 18 game against the Chicago Cubs with the score tied, 2–2, in the bottom of the ninth. The Pirates scored twice in the 13th and Face was 11–0. He pitched to 18 batters in five innings, striking out four and reducing his ERA to 1.34.

On June 25, the Pirates and Giants were locked in a 1–1 pitching duel between Harvey Haddix and Stu

Vern "Deacon" Law, the dean of the Pirates starting staff with an 18–9 record. Roy Face won six games started by Law.

Miller. Face kept the Giants off the scoreboard by retiring seven of the first eight batters that he faced, with his lone hiccup a two-out walk to Darryl Spencer in the 11th inning. Roman Mejias delivered a two-run home run in the top of the 12th off Eddie Fisher to provide the winning edge for the Bucs, and Face held off the Giants despite giving up two singles and a walk. His ERA dropped to 1.18.

In the second game of a doubleheader against the Phillies on August 30, Face relieved Don Gross in the 10th inning of a 5–5 tie. He gave up a home run, but Dick Stuart kept Face's victory streak intact when he doubled home Don Hoak and Bill Virdon to provide the margin of victory in a 7–6 win.

Face picked up his only loss of the 1959 campaign against the Dodgers in the first game of a double-header on September 11. Eight days later, he came in against the Reds with the score tied, 2–2, in the ninth inning. Face pitched to 15 batters over four innings, giving up the go-ahead run to the Reds in the 12th. The Pirates bailed out their relief ace by scoring twice in the bottom half to claim a 4–3 victory.

The 1959 Pittsburgh Pirates. Roy Face is the first man on the far right of the chair-seated row.

Harvey Haddix, the winner of one-half of his 24 decisions in 1959. Face saved three of those wins.

MORE EXTRA-INNING WINS

Seven of the 11 extra-inning wins required a single extra frame, while the other four went 11, 12, 12, and 13. Eight of the extra-innings victories were at Forbes Field, a pretty strong number of walk-off wins. The seven games (May 3, May 7, June 8, June 18, June 25, August 30, September 19) Face won after entering a tie game that also went extra innings are detailed above. The other four games are discussed in this section.

On July 9, he came on in the ninth inning against the Cubs and gave up the tying run. Harry Bright, pinch-hitting for Virdon, singled in Roberto Clemente to win the game in the bottom of the 10th.

In the first game of a July 12 doubleheader against the St. Louis Cardinals, Face entered in the top of the eighth after Haddix, who'd started the inning with a 5–1 lead, gave up three runs. In the top of the ninth, Face gave up a run-scoring single to tie the score. Clemente singled in Dick Schofield with the bases loaded in the bottom of the 10th to give Face his 14th win.

Face relieved Law in the eighth inning at Wrigley Field on August 9 with the Cubs leading, 2–1. He gave up one run but Bob Skinner threw out Jim Marshall with another would-be tally at the plate. The Pirates scored two in the ninth to tie the game, 3–3, and then took a two-run lead in the top of the 10th inning on three hits and two walks. Face pitched to 13 batters and notched win number 15.

In the second game of an August 23 Sunday doubleheader against the Dodgers at Forbes Field, Face entered in the top of the ninth inning with the Dodgers leading, 3–2. Stuart singled in the tying run in the bottom of the ninth with two outs. In the top of the 10th, Face loaded the bases before getting pinch-hitter Carl Furillo to line out to left field. Face picked up win number 16 when Dick Groat singled off Don Drysdale to drive in Virdon with the winning run.

THE OTHER FIVE WINS

Face entered the April 24 game against the Phillies in the bottom of the seventh inning with the Pirates leading, 4–3, and retired one batter. The Phillies scored two in the eighth to take the lead, but the Pirates scored four in the top of the ninth to go ahead, 8–5. Although Face gave up two hits in the bottom of the ninth, the Phillies couldn't score and Face won his second game of the season.

On May 13, he came on against the Dodgers at the Los Angeles Coliseum in the bottom of the seventh inning with the Dodgers leading 4–3 and retired three of the four batters that he faced. In the top of the eighth, the Pirates scored three on a two-run homer by Stuart and a double by Mazeroski that scored Skinner. Face gave up two singles to begin the eighth inning before retiring the next three batters. In the bottom of the ninth, Face walked two Dodgers but finished off the next three to record his fifth win of the season.

The following evening, he entered the game in the bottom of the eighth with one out, runners on first and third, and the Pirates ahead, 6–3. The Dodgers quickly tied the game. In the top of the ninth, Stuart homered, and Face retired the Dodgers in order to close out the game and notch his sixth win.

In the second game of a May 31 Sunday doubleheader at Crosley Field, Face entered the game against the Reds in the bottom of the seventh inning of a slugfest with the Pirates ahead, 14–11. He earned the win as the most effective Pirates pitcher, retiring nine of the 10 batters he faced over the final three innings.

SOME DETAILS

One-third of Face's 18 wins came in games started by Law, the ace of Pittsburgh's starting staff. Ron Kline started four of the games Face eventually won. Haddix and Bob Friend each started two of the games Face ultimately won. His other four were in games started by Bennie Daniels, Dick Hall, Al Jackson, and Red Witt.

Face spread out his wins relatively evenly through the National League with one exception. He failed to record a decision against the Milwaukee Braves. Face recorded his most wins, four, over the Dodgers, the team that provided the reliever with his sole loss. He won three games each against the Cubs, Reds, Phillies, and Giants. He got only two wins against the Cardinals.

He was stronger during the first three months of the season. After struggling in his two April outings, which still produced victories, he won five games in both May and June. At the end of those three months, Face had a 1.17 ERA. He encountered some difficulty in July, when he recorded just two wins and his ERA increased to 1.61. His combined ERA for August and September was 5.13, and he completed the season at 2.60.

Nine of Face's 18 wins ended as one-run victories as did his loss, a 5–4 defeat to the Dodgers. Four of the wins were decided by two runs, with five more being three-run victories. In only one of the games, the June 25 win over the Giants, was the Pirates' opponent held to one run.

Eight of Face's 10 saves were bunched in May and June. Unlike his efforts in wins, which involved six games started by Law, Face saved only one of Law's starts. Haddix was the beneficiary of three of Face's saves while Daniels, Friend, and Kline won two games apiece that Face saved.

CONCLUSION

Roy Face's incredible 1959 season was the result of effective pitching and good luck. His 18 wins and 10 saves contributed to 36 percent of the games the Pirates won in 1959. The Pirates' fielding was strong in supporting the relief ace; only one of Face's 28 runs was unearned. He gave up but five home runs in 93⅓ innings. In 38 of his 57 appearances, Face did not give up a run. The Pittsburgh staff ERA was 3.90. Only Law and Face recorded an ERA below 3.00. Although the Pirates finished the season barely over .500, the 1959 season provided the foundation for the 1960 World Series champions, a 95–59 regular-season performance. ∎

Bibliography

Roy Face 1959 Pitching Game Log, Baseball-Reference.com, https://www.baseball-reference.com/players/gl.fcgi?id=facero01&t=p&year=1959.

Gary Gillette, "Roy Face," SABR Biography Project, http://sabr.org/bioproj/person/a959749b.

Retrosheet

Notes

1. Jim O'Brien, *Fantasy Camp: Living the Dream With Maz and the '60 Bucs* (Pittsburgh: James P. O'Brien, 2005), 364.

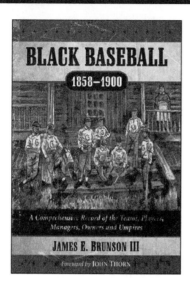
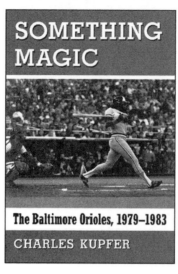
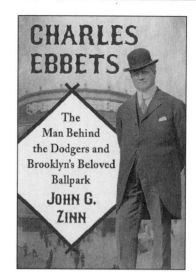
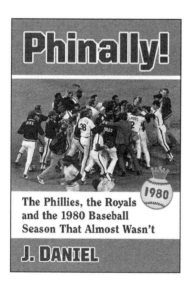
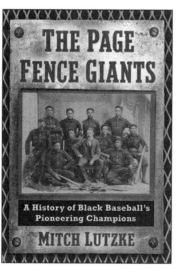

Cubs

Pirates Biggest Rivals?

William E. McMahon

L et me propose a hypothesis: The Cubs and Pirates are each other's biggest rivals. A few years ago I mentioned the idea to Cubs expert Art Ahrens (we were both in our cups), and he looked at me as if I were crazy. But I was researching the Cubs and the Pirates—my two favorite teams—and as I accumulated data, the conclusion became more and more convincing. In this paper I will recount the process which led to this conclusion.

Presumably, everyone knows what rivals and rivalry are, but let me take a moment to define terms. Free-dictionary.com gives the following definition of *rival*:

1. One who attempts to equal or surpass another, or who pursues the same object as another; a competitor.

2. One who equals or almost equals another in a particular respect.

The key conceptual features of rivalry are *competes with* and *on a (relatively) equal basis*.

The common belief is that the Cardinals and Cubs are each other's biggest rivals. As for the Pirates, who? The Phillies? For much of the history of baseball those two teams weren't competitive, and now that they aren't even in the same division, how can one call them rivals? But let me step back for a minute and consider all 15 present National League teams and evaluate them against the definition. We can eliminate the twentieth-century expansion teams, including the nearby Milwaukee Brewers, who have only been in the league a few years. We are looking at a period of at least 120 years, and teams that have entered the league since 1962 just don't count. That leaves the traditional eight teams, or six potential rivals for Pittsburgh besides the Cubs. The West Coast teams, the Dodgers and Giants, have been in another division since 1969, so they are out. Likewise the Braves.[1] The Phillies have been in another division since 1994 and, as noted above, for much of baseball history they were well below the Cubs and Pirates and therefore unable to

"rival" them. The Reds were in a different division from 1969 to 1993, so the Cubs were not really battling the Big Red Machine. So that leaves the Pirates and Cardinals as the major historical rivals of the Cubs. Let me begin, then, going era-by-era evaluating the match-ups of Cubs vs. Bucs and Cubs vs. Cardinals.

1887–1919

Before 1920, it isn't even close. The Cubs and Pirates were serious rivals, while the Cardinals were in another dimension. In 1887 the Pittsburgh team jumped from the American Association to the National League. Chicago had been in the league since 1876 and was its premier team. The St. Louis Browns, née Brown Stockings, were still in the Association. Up through 1891, the NL was either a six- or an eight-team league. From 1887 to '91, Chicago tallied the most wins, even though the club didn't win any pennants. Pittsburgh had the most losses, due to a dismal 1890, when they lost all their players to the Players League. Still, despite being a much weaker team, Pittsburgh gave Chicago a tough

Jim "Pud" Galvin won 16 and lost 11 against Chicago between 1887 and 1892.

battle on the field. The Cardinals were not in the picture yet. Still known as the Browns, they entered the National League with the merger of the NL and AA in 1892. The next era, then, is the 12-team league of 1892–99. It was not a good period for either Pittsburgh or Chicago, but they were essentially equal in mediocrity. In the standings, the Pirates were actually a shade better, eighth, while the Cubs were one place behind in ninth.[2] St. Louis? A solid 11th. After four seasons for which their average record was 37–99, the Browns' owner, Frank Robison, moved players from his other team, the Cleveland Spiders, so as to give St. Louis a respectable season in 1899.

The twentieth century begins the era when the American League became a competitor of the National. In the Deadball Era, 1901–19, Chicago and Pittsburgh were fierce competitors, while the Cardinals, as they were now called, still tail-enders. That's 25 percent of baseball history, and St. Louis isn't even in the picture.

1920–46

All three teams were pretty respectable in this era. Under Branch Rickey, the Cardinals began to improve in the '20s and won their first National League pennant and twentieth century World Series in 1926. Their greatest era was 1926–46, with nine pennants and six world championships. The Pirates won two pennants, one world championship. The Cubs had five pennants, winning every three years from 1929 to 1938 and then in 1945. However, when the Cardinals were good, the Cubs often were not, and vice versa.

The Cubs and Pirates finished first and second in the standings on three occasions, as did the Cubs and Cardinals. In overall standings, the Cubs finished closer to Pittsburgh 12 times, closer to St. Louis nine times, and five times they were equidistant. For the period of Cardinals dominance, 1926–46, the Cubs were closer to the Bucs 12 times, to the Cards six. Regarding the FAT (finished adjacent to) figure, it was Pirates 14, Cardinals eight. In head-to-head competition, the Cubs played Pittsburgh more evenly (.490) than they did St. Louis (.471). So even in this period, the strongest in Cardinals history, where all three teams were respectable, the Cubs were a bit more comparable to the Pirates.

1946–68

For me, the next baseball era goes from the end of World War II to the second expansion of the twentieth century and the beginning of divisional play. The '40s and '50s were the days of my youthful association with Cubdom. I can't recall anything being made of a

rivalry with St. Louis much before 1970, and certainly not before 1960. That's because the Cards were contenders, while the Cubs were…doormats. And what other team was comparable in doormatness? Why, Pittsburgh, of course. Who can forget those epic battles for seventh place in an eight-team league? The Cubs won in 1950, '53, '54, '57, and, after the expansion to 10 teams, in 1963. The Bucs won in 1951 and '56, and, post-expansion, tied for sixth/seventh with LA in 1964 while the Cubs were eighth. They tied for seventh in 1957. Over the period the Pirates' average finish was seventh, the Cubs' eighth, using the method to assign points to places in the standings, i.e., in an 8-team league, 8 for first, 7 for second and so on. The Cardinals were tied for third with the Braves.

The period covered so far is almost exactly two-thirds of the history of the competition among these three teams: 1887 to 1968. And the data show the Pirates to be much more significant rivals for the Cubs than the Cardinals were. To amplify this point, let us take a closer look at the data. With respect to the Cubs, the stats for the Pirates and Cardinals are:

Finished 1–2	Pirates	Cardinals
1887–1900	0	0
1901–19	3	0
1920–45	3	3
1946–68	0	0
Total	**6**	**3**

Finished 2–3	Pirates	Cardinals
1887–1900	0	0
1901–19	3	0
1920–45	2	1
1946–68	0	0
Total	**5**	**1**

Finished Adjacent To	Pirates	Cardinals
1887–1900	5	2
1901–19	10	2
1920–45	14	8
1946–68	11	5
Total	**40**	**17**

Finished Closer To	Pirates	Cardinals	Equidistant
1887–1900	6	2	1
1901–19	15	4	0
1920–45	12	9	5
1946–68	11	10	2
Total	**44**	**25**	**8**

COURTESY OF THE PITTSBURGH PIRATES

Rip Sewell led all Pirates hurlers with a 36–19 record against the Cubs.

In one other index, head-to-head competition, in all four periods, the Cubs and Pirates were closer than the Cubs and Cardinals. The overall winning average of the Cubs vs. the Pirates (.497) is closer to .500 than that of the Cubs vs. the Cards (.521). The reason for this is the Cubs' dominance over the Cardinals in 1901–19, when Chicago won 271 and lost 131. However, there is one oddity concerning the series for each season. Against the Pirates, the Cubs won the season series 33 times, Pittsburgh 34 times, and there were 15 ties. The Cubs beat the Cardinals 34 times, lost 33 times, and there were 10 ties. That would appear fairly even, except in years when one team dominated.

Again, two thirds of baseball history—and the Cubs and Pirates are unquestionably each other's biggest rivals. So what is this business about the Cubs and Cardinals? To understand that, we have to consider the last third of the history, the era of division play since 1969.

Roberto Clemente and Ernie Banks Head to Head

Through 1960	AB	H	2B	3B	HR	RBI
E. Banks	612	203	28	11	40	121
R. Clemente	389	113	13	5	7	44
After 1960	**AB**	**H**	**2B**	**3B**	**HR**	**RBI**
E. Banks	597	141	23	1	17	66
R. Clemente	777	261	35	14	34	142

1969–93

This is the period when all three teams competed in the Eastern Division. It is also the heyday for the Pirates, who won nine division titles, while the Cardinals won four and the Cubs only two. For the period, the Pirates were the best team overall in the division, while the Cards were second (they were third and fourth in the National League). Then there are the Cubs. They were clearly last in the Eastern Division, even behind the expansion Montreal Expos. Fortunately, they weren't quite last in the league, as Atlanta and San Diego in the Western Division both had worse records. The legend of a Cubs-Cardinals rivalry appears around the beginning of this era. Actually, the Cubs aren't rivals of either team except in one interesting respect: head to head. The other data:

	Pittsburgh	St. Louis
Finished 1–2	2	0
Finished 2–3	2	1
Finished Adjacent To	8	8
Finished Closer To*	10	14

*1 equidistant

But perhaps perceiving the Cards as arch-enemies spurred the Cubbies to greater effort against them. Whereas their winning average against Pittsburgh was a feeble .406, the Cubs actually came out ahead of St. Louis, winning 220 games while losing 215. In season series, the Cubs were 2–20–3 against the Pirates, 12–9–4 against the Cardinals. So the head-to-head battles were very competitive, and the Cubs played their best against the Cardinals. Hence the Cards could be regarded as main rival for this period.

1994–2017

The Central Division was created in 1994 and expanded from five teams to six in '98. Again, since the Cubs, Pirates, and Cardinals have been in the same division, same league since 1892, they are inherent rivals. But what happened after 1993 was the collapse of the Pirates, coupled with a very strong showing by the Cards. The latter have 10 division titles, the Cubs five, and Pittsburgh none. The Cubs have not really been rivals of either the Cards or Pirates. Overall, St. Louis has been the top team in the division, Chicago fourth, and Pittsburgh sixth.[3] The other data:

	Pittsburgh	St. Louis
Finished 1–2	0	2
Finished 2–3	1	1
Finished Adjacent To	8	5
Finished Closer To*	11	11

*2 equidistant

HIGHLIGHTS OF THE CUBS-PIRATES RIVALRY[4]

1886 A portent of things to come? In an exhibition game on September 24, the mediocre Alleghenies from the Association defeat the NL champion White Stockings, 10–3.

1887 Sixth place Pittsburg takes the season series from third place Chicago, 12 games to 5. Jim Galvin, one of two significant (1000 IP for the team) Pirates pitchers in the Hall of Fame, wins 6 games. John Clarkson loses 7.

1888 On June 21, George Van Haltren pitches a six-inning no-hitter against Pittsburgh.

1900 Clark Griffith pitches a 14-inning shutout on June 19 to beat Rube Waddell and the Pirates. Waddell strikes out 12.

1902 On June 22, a pitching duel between Jack Taylor of the Orphans and Deacon Phillippe of the Pirates goes 19 innings, with Chicago finally winning, 3-2. The Pirates win their second straight pennant.

1908 The Cubs win their third pennant in a row, but only by beating the Pirates on October 4, 5–2. Although the Bucs take the season series 12–10, this loss drops them to third in the league by a half-game. The Cubs are tied with New York and have to replay a game necessitated by the Merkle boner. The Cubs win and go on to win the World Series again.

1909 This time the Pirates take the pennant with 110 wins, topping 104 by the Cubs. On June 30, the teams play the first game ever at Forbes Field. The Cubs win, 3–2.

1925 The Pirates win the pennant and the World Series, over the Washington Nationals. The Cubs finish eighth but take the season series, 12–10. On Opening Day at Wrigley Field on April 14, Quin Ryan broadcasts the first Cubs regular season game on WGN. Grover Alexander beats the Pirates, lacking only a triple to hit for the cycle.

1927 The Pirates win the pennant again but are demolished by the powerful New York Yankees in the World Series. On May 30, Jimmy Cooney makes an unassisted triple play, catching Paul Waner's liner, stepping on second to double off Lloyd Waner and then tagging Clyde Barnhart coming from first. The Cubs win to stop an 11-game Pirates winning streak. On November 28, the Cubs trade Sparky Adams and Pete Scott for Kiki Cuyler.

1938 After two years of the Cubs finishing second and the Pirates fourth and third, Chicago and Pittsburgh are in a pennant race that comes down to a three-game series in Chicago in late September. On the 27th, the Cubs win, 2–1. The game of the 28th is decided by Gabby Hartnett's famous Homer in the Gloaming. The score is tied, 5–5, in the bottom of the ninth with two out and the game about to be ended by darkness. Hartnett homers off Mace Brown to win. This appears to demoralize the Bucs. They drop out of first, and the next day the Cubs earn the sweep, 10–1, behind Bill Lee. The Cubs win the pennant.

1953 Branch Rickey, believing the Pirates could lose without him as well as with him, trades Ralph Kiner to the Cubs, who also get Howie Pollet, Joe Garagiola, and George Metkovich and send Toby Atwell, Preston Ward, Bob Addis, George Freese, Gene Hermanski, and Bob Schultz to the Pirates.

1955 Sam Jones pitches a no-hitter against the Pirates on May 12. Roberto Clemente breaks into the majors but bats only .194 against Chicago.

1956 On May 19, Dale Long begins a streak of homering in eight consecutive games with a blast against the Cubs.

1958 Circumstances force Long, traded to Chicago in 1957, to become the fifth left-handed catcher in Cubs history in the first game of a doubleheader vs. the Pirates.

1959 Although the Cubs win the game on June 5, Dick Stuart hits the longest home run in Forbes Field history off Glen Hobbie. The ball sails over the 457-foot sign in center field. Earlier, Banks had hit one over the 436-foot sign in left-center.

1960 The Pirates win the pennant, beating the seventh-place Cubs 15 times. They go on to shock the Yankees in the World Series. On May 4, announcer Lou Boudreau swaps positions with Manager Charlie Grimm as the Cubs beat the Pirates, 5–1. On June 26, Ron Santo breaks in with the Cubs, leading them to a doubleheader sweep of the Pirates, going 3-for-7 with five RBIs.

1970 On June 28, in the final games at Forbes Field, the Pirates sweep a doubleheader, 3–2 and 4–1, before 40,918 fans.

1975 Rennie Stennett goes 7-for-7 in a 22–0 Pirates victory on September 16, with two doubles and a triple.

1978 The Pirates blow a 10–2 lead on September 19 but score in the 11th to win, 12–11. The winning hit is a home run by Dave Parker, who hits .478 against the Cubs, with five homers.

1980 The longest game in Cubs history by hours is a 20-inning, five-hour, 31-minute marathon at Three Rivers on July 6. It ends when Omar Moreno drives in Ed Ott. The Cubs get 13 scoreless relief innings, five by Bill Caudill.

1981 On May 25, losing 8–0 in the fourth inning, the Cubs come back to win, 10–9, in 11.

1990–92 The Pirates have the best overall record in the league and win three division titles. Their record against the second-division Cubs is 35–19. But they fail in the playoffs, to the Reds and then the Braves twice. The Pirates wouldn't have another winning season until 2013.

1998 On December 14, Chicago gets Jon Lieber from Pittsburgh for Brant Brown. Lieber wins 20 in 2001, as well as going 7–1 against the Pirates over the next four years.

2003 On July 23, the Pirates trade Aramis Ramirez, Kenny Lofton, and cash to the Cubs for Jose Hernandez, Bobby Hill, and Matt Brubeck. The additions help the Cubs to win the division.

2015 The Cardinals (100 wins), Pirates (98), and Cubs (97) finish 1–2–3 in the division. In the wild-card game, the Cubs beat the Bucs, 4–0, on a shutout by Jake Arrieta, who had gone 3-1 with an 0.75 ERA against Pittsburgh in the regular season. They go on to beat the Cards, 3–1, in the Division Series but are swept by the Mets in the NLCS.

Feisty infielder Phil Garner scored the winning run in the bottom of the 18th on August 10, 1977, as the Pirates beat the Cubs, 2–1.

Head-to-head in this era, the Cubs and Cardinals have been competitive, with Chicago winning 184 and losing 195, a winning average of .485. The Cubs have a 202–172 record against the Pirates, a fairly dominant .540. The Pirates have fared even worse against the Cards, who have beaten them to the tune of 216–157 (.579).

So there isn't a *strong* rivalry between the Cubs and either team; the Cubs have sometimes been competitive, in which case they challenge the Cardinals. But they are also prone to bad years, when they are in a

class with the Pirates. Future tendencies are unclear. The Cubs' resurgence in 2016 gave rise to talk of a dynasty, but 2017 showed that may not happen. After 20 losing seasons, the Pirates appeared to be on the rise from 2013 to 2015, but they have regressed, and the future doesn't look promising.

Nevertheless, these three teams have been rivals since the nineteenth century, and the Cubs and Pirates have at least had a bit more of an even competition than that between the Cubs and Cardinals. The point of this paper is thus to correct a somewhat mistaken perception of the Cubs' rivalries over the years.

And finally, one may note that the *psychological* dimension of all this has been ignored. What do the fans think? And the media? Do the fans think what the media want them to think? For now, I'll dodge those questions and leave you to ponder the facts as they are. ■

Appendix
The author has compiled a stats comparison of significant players of the two teams which can be found online at SABR.org (https://sabr.org/node/50354).

Notes
1. For a brief period, essentially the '50s, the Milwaukee Braves were regarded as a rival of the Cubs because of proximity. Not only was that short-lived, but as the Braves were strong and the Cubs were weak, they weren't even competitive.
2. For the benefit of Cleveland fans it may be noted that the Spiders were third. And if you take away the horrible 1899 season, they jump past Baltimore to second.
3. The fifth place team, Milwaukee, entered the division in 1998. The Houston Astros were second when they were in the division, through 2012.
4. The compilation of these data was aided considerably by two books: Art Ahrens and Eddie Gold, *Day by Day in Chicago Cubs History* (West Point, NY: Human Kinetics, 1982); Morris Eckhouse and Carl Mastrocola, *This Date in Pittsburgh Pirates History* (New York: Stein and Day, 1980).

Carlos Bernier and Roberto Clemente

Historical Links in Pittsburgh and Puerto Rico

Thomas E. Van Hyning

Carlos Bernier was 26 years old when he broke the Pittsburgh Pirates' color line on April 22, 1953, nearly one year before Curt Roberts played his first game with the Pirates.[1] The controversial and temperamental outfielder was one of two Bucs, with Lino Donoso, a Cuban pitcher, who encouraged Roberto Clemente to refrain from emotional outbursts and temper tantrums in Fort Myers, Florida, during spring training in 1955. Bernier recognized Clemente's special baseball skills, having played against him in Puerto Rico winter ball the prior three seasons when Bernier's Mayagüez Indians faced Clemente's Santurce Crabbers.

The 20-year-old Clemente had a splendid 1954–55 season with Santurce, winners of the 1955 Caribbean Series in Caracas, Venezuela. Clemente played left field, with Willie Mays in center and Bob Thurman in right field. George Crowe, Ronnie Samford, Buster Clarkson, and Don Zimmer were a formidable infield. Harry Chiti or Valmy Thomas did the catching. Sam Jones, Rubén Gómez, and Bill Greason were the key starting pitchers. Clemente became property of the Pittsburgh Pirates via the Rule 5 draft on November 22, 1954. Branch Rickey—who saw Clemente play in Puerto Rico—wrote Clemente a letter dated November 30, 1954, saying that he "had a habit of taking an extra step or so before throwing the ball, and this should be corrected."[2] Clemente, Mays, and batboy Orlando Cepeda joined Santurce manager Herman Franks for 11AM practices to work on Clemente's throwing approach. These practices created a bond between Clemente and Mays.

BERNIER AND CLEMENTE'S CONNECTION TO NEGRO LEAGUERS

Was Bernier a black Puerto Rican? The literature review says yes. Pedrín Zorrilla, owner of the Santurce Crabbers from 1939 to 1956, alleged in August 1949 that the Negro Leagues transferred several contracts to organized-baseball clubs without the consent of these players' organizations in Puerto Rico. Zorrilla specifically referred to the cases of pitcher José Guillermo Santiago with Dayton and Carlos Bernier—"the flashy Mayagüez outfielder"—under contract with Bristol of the Colonial League. Santiago pitched for the 1947 and '48 New York Cubans. Bernier joined Bristol in 1949, then played in two games for Indianapolis, a Pittsburgh farm team, before returning to Bristol.[3]

Bernier dropped out of school in the sixth grade in Juana Díaz, a municipality nine miles east of Ponce and 26 miles west of Guayama. Cefo Conde, a star pitcher for the Guayama Witches with Satchel Paige in the late '30s and early '40s, was from Juana Díaz and was a mentor to Bernier. Conde brought the 19-year-old Bernier to Mayagüez in 1946 after the outfielder had been a plumber's aide, cut sugar cane, and served in the Army. Bernier looked up to Mayagüez teammates in the late 1940s, including Negro Leaguers Artie Wilson, Alonzo Perry, Wilmer Fields, Johnny Davis, and Luke Easter. A highlight of Bernier's 1948–49 postseason was the February trip to Havana, Cuba, for the first-ever Caribbean Series, where the host team won it all with Monte Irvin.

Clemente idolized Irvin and Larry Doby when they starred for the San Juan Senators in 1945–46 and 1946–47, when Clemente was 11 and 12.[4] He would take the bus from Carolina to Sixto Escobar Stadium, home of the Senators and the Crabbers. Six years later, Clemente, a Santurce rookie, was summoned by player-manager Clarkson to pinch-hit for Thurman in the eighth inning of a tie game in Caguas. Clemente's two-run double won it. When Thurman congratulated him it was his biggest thrill in pro baseball to that point. Clemente was an 18-year-old high schooler while Thurman was a hitting star for Santurce.[5]

BERNIER MAKES IT TO PITTSBURGH

The Pacific Coast League Hollywood Stars, not Pittsburgh, drafted Bernier on December 3, 1951, in the minor-league draft.[6] The 5-foot-8 Bernier, nicknamed "Bandit" and "Comet," batted .301 with nine home runs and 79 RBIs with the 1952 Stars, with a league-leading 105 runs and 65 stolen bases for manager Fred Haney. Groucho Marx spoke for the universe of Stars fans when he said, "Sending Bernier from the first-place Stars to the last-place Pirates would be a

Pittsburgh's two outfielders from Puerto Rico—Carlos Bernier, 1953 season (top), and Roberto Clemente, 1971 season (bottom).

demotion."[7] Bernier and pitcher Johnny Lindell were sold to Pittsburgh under a working agreement between the two clubs.

Bernier was fortunate the 1953 Pirates held their spring training in Havana. Rickey wanted the club to relocate away from Florida due to its 40–112 season in 1952. Havana was a better venue than Florida for Bernier because it had less racial tension and offered him a level of comfort as a Spanish-speaking Caribbean island. Cuban fans loved to bet on baseball games but were frustrated when Pirates manager Haney removed starting players early in games against the Philadelphia Athletics and a Cuban All-Star team.[8] Haney was impressed with Bernier, saying, "He can run, throw and go get a ball. ...first time I saw him last spring, I didn't think he could hit, but he fooled me. Once he gets on base, he's hard to stop. He's a streak."[9]

Bernier's 1953 highlight was three triples in a game against Cincinnati on May 2, 10 days after his debut. A hitting slump from mid-May to June 30 affected Bernier's playing time. Rickey weighed in on Bernier in late July: "He's a first-year player, strange to the language, nervous in the big leagues. He simply needs orientation."[10] For the season, Bernier batted .213 and stole 15 bases.

He had a fine 1953–54 winter season for Mayagüez. He was chosen over Santurce's Clemente to reinforce the Caguas Criollos in left field for the Caribbean Series, won by Caguas under player-manager Mickey Owen. Caguas bested Cuba, Panama, and Venezuela at Sixto Escobar Stadium. Bernier was cut by the 1954 Pirates in spring training and Swarthmore College graduate Dick Hall made the parent club instead. Bernier never played another regular-season game in the major leagues. He spent the next four years with the Hollywood Stars.

CLEMENTE, PITTSBURGH'S NEXT OUTFIELDER FROM PUERTO RICO

Fort Myers was intimidating and difficult for black players in 1955. Luis Arroyo, a St. Louis Cardinals pitcher, traveled with Clemente from Puerto Rico to ensure Roberto got situated before Arroyo went on to St. Petersburg. Clemente and other black players lived in the black Dunbar Heights neighborhood of Fort Myers, across the railroad tracks on the town's east side.[11]

Pittsburgh had six black players in camp: outfielders Bernier, Clemente, and Cuban Román Mejías, plus second baseman Roberts and pitchers Donoso and Domingo Rosselló. The Bernier-Clemente-Mejías trio made up the first black, all-Caribbean outfield in the majors when Pittsburgh visited the Phillies at Clearwater on March 13, 1955.[12]

Clemente impressed Rickey, manager Haney, and sportswriter Al Abrams, who wrote in the March 14, 1955, *Pittsburgh Post-Gazette*, "Clemente is an outfielder with the verve and showmanship of a Willie Mays, a player he imitates to quite a degree. ...Clemente will be the right Forbes Field ticket. The dusky Puerto Rican was the delight of more than 2,500 Floridians, transplanted Pittsburghers and just plain tourists. ...every time we looked up there was Roberto showing his flashing heels and gleaming white teeth to the loud screams of bleacher fans."[13] Clemente was guaranteed a roster spot on the 1955 Pirates, and followed Bernier's advice to focus on baseball.

TALENT, CONTROVERSIES, AND FINES

Clemente duplicated Bernier's three-triple game against Cincinnati on September 8, 1958, in his fourth big-league season.[14] He had a marvelous Caribbean Series for the 1957–58 Caguas Criollos, batting .391 in the 1958 classic hosted by Puerto Rico.[15] Clemente's career Caribbean Series batting average was .327, but his slugging average was more impressive.

Table 1. Top 10 Caribbean Series Slugging Average, 50+ Plate Appearances

Player	Country	SLG
Wilmer Fields*	Puerto Rico/Venezuela	.679
Armando Rios	Puerto Rico	.649
Willard Brown	Puerto Rico	.627
Roberto Clemente	Puerto Rico	.592
Carmelo Martínez	Puerto Rico	.589
Bob Thurman	Puerto Rico	.587
Héctor Rodríguez	Cuba	.583
David Ortíz	Dominican Republic	.579
Tony Pérez*	Puerto Rico	.576
Candy Maldonado	Puerto Rico	.573

* Wilmer Fields played two series for Puerto Rico and one for Venezuela. Tony Pérez is from Cuba but represented Puerto Rico in the Caribbean Series.

Bernier played for the Hollywood Stars in 1954–57; the Salt Lake City Bees in 1958–59; the Columbus Jets and Indianapolis Indians in 1960–61; and the Hawaii Islanders in 1961–64. He spent 1965 with the Reynosa Broncs in the Class AA Mexican League before a farewell winter with the 1965–66 Arecibo Lobos.[16] He was a superb player, though one with many suspensions and fines. Fans in Puerto Rico compared his hard-nosed, spikes-high style to that of Ty Cobb. His June 1954 fight with Los Angeles Angels infielder Bud Hardin resulted in a $50 fine and a suspension. Two months later, on August 11, Bernier was suspended for the rest of the season after slapping umpire Chris

Valenti. He admitted he was "not well; was beaned in 1948 and have been nervous and aching in the head ever since."[17] After the game, a tearful Bernier apologized to Valenti and they shook hands.[18] Bernier frequently scuffled with Angels second baseman Gene Mauch, who claimed Bernier would steal bases with Hollywood way ahead. Mauch repeatedly picked up dirt and threw it into Bernier's face after Bernier slid into second.[19] One prominent fight happened in Puerto Rico on November 5, 1955, when Mayagüez played Caguas. Gary Blaylock, pitching for Mayagüez, hit Vic Power with a pitch. Mayagüez's Jim Gentile was beaned by Tom Lasorda and a fight broke out. Bernier joined the fracas and got a black eye. Lasorda's uniform was ripped.[20]

Clemente, with San Juan, was involved in a dispute at first base in the tiebreaker game for fourth place at the end of the 1961–62 regular season. Umpire Mel Steiner called Clemente out at first on a close call on a grounder to Arecibo shortstop Germán Rivera. Clemente was cleared when he testified at a league hearing that he argued with Steiner, whose angle "was not a good one," adding, "My teammate Chico Ruiz grabbed me to keep Steiner from giving me the heave. ...If I had said something vulgar or even hit Steiner, he would have thumbed me out of the game." Doug Harvey, the umpire who handed Clemente the ball after hit number 3,000 with Pittsburgh on September 30, 1972, was at this hearing. He was an arbiter in the Arecibo-San Juan contest.[21]

Clemente showed less restraint in a May 1963 Pirates home game against Philadelphia. After first base umpire Bill Jackowski called him out on a double-play grounder, Clemente's five-minute rant included twice bumping Jackowski. National League President Warren Giles sent Clemente a telegram announcing his five-game suspension along with a $250 fine, calling his actions "the most serious reported to our office in several years."[22]

BERNIER AND CLEMENTE AS SAN JUAN SENATORS TEAMMATES

Bernier and Clemente were San Juan teammates in 1959–60 and 1960–61. The first of those teams went 41–23 in the regular season prior to a semifinal series win and a best-of-nine-finals loss to Caguas. Clemente batted .330, third in the batting race. Power, Caguas player-manager and batting champ, was not sure Clemente was going to be the superstar he became with Pittsburgh from 1960 on because of a bad back, but he never questioned Clemente's effort. Bernier's 21 stolen bases in 1959–60 were second to Caguas's Félix Mantilla, who stole 23. Clemente and Bernier finished second and third in triples with six and five, behind teammate Nino Escalera's seven.[23]

The 1960–61 San Juan club won the league finals over Caguas. Bob Leith, San Juan's owner, did not send player contracts out by the June 1, 1960, deadline, but Clemente agreed to $1,500 per month, the same salary from a year earlier. Bernier signed with San Juan but sat out 1961–62 due to a salary dispute. San Juan's imports, or stateside players, wanted more money to play in the February 1961 Interamerican Series, a four-team round-robin tournament hosted by Venezuela. Clemente displayed his leadership skills in a 10-minute closed-door meeting when he affirmed all players would receive the same salary stipulated in their contract, and he would call Commissioner Ford Frick if they refused to honor their contracts.[24] San Juan fell short, with two losses to Bob Gibson of the Valencia Industrialists. Valencia won this event over Puerto Rico, Panama, and a second team from Venezuela.

BERNIER'S BASEBALL LEGACY

In 11 seasons in the Pacific Coast League, Bernier played in 1,571 games, batted .302 with 147 home runs and 777 RBIs, scored 1,005 runs, and stole 308 bases.[25] He was inducted into the PCL Hall of Fame in 2004. His single-season record of 41 stolen bases in Puerto Rico, set in 1949–50, was eclipsed by Rickey Henderson's 44 in 1980–81 for the Ponce Lions.[26] Bernier's 69 stolen bases in back-to-back Puerto Rico seasons (1949–50 and 1950–51) are a record, ahead of Henderson's 63 in 1979–80 and 1980–81. Rogers Hornsby, Ponce's manager in 1950–51, tried to acquire Bernier in a trade with Mayagüez, according to Wayne Blackburn, Mayagüez's manager. Bernier was inducted into the Puerto Rico Professional Baseball Hall of Fame in 1992.

TESTIMONIALS FROM FANS AND PLAYERS

Jim Lyons was born in Hollywood, California, and became a Stars fan in 1954. In a November 2014 blog post, he wrote: "Before games, the team let kids go near the dugouts to get autographs. Many players like Bobby Del Greco would come out and sign for five or 10 minutes. Bernier would sign for a half hour or longer. He would personalize the autograph: 'To my friend Jimmy from Carlos Bernier.' He would talk to you and look at you. He is my all-time favorite player. My oldest son has the middle name Carlos."[27]

Clemente, as a young player, "found relief with the fans, and after games, loved nothing more than to stand surrounded by admiring strangers, and sign his autograph on their scorecards and baseballs for as long as they wished."[28] Mario Mendoza was befriended by Clemente in Bradenton, Florida, during spring training in 1971. Mendoza and other minor leaguers came in for dinner at 5:30 PM and left an hour later when the big leaguers entered. Clemente stayed outside the dining hall, chatting with Mendoza and the others until the last call was made for big leaguers to eat. Clemente told the youngsters: "The heck with the meal. I'll eat somewhere else later in the evening. Let's keep talking." After the Pirates won the 1971 World Series, Clemente was asked if he had ever played with such a powerful team. He said, "Yes, when the Santurce Crabbers won the [1955] Caribbean Series."[29] ■

Acknowledgments

Grateful acknowledgment to Jorge Colón Delgado for insights on Carlos Bernier and Roberto Clemente. Thanks to these former players who played with or against Bernier and Clemente: Mario Mendoza, Ozzie Virgil Sr., Rubén Gómez (deceased) and Vic Power (deceased). Thanks to Wayne Blackburn (deceased), who managed Bernier at Mayagüez, and to Rickey Henderson, all-time major-league stolen base leader and single-season Puerto Rico stolen base record-holder.

Sources

Books

Stew Thornley, "Roberto Clemente," in *Puerto Rico and Baseball: 60 Biographies*, Bill Nowlin and Edwin Fernández, eds (Phoenix: SABR Digital Library, 2017), 87–103. https://sabr.org/bioproj/person/8b153bc4.

Thomas E. Van Hyning, "Rubén Gómez" in Puerto Rico and Baseball, 146–56. https://sabr.org/bioproj/person/7d94a891.

Lloyd Johnson and Miles Wolff, eds., *Encyclopedia of Minor League Baseball*, Third Edition (Durham: Baseball America, 2007).

Rafael Costas, *Enciclopedia Beisbol Ponce Leones 1938–1987* (Santo Domingo: Editora Coripio, 1987).

Rick Swaine, *The Integration of Major League Baseball: A Team by Team History* (Jefferson, NC: McFarland, 2009), 116.

Thomas E. Van Hyning, *The Santurce Crabbers* (Jefferson, NC, McFarland, 1999).

Internet Resources/Websites

"Carlos Bernier," Baseball Reference, https://www.baseball-reference.com/players/b/bernica01.shtml.

Burly, "The Pacific Coast League's First Black Baseball Stars, Part III," Burly's Baseball Musings, July 19, 2013. https://notanotherbaseballblog.wordpress.com/2013/07/19/the-pacific-coast-leagues-first-black-stars-part-iii. Accessed December 31, 2017.

Journal, Magazine, and Newspaper Articles

"Bucs Sell Four Players, Option Two to Hollywood," *Pittsburgh Post-Gazette*, April 7, 1954.

"Claims Negro Leagues Raid Puerto Rico and Sell Stars to Majors," *New York Age*, August 6, 1949.

David Wharton and Lance Pugmire, "Park Place," *Los Angeles Times*, October 27, 2002. http://articles.latimes.com/2002/oct/27/sports/sp-wrigley27/2. Accessed July 7, 2017.

Frank Deford, "Liege Lord of Latin Hopes," *Sports Illustrated*, December 24, 1973. https://www.si.com/vault/1973/12/24/618486/liege-lord-of-latin-hopes. Accessed April 30, 2018.

Jack Hernon, "Haney's Size-up on Bob Clemente 'Much to Learn,'" *The Sporting News*, March 16, 1955.

John Schulian, "Of Stars and Angels" *Sports Illustrated*, June 21, 1993. https://www.si.com/vault/1993/06/21/128782/of-stars-and-angels-once-upon-a-time-tinseltown-was-a-heavely-place-to-watch-minor-league-baseball. Accessed January 5, 2018.

Thomas E. Van Hyning, "Hall of Famers Shine in Puerto Rico," *The National Pastime* 12 (1992), 14–16.

Xavier F. Totti, "The Case for Carlos Bernier: Baseball's Historic Omission," Centro Voices, February 5, 2016. https://centropr.hunter.cuny.edu/centrovoices/chronicles/case-carlos-bernier-baseballs-historic-omission. Accessed December 27, 2017.

Personal Interviews

Mario Mendoza, in-person interview, Smith-Wills Stadium, Jackson, Mississippi, July 1994.

Ozzie Virgil Sr., telephone interview, January 1993.

Rickey Henderson, in-person interview, Camden Yards, Baltimore, May 19, 1992.

Rubén Gómez, in-person interview, Hiram Bithorn Stadium, San Juan, Puerto Rico, January 1992.

Vic Power (Víctor Pellot), in-person interview, Ponce, Puerto Rico, October 20, 1991.

Wayne Blackburn, telephone interview, April 1992.

Notes

1. Cliff Corcoran, "Sons of Jackie Robinson," SI.com, April 15, 2014. https://www.si.com/mlb/strike-zone/2014/04/15/jackie-robinson-day-mlb-integration-ernie-banks-elston-howard-larry-doby. Accessed April 30, 2018. Respected historians and sportswriters from the 1950s through today, plus Puerto Rican, Cuban, and Dominican ballplayers who played with and against Bernier, believe or believed Bernier should be considered the first black player in Pirates history. This includes writers from African American publications; Larry Lester, Negro Leagues historian and co-founder of the Negro Leagues Museum; Jorge Colón Delgado, historian, Roberto Clemente Professional Baseball League; Rubén Gómez, Vic Power (Víctor Pellot), Ozzie Virgil Sr; Joe Guzzardi, Xavier F. Totti, and Bernier's son, Néstor Collazo Bernier.

2. Jorge Colón Delgado, *La Maquinaria Perfecta: Santurce Cangrejeros 1954–55* (San Juan: Historical Sports Research, 2007), 73–76. The Puerto Rico Winter League was renamed after Roberto Clemente in May 2012.

3. Bernier was considered a black player in organized baseball in 1948, when he played for Port Chester. Two other black Puerto Ricans—Rubén Gómez and Nino Escalera—were Bernier's teammates with the 1949 Bristol Owls, Colonial League champions. Bernier and Gómez were teammates with St. Jean (Canada), Provincial League, after the Colonial League folded. Bernier played in the Manitoba-Dakota League, a Canadian Negro League, circa 1947. Gómez told the author Bernier was considered a black player when they were teammates. Ozzie Virgil Sr., Detroit's first black player in 1958, had a complection similar to Bernier's. He told the author: "Bernier (as a Mayagüez teammate and in the minors) had a compact swing and a good 'inside-outside' stroke to right field."

4. Clemente and Irvin were inducted into the National Baseball Hall of Fame in the 1973 ceremony. Clemente is in the Puerto Rico Professional Baseball Hall of Fame (1991), Marine Corps Sports Hall of Fame (2003), and others.

5. Bob Thurman was the first African American player with the San Francisco Seals of the Pacific Coast League in 1951 and played for the 1952 Seals. Thurman is the all-time Puerto Rico League career home run leader with 120.

6. "Carlos Bernier: Hollywood Bought and Sold," Unknown Transaction, July 10, 2015. Located at http://unknowntransaction.blogspot.com/2015/07/carlos-bernier-hollywood-bought-and-sold.html. Accessed April 30, 2018. Bernier was the first black player to play for the Hollywood Stars in 1952. He had a stellar season with the 1951 Tampa Bay Smokers, managed by Ben Chapman, in the Class B Florida International League. Bernier was the first Afro-Caribbean player for the Smokers, preceding Cuban outfielder Claro Duany and others.

7. Joe Guzzardi, "Carlos Bernier, more than a footnote," *Pittsburgh Post-Gazette*, April 14, 2013. http://www.post-gazette.com/opinion/Op-Ed/2013/04/14/Carlos-Bernier-more-than-a-footnote/stories/201304140150. Accessed April 30, 2018.

8. Guzzardi, "Playing ball in Cuba," *Pittsburgh Post-Gazette*, March 29, 2014. http://www.post-gazette.com/opinion/Op-Ed/2014/03/30/Pirates-playing-ball-in-Cuba-JOE-GUZZARDI/stories/201403300161. Accessed April 30, 2018.

9. J.G. Preston, "One and Done: The Sparky Anderson All-Stars," J.G. Preston Experience, April 9, 2013. https://prestonjg.wordpress.com/2013/o4/09/one-and-done-the-sparky-anderson-all-stars. Accessed July 31, 2017.

10. C.C. Johnson Spink, "The Low Down on Majors' Big Shots," *The Sporting News*, January 6, 1954. The story calls Bernier the "most temperamental Pirate." Some other "temperamental" players: Larry Doby (Cleveland), Ted Williams (Boston), Satchel Paige (St. Louis Browns), Eddie Mathews (Milwaukee), and Eddie Stanky (St. Louis Cardinals).

11. David Maraniss, *Clemente: The Passion and Grace of Baseball's Last Hero* (New York: Simon & Schuster, 2006), 67. Pittsburgh's white players stayed at the downtown Bradford Hotel. Clemente lived in a room of a widow's house on Lime Street. This was the second spring training in Florida for Clemente and Bernier.

12. Charles F. Faber, "Carlos Bernier," in *Puerto Rico and Baseball: 60 Biographies*, Bill Nowlin and Edwin Fernández, eds (Phoenix: SABR Digital Library, 2017), 49. Faber's excellent bio initially stated this perhaps was the first all-Puerto Rico outfield in a major-league game, but Román Mejías is Cuban. The 1973 St. Louis Cardinals had three Cruz brothers from Puerto Rico—José, Héctor and Cirilo "Tommy"—but they were not in the outfield at the same time in a major-league game. Héctor Cruz, Jerry Morales and Carlos Lezcano did play the outfield together in a regular-season game for the 1981 Chicago Cubs.

13. Al Abrams, "Sidelights on Sports," *Pittsburgh Post-Gazette*, March 14, 1955.

14. Through the 2017 season, three triples in one game had been done 26 times by 25 players in the National League since 1899, including five times by Pirates players: In addition to Bernier and Clemente, the other three were Ginger Beaumont on August 9, 1899; Dave Brain on August 8, 1905; and Chief Wilson on July 24, 1911. http://www.baseball-almanac.com/recbooks/rb_trip1.shtml.

15. Tony Piña Cámpora, "Serie del Caribe: Historia de la Confederación," 2014. http://www.beisboldelcaribe.com/home/documentos/SCARIBEHISTORIA.pdf. Accessed April 30, 2018. Clemente had 16 hits in 49 at-bats for the combined 1955 and 1958 Caribbean Series. His 29 total bases included two home runs, a double, and three triples. Clemente was the All-Star center fielder of the 1958 Caribbean Series; Mays was the All-Star center fielder in 1955. Clemente was inducted into the Caribbean Baseball Hall of Fame in 2015, a decade after Mays. Phase I, Caribbean Series, 1949–60, was with Cuba, Panama, Puerto Rico, and Venezuela. Phase II is 1970 to the present. Current teams are Cuba, Dominican Republic, Mexico, Puerto Rico, and Venezuela. The Interamerican Series took place 1961–64.

16. "Carlos Bernier," Baseball-Reference.com, https://www.baseball-reference.com/register/player.fcgi?id=bernie001car. Full name: Carlos Eugene Bernier Rodríguez. Born in Juana Díaz on January 28, 1927; died in Juana Díaz on April 6, 1989.

17. Preston, "One and Done."

18. Faber, "Carlos Bernier," 49.

19. Steve Treder, "Carlos Bernier," *Hardball Times*, August 25, 2004. https://www.fangraphs.com/tht/carlos-bernier. Accessed December 27, 2017.

20. Héctor Barea, *Historia de los Criollos* (San Juan: Ana G. Méndez University System, 1997).

21. Thomas E. Van Hyning, *Puerto Rico's Winter League* (Jefferson, NC: McFarland, 1995), 64.

22. Maraniss, *Clemente*, 202. Clemente was particularly sensitive to close plays at first base and on plays called errors by official scorers that might have been infield hits.

23. José A. Crescioni Benítez, *El Béisbol Profesional Boricua* (San Juan: First Book Publishing of Puerto Rico, 1997), 101–2, 236, 241, 351, 354. Bernier stole 286 bases in 19 seasons, the most all-time. He led the league five times and was runner-up nine times. Bernier's 85 career triples in Puerto Rico are the standard. His lifetime batting average was .268, 4,126 at-bats, 739 runs, 1,107 hits, 151 doubles, 48 home runs, 415 RBI. Clemente has the fourth-highest league batting average: .324, behind Willard Brown at .350; "Pancho" Coimbre's .337; and Perucho Cepeda's .325. Clemente had 1,917 at-bats, 302 runs, 621 hits, 100 doubles, 25 triples, 35 home runs, 268 RBI, and 32 stolen bases.

24. Van Hyning, *Puerto Rico's Winter League*, 62.

25. "Carlos Bernier," MILB.com, http://www.milb.com/content/page.jsp?sid=l112&ymd= 20110503&content_id=18574638&vkey=league3.

26. Van Hyning, "Henderson Runs Past Cobb and Bernier," *Baseball Research Journal*, 21 (1992), 20–21. Rickey Henderson agreed to an interview by the author in the Camden Yards visitor clubhouse upon hearing he still held Puerto Rico's single-season stolen base mark. Henderson stole 44 bases in 48 games for Ponce in 1980–81 during a 60-game season. Bernier stole 41 bases during an 80-game season in 1949–50.

27. Treder, "Carlos Bernier."

28. Maraniss, *Clemente*, 87.

29. Colón Delgado, *La Maquinaria Perfecta*, back cover. The 1954–55 Santurce Crabbers were considered the best Caribbean, Central, or South American Winter League team ever assembled, per sportswriters, fans, and players.

Roberto Clemente and *The Odd Couple*

Two Different Stories

Rob Edelman

U nlike major leaguers from the Bambino to Turkey Mike, Roberto Clemente never forged a career on the silver screen. But his one celluloid connection is worth probing because of his legend—and because it is a textbook example of the manner in which simple anecdotes and truths of any kind may be twisted beyond recognition.

The film in question is *The Odd Couple*, the screen version of Neil Simon's hit Broadway play. While not a standard "baseball story," the film features the sport in a sequence that is linked both to Clemente and his Pittsburgh Pirates.

One half of the title "odd couple" is Oscar Madison, New York sportswriter and slob-extraordinaire, a character created by Walter Matthau onstage in 1965. Matthau replayed Madison on-screen and, at one point, he is covering a Pirates-New York Mets contest at Shea Stadium. The sequence was filmed at the ballyard on June 27, 1967, prior to a real Mets-Pirates fray. In the fictional game, the Mets are up by a run in the ninth inning. Pittsburgh loads the bases and one of their top hitters comes to the plate. "Well, that's the ballgame," predicts Heywood Hale Broun, cast in a cameo as a fellow scribe. "It's not over yet" is Oscar's rejoinder. "What's a matta, you never hoid of a triple play?" Oscar then takes an "emergency" phone call from his roommate, fussy Felix Ungar (Jack Lemmon), who implores him not to consume any frankfurters because of the franks-and-beans dinner he is preparing. Meanwhile, the Pirate at bat smacks into a triple play, ending the game. "Greatest fielding play I ever saw," Broun tells Madison, "and you missed it."

The on-screen Pirates batter is Bill Mazeroski. Originally, it was supposed to be Clemente, but he is not to be found here. Two diametrically opposite stories exist regarding his involvement with *The Odd Couple*. The first is an affirmation of Clemente's solemnity and athleticism: He *never* would agree to hit into a triple play, even in an all-in-good-fun entertainment. After all, according to biographer David Maraniss, Clemente "ran everything out, first of all, full speed, head down, every feeble tap back to the pitcher, and he worked so hard at running. ...When Clemente was on the go, it seemed not so much that he was trying to get to a base as to escape from some unspeakable phantasmal terror."[1]

This resolve also is emphasized in Jon Volkmer's Clemente history. Volkmer noted that a "man showed up and asked Roberto to take a small part in a movie," adding: "They told him it was a benefit for children, and that's why they could pay him only a token $100 for his appearance. Roberto was always ready to help children. He said 'Yes, sure.'" It wasn't until he arrived at Shea that he realized this was no kiddie film. Additionally, upon learning that he was to hit into a triple play, he "walked off the field, mad as a hornet." He was "still mad when the game began" but came to appreciate the irony of the situation later on when he reported that, during the game, he "took a pitch, and...hit it 440 feet over the fence. I knew where that movie producer was sitting. As I went by I yelled to him, 'Take a picture of *that* for your stinking movie.'"[2]

Volkmer's anecdote is embellished by Bruce Markusen, another Clemente profiler. According to Markusen, the ballplayer reported the $100 fee to teammate Matty Alou. "He says I am foolish," Clemente told Jerry Lisker in the *New York Daily News*, declaring that his payment should be nothing less than $1,000. "They insult me," he added. "One hundred dollars, that's what they want to pay me. Who they think they try and fool? They think Roberto Clemente was born last week?" He continued, "What would fans in Latin America say if they see me hit into triple play? They would not understand." Markusen added that Clemente's 440-foot drive occurred not in-game but during batting practice: "As the ball soared toward the outer limits of Shea Stadium, Roberto yelled in the direction of a cameraman. 'Hey movie man,' Roberto exclaimed, 'take a picture of that home run and put it in your stinking picture. You can have it for nothing.'"[3]

Lisker's July 30, 1967, *Daily News* piece (published over a month after the filming) also included this anecdote: "A director with a megaphone and a baseball cap on his head strutted up to Clemente. He put his arm

COURTESY OF THE PITTSBURGH PIRATES

Roberto Clemente, rounding third base.

around Roberto's shoulder and gave him a typical Hollywood greeting: 'Hiya, Roberto, how's my old buddy?'[4] Roberto looked the guy square in the eye. 'I am not old,' Clemente said coldly, 'and I ain't gonna be in your stinkin' movie. How you like that, old buddy?'" (In a conflicting observation, writer John McCollister claimed that Clemente was in fact offered $1,000 but "politely thanked the filmmakers" before turning it down.[5] Additionally, Tom Smith reported in a piece on the Roberto Clemente Museum in Lawrenceville, Pennsylvania, that the ballplayer's refusal was for *The Odd Couple* television series!)[6]

Barney Kremenko, writing in *The Sporting News* that July, reported that "Mazeroski was pinch-hitting for Roberto Clemente, who pulled out of the movie the night before." No explanation is given.[7] It was noted in *Sports Illustrated* that Clemente "huffed out, offended at the mere $100 Paramount would pay" to participate in the "Boyer-to-Buchek-to-Kranepool job."[8] *The New York Times* also covered the filming; here, the story was penned by Vincent Canby, the paper's film critic. Canby described Mazeroski as "a pinch hitter for Roberto Clemente," adding that the outfielder "bowed out when he learned the film sequence was for a big budget Hollywood picture, rather than for a promotional film. He felt the $100 fee, the Screen Actors Guild minimum for acting ball players, was an insult."[9] Still another angle was reported in the *Pittsburgh Press*. Here, Clemente declared, "I will do it either for nothing or for much more than $100. …They will use my name in the movie and exploit me for $100. Not for me."[10]

(*New York Post* sportswriter Maury Allen once claimed that, for $100, Clemente not only wouldn't agree to hit into a triple play but rejected switching the scene to a double play.[11] One only can speculate on the veracity of Allen's tale. However, one blatant—not to mention sloppy—error is found in the American Film Institute's *AFI Catalog of Feature Films*: "Pittsburgh player Maury Wills and Mets player Roberto Clemente declined to appear for the $100 Screen Actors Guild [SAG] fee offered them.")[12]

In the stands on the day of the shoot was 15-year-old Steve Kallas, who attended with his father. "We got there early, as we always did, for batting practice. We had no idea that they'd be shooting a movie," Kallas recalled. "Well, they had to do four or five takes for this scene. I remember there was booing between takes, a real New York kind of boo because the scene was so contrived. The batter had to run slower and slower every take." That batter was *not* Roberto Clemente. "The movie's great, but that scene's awful," Kallas said. "Clemente would've made the scene that much more ridiculous. Even in the context of a fantasy, Clemente made the right call."[13]

* * *

The second scenario differs markedly from the first. Here, Clemente actually filmed the scene. The Turner Classic Movies cast list cites various real-life *Odd Couple* ballplayers, including Alou, Wills, Vernon Law, Ken Boyer, Bud Harrelson, Jerry Buchek, Ed Kranepool—and Roberto Clemente![14] According to the Internet Movie Database "Trivia" link for *The Odd Couple*: "The fleet-footed Pirate kept beating the throw to first base. After several takes, Clemente slowed so much he appeared to be walking. Bill Mazeroski, a more lead-footed athlete, was offered the part instead."[15]

A fan who refers to himself as Joey D. offered a similar memory on MetsMerizedOnline.com: "The fleet-footed Clemente did about six takes but despite trying to run slower, he kept beating the throw to first base, so they went with the much slower Maz," he wrote, adding: "I was there sitting in the upper deck behind home plate when they filmed it, getting in free with a dozen box tops from Borden milk products!"[16]

Bill De Cicco, a Shea Stadium batboy, also was present that day and reported versions of both stories in his memoir. In the first, Clemente agreed to appear but was "too fast running to first base. …After three or four takes, (he) slowed down his running to make it happen, but it looked unnatural so they couldn't use it." In the second, Clemente refused to participate "because it made him look bad. When Mazeroski heard this and that he would get a hundred dollars to hit a ground ball, he jumped at the chance. It took three or so takes to get it right."[17]

Further insight into Clemente and *The Odd Couple* is offered by Mike Frassinelli, writing in the Allentown, Pennsylvania, *Morning Call* on the 30th anniversary of the ballplayer's death. "Not only would it be nearly impossible for the speedy outfielder to hit into a triple play, he didn't want to fuel the stereotype of the lazy Puerto Rican," Frassinelli wrote. "Even when it came to a seemingly harmless comedy movie, Clemente wanted to be seen as more than a punchline. He wanted to be seen as a dignified credit to his race—the human race."[18] ■

Notes

1. David Maraniss, *Clemente: The Passion and Grace of Baseball's Last Hero* (New York: Simon & Schuster, 2006), 189–90.
2. Jon Volkmer, *Roberto Clemente: The Story of a Champion* (West Berlin, NJ: Townsend Press, 2008).
3. Bruce Markusen, *Roberto Clemente: The Great One* (New York: Sports Publishing, 2001).
4. "What They Were Saying," *New York Daily News*, September 18, 2005. http://www.nydailynews.com/archives/nydn-features/-article-1.629880.
5. John McCollister, *Tales From the Pittsburgh Pirates Dugout: A Collection of the Greatest Pirates Stories Ever Told* (New York: Sports Publishing, 2003).
6. Tom Smith, "Roberto Clemente Museum: The Great One Would Be Proud," Rum Bunter, November 16, 2009. https://rumbunter.com/2009/11/16/roberto-clemente-museum-the-great-one-would-be-proud.
7. Barney Kremenko, "Maz Raps Into Triple Play, But It's Only for Hollywood," *The Sporting News*, July 15, 1967.
8. "People," *Sports Illustrated*, July 19, 1967. https://www.si.com/vault/1967/07/17/610100/people.
9. Vincent Canby, "Mazeroski Hits Into Triple Play In 'Odd Couple' Filming at Shea," *The New York Times*, June 28, 1967.
10. "The Scoreboard: Mets' Shaw Irritating," *Pittsburgh Press*, June 28, 1967.
11. Greg Gutes, "Oddly enough, game-ending triple play involving Mets has been turned before," *Newsday*, August 23, 2009. https://www.newsday.com/sports/baseball/mets/oddly-enough-game-ending-triple-play-involving-mets-has-been-turned-before-1.1389302.
12. "The Odd Couple," *AFI Catalog of Feature Films: The First 100 Years 1893–1993*, https://catalog.afi.com/Catalog/moviedetails/23870.
13. Phil Mushnick, "Clemente Still Sets Example: Pirates Great Always Played Game Right Way," *New York Post*, December 15, 2002. https://nypost.com/2002/12/15/clemente-still-sets-example-pirates-great-always-played-game-right-way.
14. "The Odd Couple (1968)," Turner Classic Movies. http://www.tcm.com/tcmdb/title/4740/The-Odd-Couple.
15. "The Odd Couple," *AFI Catalog of Feature Films: The First 100 Years 1893–1993*, https://catalog.afi.com/Catalog/moviedetails/23870.
16. Phil Mushnick, "Clemente Still Sets Example: Pirates Great Always Played Game Right Way," *New York Post*, December 15, 2002. https://nypost.com/2002/12/15/clemente-still-sets-example-pirates-great-always-played-game-right-way.
17. "The Odd Couple (1968)," Turner Classic Movies. http://www.tcm.com/tcmdb/title/4740/The-Odd-Couple.
18. "The Odd Couple (1968): Trivia," IMDB. http://www.imdb.com/title/tt0063374/trivia.
19. Joey D., "50 Years Ago Today: Classic Shea Stadium Scene In *Odd Couple*," June 27, 2017. https://metsmerizedonline.com/2017/06/50-years-ago-today-classic-shea-stadium-scene-in-odd-couple.html.
20. Bill De Cicco, *My Amazing Journey: Shea Believer* (Bloomington, IN: WestBow Press, 2015).
21. Mike Frassinelli, "Roberto Clemente still a legend 30 years after death," Morning Call (Allentown, PA), December 30, 2002. http://articles.mcall.com/2002-12-30/news/3426164_1_roberto-clemente-plane-crash-puerto-rican.

Land of the Free, Home of the Brave

Mudcat Grant's Odyssey to Sing the National Anthem

Dan VanDeMortel

When San Francisco 49ers quarterback Colin Kaepernick refused to stand for the national anthem during a 2016 preseason game to protest police violence against black people in America, all hell broke loose. Voices of praise and condemnation rained down. Passion often trumped reason. The "conversation" remains heated, while complicated criminal justice problems remain unsolved.

Is there a way for collectively honoring a song that symbolizes Home while Home leaves some citizens vulnerable with little political or legal recourse? Football and basketball players, owners, and fans have struggled to find that balance. Meanwhile, baseball remains cloaked in timidity, virtually silent in words and deeds on the field and off.[1] Its fans are thus left to a difficult search through history for any semblance of a clue or role model. Yet relevant history does exist: October 4, 1970, at newly opened Three Rivers Stadium in Pittsburgh, when, moments before the Pirates hosted the Cincinnati Reds in National League Championship Series Game Two, black Pirates relief pitcher James "Mudcat" Grant—sporting muttonchop sideburns and an immaculate white pin-striped suit—took the microphone to sing the anthem.

Why was Grant singing the anthem? And how is that relevant today? The answers offer insight into a unique blend of accomplishment in both baseball and singing, both while navigating our country's civil rights struggles.

Grant was born in 1935 in Lacoochee, Florida, a rural lumber-mill town north of Tampa. Just two when his father died, James and his five siblings were raised by their mother, who worked at a citrus canning factory and as a domestic worker. Excelling at sports, James eventually competed with a semipro team, which stationed him at third base. He earned an athletic scholarship to Florida A&M University but soon left due to family financial hardships. Baseball fortuitously offered rescue in 1954, when bird-dog scout Fred Merkle, having previously watched Grant in high school, invited him to a Daytona Beach tryout with the Cleveland Indians. Once there, Grant's black skin and ragged uniform prompted a fellow invitee to haze him with the nickname "Mudcat," claiming he was as ugly as a Mississippi catfish. The nickname stuck; a "brand" was born. Impressed with his live arm, and seeing his potential as a pitcher, the Tribe signed "Mudcat" days later.

In essence, a happy ending. But, harsher truths abounded, challenging Grant's Baptist upbringing. His family's dilapidated shack lacked electricity, hot water, and toilets. He studied from shabby schoolbooks, disdainfully discarded from white schools, by kerosene lamp or firelight. His mother once collapsed from exhaustion, falling on the stove and burning her face and arms. To help, the teenage Grant lied about his age to gain work in the lumber mill.

Even worse, segregation provided constant intimidation and danger. The family had a trapdoor in the floor, a refuge for when marauding white bands invaded, shooting into houses during what Grant described as "n*****-shooting time."[2] He was verbally and physically harassed by local authorities, and whites pelted him with rocks when he ventured outside "colored" areas. A childhood friend was killed for violating racial protocol.[3] As Grant recalled, "As a black person, if you tried to think about the worst thing that could happen to you, it could happen that day. And something worse could happen to you the next day. …These became almost everyday things. … We were terrorized for 300 years. But we didn't call it terror."[4]

Two women kept Grant focused. His mother, a church choir director, instilled a religious belief that he could succeed, that he had "come into the world for many missions."[5] She helped forge the endurance needed to handle racism and encouraged him to release anger in an unharmful way. Inspiration also came from teacher Vera Lucas Goodwin, a woman of culture and music in barren circumstances. She found in Grant a talented spirit: a "bathtub singer" since his mother taught him at five. Grant eagerly devoured her knowledge and recordings of Johann Strauss, Eddy Arnold, John Lee Hooker, and others she passed along.[6]

Grant graduated to the Indians in 1958, where he became the American League's only black starting pitcher. "You were always aware of the fact that you were black because there were stares, there were people that took your money at the counter [who] didn't want to touch your hand," he wrote, adding, "Pain always showed up, every day, in terms of something that happened."[7]

In 1960 Grant had offered two dramatic opportunities to deal with the pain. On the morning of September 5, his Detroit hotel phone rang. An aide for presidential candidate John F. Kennedy said Kennedy wanted to meet him for breakfast. Grant hung up, figuring the call a prank. Minutes later, though, Kennedy's aides appeared at his door, and soon he *was* having breakfast with the Massachusetts senator. They talked for an hour, covering baseball and Kennedy's admiration for him and the sport's black pioneers. But Grant also kept it real, covering his upbringing, both good and ill. Their conversation springboarded Grant to a future White House meeting, where Grant asked for and received aid for Lacoochee.

Eleven days later in Cleveland, opportunity took a darker turn. Egged on by bullpen teammates and frustrated by obstructed efforts to integrate Southern lunch counters, Grant's tolerance boiled over as he sang along with the anthem. As the song reached its ascending conclusion, Grant ad-libbed, "And this land is not so free, 'cause I can't even go to Mississipp-ee," or words to that effect.[8] Pitching coach and Texas resident Ted Wilks overheard. "If you don't like our country, why in the hell don't you get out," he thundered. "Well, I can get out of the country," Grant replied. "All I have to do is go to Texas. That's worse than Russia." Wilks lit the match: "Well, if we catch your black n***** ass in Texas, we're going to hang you from the nearest tree."[9] Grant threw a punch that dropped Wilks to the ground. Pushing and shoving ensued until teammates separated them. Angered and unable to think clearly, Grant fled the park without alerting manager Jimmy Dykes, for which he was suspended for the rest of the season.

Some accounts indicate Wilks apologized. "Are you kidding me?" Grant recently scoffed. "He was a racist. …There was no way he was going to apologize because [racism] was too strong back in those days."[10] To the team's credit, it quickly reassigned Wilks to the minor leagues and kept Grant on.[11] But letters filled his mailbox, some complimentary, many not. He burned all but one he considered "funny" from a war veteran: "Dear black SOB, you got a lot of nerve," it read. "After all we've done for you. …We ought to ship all you

N****** and Jews back to Africa."[12] Grant expected other players to follow his protest, but no one did.

Over time, unlike Kaepernick, Grant's career thrived, especially after he completed Army duty in 1962. He developed a sinker, "Comet Ball," "fast curve," "Hop and a Jumper," and a discussed-but-never-thrown "Cloud Ball that got a little wet from the air"/ "razzafratz"/"soapball" spitball.[13] Everything climaxed in 1965, after he was traded to the Minnesota Twins and became the first black American Leaguer to lead the league in wins, shutouts, and winning percentage.

Another career also blossomed: entertainment. Using presentation skills forged at baseball community-relations events, Grant pursued a singing career, debuting in 1962 at a benefit banquet. That led to more appearances, solo and with assorted groups, where he pleased fans with autographed pictures and handouts of his poem "Life," which compared life to baseball.[14]

His baseball success in 1965 rocketed Grant's music act to the big leagues, highlighted by appearances on Johnny Carson's and Mike Douglas's television shows.[15] Influenced by Duke Ellington, Ella Fitzgerald, Count Basie, and others, Grant formed Mudcat and the Kittens. The group focused on blues, with touches of R&B, jazz, pop, soul, gospel, and pure showbiz. Grant contributed fame, a melodious baritone voice, sartorial perfection that could make a tuxedo cat smile, a dancer's grace, and an ability to read an audience

PUBLICITY PHOTO

Grant's band, Mudcat and the Kittens, featured talented musicians and, as seen here, choreographer/dancer Frank Hatchett and a group of sexily-clad "Kittens" who provided backup vocal harmony and dancing.

like nobody's business. The Kittens brought groove. A choreographer, drummer, guitar player, and bass player joined a group of sexily clad female "Kittens"—all accomplished church singers with curves and harmony.

The group's work ethic was pure baseball. "It was like baseball: The more you practiced the better you got at it. You had to rehearse or it would be like going on the field with nine players who had never played with each other," Grant explained.[16] Attending sessions of and receiving feedback from legends such as Marvin Gaye and Gladys Knight and the Pips, the band honed its craft until magic happened: "the time of night when everybody had a few drinks and thought maybe we were Sinatra!"[17] With or without Kittens, Grant performed nationwide, in Canada, Europe, and the Caribbean, and three times joined fellow baseball players on goodwill tours of Vietnam.

As the 1960s wore on, though, Grant continued to confront racial impediments. His skin limited endorsement possibilities open to baseball's white stars. Gradually embroiled in the Twins' increasing racial divisions and embittered by acrimonious contract negotiations, Grant was traded after the 1967 season. "My mind was so perverted. I was crawling with hate," he later reflected.[18] For two years, he drifted from team to team, relegated to the bullpen while struggling with age and injuries. He flirted with racial danger by attending civil rights rallies and sneaking encounters with a white Austrian woman, which did not fly well with white team owners.[19] His singing career, although busy, no longer commanded the national spotlight. Meanwhile, the country also struggled. His acquaintances and idols Martin Luther King Jr. and Robert Kennedy were assassinated. And American strife went global at the 1968 Olympics when two black track medalists raised gloved fists in a Black Power salute as the U.S. national anthem played during the medals ceremony.

Landing with the Oakland A's in 1970 resuscitated Grant, who became a relief specialist, racking up 80 appearances, 24 saves, and a 1.82 ERA for the season with Oakland and, late in the year, Pittsburgh.[20] Performance-wise, as one of the two players chosen to represent the A's, he sang the anthem soul style and played in a March 28 exhibition all-star game at Dodger Stadium to benefit King-related causes.[21] Days later, A's owner Charlie Finley, who was open to any promotional event, appointed Grant to sing the anthem, in uniform, on Opening Day, the first time a participating player had been so honored in any regular-season game.[22]

When the A's pennant hopes dwindled in August, they traded Grant to the contending Pirates.[23] Although

COURTESY OF THE PITTSBURGH PIRATES

Mudcat Grant, circa 1971. Note the distinctive mutton-chop sideburns, Grant's signature facial hair look of the time.

he was upset with another address change, once he focused forward, he sang a different tune, fitting in like a glove, or more like a musical ambassador. "In the clubhouse they always wanted me to perform. I went ahead and did that, at no charge," he quipped.[24] On the road, Grant escorted teammates, including Roberto Clemente and Manny Sanguillen, to landmarks such as the Apollo Theater in New York, where baseball was revered. The musicians "would get taking pictures with the Pirates and before you know it, you've got 10 to 15 people that want their pictures taken with my teammates. You'd have more people watching the ballplayers than the performers!"[25] And for extra laughs, Grant roomed with star pitcher Dock Ellis.[26]

Grant helped the Bucs win the NL's Eastern Division, but his late arrival prohibited playoff participation.[27] Game Two brought a chance to shine when General Manager Joe L. Brown asked him to sing the anthem. Grant immediately accepted, troubled past notwithstanding. "I would never have sung it publicly in a protest circumstance where it would be used for anything other than the anthem," he said years later.[28] His nationally televised semi-rock rendition—backed by organ, trap drum, and trombone— before 39,317 fans marked the first time a participating team's player sang the anthem before a playoff game.[29] Inexcusably, the only notable "analysis" of this milestone came in the form of a *Tampa Tribune* columnist writing that Wilks, by not forgiving or forgetting Grant's 1960 rendition of the anthem, "helped Grant learn a lesson.[30] *That's* fake news.

Marvin Gaye's classic "What's Going On" album, which lamented "trigger happy policing," among other societal problems, came out in 1971. Grant remained a popular Pirate, entertaining a Pirates Wives team-packaged event in Pittsburgh and a teen-night crowd in St. Louis before a game. But his pitching slipped, so in August he was ping-ponged back to the A's.

COURTESY OF THE PITTSBURGH PIRATES

Pirates star pitcher Dock Ellis, circa 1971. When Mudcat Grant was traded to the Pirates, he and Ellis became roommates. They shared many interests, including traveling to music venues to check out the latest acts at clubs such as the Apollo in New York City.

"Baseball is a business. Maybe I'm just another one of its saleable items," he said with resignation.[31]

Recording three saves and a win, Grant pushed the A's to the League Championship Series. When Oakland returned home for Game Three after losing the first two to the Orioles in Baltimore, Finley once more selected Grant to sing the national anthem, which he did before 33,176 fans. His "slow, Billy Eckstine" voice could not prevent another loss, however, freeing him for the Kittens and the running of Mudcat Incorporated, a cosmetic company specializing in, appropriately, Mud for Cats complexion cream.[32]

The A's released Grant the following spring. His efforts to return to the majors failed. "Baseball players are like streetcars: They just come and go," Grant once remarked, and his career was quickly gone.[33]

Grant soon broke up the Kittens to focus on solo gigs. Since his retirement as a player, he has held various positions inside and outside baseball and has sung the anthem repeatedly, including at Frank Robinson's color barrier-breaking managerial debut in 1975. In 2007, he authored *The Black Aces*—a profile of baseball's black 20-game winners—and was honored with black leaders at the White House, where President George W. Bush commended his "courage, character, and perseverance."[34] Free of past anger, his mission

remains true: "Feel the pulse of your community and see what you can do to alleviate some of the problems that have been tagging us for a long time."[35]

When asked recently about Kaepernick's protest, which he supports, Grant said, "Racism gnaws at your guts. You either want to say something or you don't want to say anything. And one morning you wake up and say, 'I gotta say something.' But some people will understand it and some people won't. But you sure are going to catch hell because some people don't want to hear it."[36] Making such a choice in the public eye is indeed difficult, with Grant the closest embodiment baseball has to straddling the line where sports, social justice, speaking out, and patriotism intersect. ∎

Acknowledgments

Many thanks to James "Mudcat" Grant for granting an interview to discuss his singing and baseball career. A tip of the cap goes to the Hall of Fame staff for research assistance and to Ken Manyin, Ryan McEwan, and Kyla Gibboney for helpful editing. Truly missed while working on this article was the presence of Greg Erion (1947–2017), longtime SABR author, editor, organizer, and mentor extraordinaire.

Notes

1. Few baseball players have commented on Kaepernick's protest, let alone publicly supported it. On September 23, 2017, in Oakland, A's rookie catcher Bruce Maxwell kneeled while the anthem played. He was not joined or followed in that action by any baseball player. The dearth of blacks across the sport—on the field, in the stands, and in management and ownership—plays a tremendous role in creating a culture of avoidance. As socially conscious Tampa Bay Rays reliever Chris Archer, who is black, observed: "Just from the feedback that I've gotten from my teammates I don't think it would be the best thing to do for me at this time." Daniel Russell, "Chris Archer: Baseball Players Face 'Harsher Criticism' for Protesting," SBNation.com, September 25, 2017; Alvin Chang, "This is Why Baseball Is so White," Vox, October 24, 2017. https://www.vox.com/2016/10/27/13416798/cubs-dodgers-baseball-white-diverse.

2. John Florio and Ousie Shapiro, *One Nation Under Baseball* (Lincoln: University of Nebraska Press, 2017), 3.

3. The "crime" for which he was tied to railroad tracks and killed: carrying groceries from the lumber mill store to the front door, not the back door, of a white woman's home.

4. Billy Staples and Rich Herschalag, *Before the Glory* (Deerfield Beach, FL: Health Communications, 2007), 193.

5. Jim "Mudcat" Grant, *The Black Aces* (Farmingdale, NY: Aventine Press, 2007), 11.

6. Goodwin even arranged a 1949 gig for James and a local choir to sing on Tampa television.

7. Grant, *The Black Aces*, 210.

8. Steve Jacobson, *Carrying Jackie's Torch* (Chicago: Lawrence Hill Books, 2007), 57.

9. Grant, *The Black Aces*, 219.

10. James Grant, telephone interview, January 31, 2018.

11. The black press at the time reported that in 1947 Wilks, then a St. Louis Cardinals pitcher, tried to organize a boycott to prevent having to play against Jackie Robinson and the Brooklyn Dodgers, and regularly threw at the heads of black batters. Sam Lacy, "'Just Didn't Jump High Enough,' Says Thomas," *Baltimore Afro-American*, September 20, 1960. https://news.google.com/newspapers?nid=2205&dat=19600920&id=RWZGAAAAIBAJ&sjid=guUMAAAAIBAJ&pg=992,5140986&hl=en.

12. Steve Jacobson, "[Illegible] Due, but Does Grant?" *Newsday*, October 19, 1965.

13. Grant, telephone interview; Frank Deford, "Coochee Coos Another Tune," *Sports Illustrated*, April 8, 1968, https://www.si.com/vault/1968/04/08/614231/coochee-coos-another-tune; Jay Johnstone and Rick Talley, *Over the Edge* (Chicago: Contemporary Books, 1987), 80; Grant, *The Black Aces*, 212. Despite reports to the contrary, Grant denies throwing a spitball.

14. Grant, "Life," Baseball Almanac, March 2002. http://www.baseball-almanac.com/poetry/po_mud.shtml.

15. Grant even hosted a Minneapolis variety television program in 1965, *The Jim Grant Show*, viewable via the Walter J. Brown Media Archives & Peabody Awards Collection, http://dbs.galib.uga.edu/cgi-bin/parc.cgi?userid=galileo&query=id%3A1965_65008_ent_1-2&_cc=1.

16. Grant, telephone interview.

17. Grant, telephone interview.

18. Deford, "Coochee Coos Another Tune."

19. Grant met this woman, Gertrude, in 1957, and for a time they were romantically involved. Cleveland management balked at the situation, so they broke things off but stayed in touch discreetly over the years, trying their best to circumvent disfavor from subsequent ownerships. By 1975, when Grant and Gertrude were both divorced from prior partners, they married. They remain together and live in Los Angeles.

20. Grant's 80 appearances were the sixth highest in baseball history at the time.

21. "East-West All Stars to Play Benefit Game," *The Sporting News*, February 21, 1970; Dwight Chapin, "King Game Great—Even for Losers," *Los Angeles Times*, March 29, 1970. Grant sang in a white suit before 31,694 fans. The exhibition featured some of baseball's best players—black and white—and was held to raise funds to benefit King's Southern Christian Leadership Conference and a memorial center planned for Atlanta. Each major-league team sent two representatives, who were divided into East and West All-Star squads. The Joe DiMaggio-managed East emerged with a 5–1 victory over Roy Campanella's West. Grant pitched one inning, giving up four hits and three runs.

22. Pat Harmon, "Mudcat and His Kittens," *Cincinnati Post*, October 7, 1970. Grant performed while surrounded by a mascot mule, clowns, gold bases, a Dixieland band, and mounted patrols. After checking comparable rates for other entertainers who had performed the anthem, Grant calculated and sent Finley a bill for $300. The notoriously cheap Finley refused to pay for quite some time, arguing that he thought Grant would perform this distinctive act for free. Grant held firm until Finley paid. "If he'd just bought me a steak dinner at the time I sang, I'd have called it even. But, the longer I waited, the better my price got," Grant said.

23. "Hi, There, Waiver Boy!" *The Sporting News*, October 10, 1970; "Let's Outlaw Those Late-Season Waiver Deals," *Baseball Sports Stars*, 1971. Grant was traded for a player to be named later: young outfielder Angel Mangual. The 1970 trading deadline was June 15. A loophole allowed players such as Grant to be traded if they cleared the $20,000 waiver price from every team, which was practically a certainty given his high salary (about $50,000–$60,000). And even if a waiver claim had been filed, the waiver offer would likely have been revoked. Once clear, clubs could then trade the player(s) in question at "undisclosed" prices, although likely far above the waiver stipend. Waiver-related deals such as this elicited howls from some that teams were attempting to buy a pennant.

24. Grant, telephone interview.

25. Grant, telephone interview.

26. Ellis, who combined pitching prowess with a free spirit attitude and a rarely used edit button when discussing race or anything else, earlier in 1970 had thrown a no-hitter while on LSD.

27. Grant pitched in eight games for the Pirates, going 2–1 with a 2.25 ERA in 12 innings.

28. Grant, telephone interview.

29. Dean A. Sullivan, ed., *Late Innings* (Lincoln: University of Nebraska Press, 2002), 267. The identification of Grant's 1970 "firsts"—singing the anthem at a regular-season game and at Game Two of the NLCS—is based on personal research and correspondence with Matt Rothenberg, manager of the Giamatti Research Center at the National Baseball Hall of Fame, based on available records.

30. Frank Klein, "Making His Point," *Tampa Times*, October 5, 1970. In 2015, voluminous coverage and commentary surrounded Serena Williams's decision to end a 14-year boycott and return to the Indian Wells tennis tournament after she'd experienced racial taunts and criticism there in 2001. How would Grant's anthem performance have been reported in the modern media? An intriguing question.

31. Milton Richman, "Mudcat Getting Dizzy," *Berkeley Daily Gazette*, August 18, 1971; Russell Schneider, "Home Sweet Home is Mudcat's Theme as Indian Hopeful," *The Sporting News*, March 11, 1972. The Pirates went on to win the 1971 World Series. Grant would have received an approximately $18,000 winner's share if he had stayed with the team.

32. Jack Smith, "Reggie: O's Great," *San Francisco Chronicle*, October 6, 1971; Richman, "Mudcat Getting Dizzy;" Grant, telephone interview. Mud for Cats, alas, is not currently available at Sephora or via an old jar on eBay. "Oh, that goes waaaaay back," Grant guffawed when recently reminded of a cream he had not thought about in years. "You got one of the jars of that stuff, man? I thought that was going to take off, but it never did!"

33. Deford, "Coochee Coos Another Tune."

34. George W. Bush, "Remarks at a Celebration of African American History Month," The American Presidency Project, February 12, 2007, http://www.presidency.ucsb.edu/ws/?pid=24522.

35. Mark Sheldon, "Grant a Walking History Lesson," MLB.com. Accessed at http://www.fergiejenkinsfoundation.org/13black_aces_files/mudcat.htm.

36. Grant, telephone interview; Matt Baker, "Lacoochee's Mudcat Grant on His 1960s Anthem Moment: 'Those Were Trying Times,'" *Tampa Bay Times*, October 13, 2017. http://www.tampabay.com/sports/baseball/rays/lacoochees-mudcat-grant-on-his-1960s-anthem-moment-those-were-trying-times/2340934?curator=SportsREDEF.

1971: Willie Stargell's Pivotal Season

Blake W. Sherry

I wish that someone had told me when I was 15 years old that Willie Stargell was starting a five-year tear that would transform him from a good home run hitter to one of baseball's superstars. If they had, I would have taken more mental snapshots of the man who was not yet "Pops." While 1971 will always be remembered most for Roberto Clemente's World Series heroics, it was also the year Stargell emerged from Clemente's shadow and came into the national spotlight.

Stargell showed great promise as early as 1964, when he was named to his first All-Star Game. In 1965 he reached new highs with 27 homers and 107 RBIs. He demonstrated it was no fluke in 1966, hitting .315 with 33 homers, 102 RBIs, and a third consecutive All-Star selection. Two years later, in 1968, his average dipped to .237 with 24 homers. An eye injury resulting from crashing into the scoreboard in left field at Forbes Field may have been the cause. Later, Stargell said, "I don't think I should have played after that accident," which at times gave him double vision. "I probably would have been better sitting out the rest of the season."[1]

He re-established himself with productive though not stellar seasons in 1969 and '70. During the 1970 season, he began dealing with his daughter's illness, diagnosed as sickle cell anemia. It became his cause to fight. He would set up a foundation to help those with the disease. After that season he participated in a trip with broadcaster Bob Prince to visit soldiers in Vietnam. It was life-changing. Seeing the horrors of war refined his definition of what a hero really was. It was no longer a man in a ball cap, but a person in fatigues serving his country for freedom.[2]

But with his 100-RBI seasons now four years removed, many felt that he had been a disappointment. Fans were still waiting for his breakout year. And now that he was 31 years old it seemed doubtful to happen. Later studies from experts like Bill James have indicated that players in their 30s tend to experience gradual production declines, not breakouts.[3]

Stargell showed up a different man for the 1971 season. He reported to training camp 20 pounds lighter than at the end of 1970. While part of that weight loss was due to his trip to hot, humid Vietnam, it also was the result of working harder on his fitness over the winter.[4] This included long walks down a path, nearly four miles long, in a nearby graveyard.[5] Arriving at camp in playing shape enabled Stargell to spend more time in the batting cage getting ready for the season rather than running in the outfield to shed the winter pounds.[6]

Stargell got off to a torrid start. He batted .347 in April, along with an .813 slugging average, a 1.211 OPS, 27 RBIs, and 11 home runs, breaking the previous April record of 10, shared by Tony Perez and Frank Robinson. The hot start yielded Stargell a Player of the Month Award. Yet despite his explosive month at the plate, the Pirates got off to a mediocre 12–10 start, including shutout losses in both games Stargell was out of the lineup with a virus.[7]

During that scorching April, Stargell, with his rocking and windmilling motion as he awaited the next pitch, had two three-homer games, both against the Braves. Three home runs in a game was not a new thing for Stargell. He first did it on June 24, 1965, in Los Angeles, then did it again on May 22, 1968, in Chicago.[8]

He cooled off a bit in May but was red-hot again in June, with a 1.193 OPS and 11 more homers, and the Pirates as a team began to follow his lead. They arrived at the All-Star break riding a six-game winning streak, leading the NL East by nine games over the Mets. Stargell was again named Player of the Month for June. He had 30 home runs and 87 RBIs while batting .320 going into the All-Star Game. The benefits of reporting to camp lighter seemed to be paying off. Manager Danny Murtaugh understood the hard work Stargell had endured in the offseason. "It is the kind of sacrifice that makes Stargell a champion," Murtaugh said. "There's no telling what he can accomplish now."[9] The manager was right. Stargell's string of five consecutive Top-10 MVP finishes was just about to begin.

After the break, the Pirates won their first five, giving them an 11.5-game lead in the East. Stargell kept hitting. He hit two home runs in a game against the Giants on July 31 at Candlestick Park and then hit two more in the nightcap of a doubleheader the next day. At that point, Stargell already had 38 homers and 100 RBIs with two months to play. He was asked about Roger Maris and his record 61-homer season continually. But just as he'd been uninterested in celebrating his 11 home runs in April, he was uninterested in talking about Maris.[10]

Stargell, already a veteran of two knee surgeries, played much of that season with his left knee aching. Murtaugh was aware of the pain, and at one point he and the doctors suggested Stargell undergo immediate surgery to repair it, but he declined and pushed surgery to the offseason. As Stargell remembered in his autobiography, "There was no way I was going to miss the '71 season. I knew that something very special was waiting for us just around the corner."[11]

Nationally, Stargell and the Pirates were making headline news as well. Stargell was chosen for the cover of *Sports Illustrated* in August, and the article celebrated the Pirates' melting pot of diverse ethnicity "in full active harmony at Three Rivers."[12] During this time, Stargell's presence in the clubhouse continued to grow.

Murtaugh had a close and trusted relationship with the players. On top of that, Stargell explained, both Clemente and Bill Mazeroski were strong contributors to the team's winning attitude. They'd both been in pennant races before and both led by example. But it "was Roberto that kept our competitive spirit finely tuned. He was a fierce competitor who wasn't afraid to kick you in the behind if your performance slipped." Stargell added, "Each one of us wanted to be like Roberto. He taught us to take pride in ourselves, our team and our profession."[13]

While this was no doubt Clemente's team, Stargell continued to emerge as a leader in his own way. He made it a point to keep everyone loose and keep the locker room inclusive. In his autobiography, he wrote that "a lot of us were pranksters, so my job wasn't terribly difficult. But the players who needed my attention were not the veterans, but the rookies, who were often excluded from clubhouse pranks and camaraderie. I took it upon myself to make them feel a part of the team." But he added, "Everyone needs a pat on the back occasionally, even veterans, and when they needed it, I gave it to them."[14]

As Jim O'Brien, author of the "Pittsburgh Proud" series, put it, "If Clemente was the soul of the 1971 World Champion Pirates, then Stargell was its heart."[15] As the end of the decade neared, in 1979, Stargell was both the Pirates' heart and its soul.

A young Willie Stargell started showing his great potential as early as the 1964 season, when he was selected to his first of seven All Star Games.

It was an eventful stretch run for the Bucs on many accounts. On August 14, Bob Gibson threw a no-hitter at Three Rivers Stadium, the first in Pittsburgh since 1907, with Stargell striking out looking for the final out. Though the Bucs trailed, 11–0, in the ninth, I remember rooting for Stargell to hit one out and end the no-hitter. It was another moment I wish someone had told me to just appreciate history and savor witnessing a Hall of Fame pitcher tossing a gem like that. But instead, I left the park dejected as the Cardinals gained another game on the Pirates. The following day, despite another multi-homer game by Stargell, the Cardinals completed the four-game series sweep to close the Pirates' lead to 4 games. The next night, Stargell's four-hit, four-RBI performance against the Astros got the Pirates winning again.

Stargell had help along the way. Dock Ellis won 19 games. Clemente batted .341 in 132 games, All-Star catcher Manny Sanguillen batted .319, and Bob Robertson added 26 home runs. A young Al Oliver continued his solid hitting and center-field play as well. On August 23, Oliver had a monster game with a 6-4-5-5 line in the box score. He hit two home runs and a triple while helping the Pirates whip the Braves, 15–4.

On September 1, in a game at Three Rivers Stadium that spawned a book published in 2006, *The Team That Changed Baseball* by Bruce Markusen, and a 2017 MLB Network documentary, *The Forever Brothers*, Stargell participated in history. He was the starting left fielder in the game in which Murtaugh sent out a lineup of all black and Latino players for the first time in major-league history. Stargell contributed a single, double, and sacrifice fly as the Pirates beat the Phillies, 10–7.

A few days later, on September 6, Stargell hit his second grand slam of the season in a win over the Cubs. The first slam, hit on June 20, was in the second game of a doubleheader. In the opener, he'd blasted one into Three Rivers' upper deck for only the third time in the stadium's short history.[16]

However, during much of the second half, Stargell played through the pain of his aggravated knee, likely impacting his ability to hit 50 home runs for the season. It eventually forced him to miss five straight games starting September 15. Murtaugh wanted Stargell healthy for the postseason.

He came back in time to help the Bucs clinch the pennant on September 22. The 5–1 win put the pesky Cardinals away for the season. The next day, the Pirates put an exclamation point on it with Stargell's two-run homer, pulling him even at 46 with Hank Aaron for the league lead. It supported Nellie Briles's six-hit shutout.

When the regular season ended, Stargell sat atop the league in home runs, extra-base hits, and (the yet-to-be-invented) wins above replacement for non-pitchers with 48, 74, and 7.9 respectively. His home-run total edged Aaron's by just one. He also had a .295 batting average and drove in 125 runs. While this performance helped the Pirates finish with the best record in the National League and win the East by seven games, Joe Torre of the Cardinals trumped him in winning the NL MVP with a stellar .363 batting average while driving in 137 runs, both league-leading marks.

Still, it added up to Stargell's best season so far. He'd become a real superstar in the eyes of the baseball nation. But his turning-point season was not without frustration and disappointment. After his MVP-caliber year, he had a miserable NLCS, going 0-for-14 as the Pirates beat the Giants three games to one to head to the World Series against Baltimore. Stargell rebounded only slightly in the Fall Classic, batting .208. He also drew seven walks for a .387 on-base percentage. It was Clemente's year to shine on the national stage. And as has been well documented, MVP Clemente dominated all aspects of the Series at age 37, with timely hits, a .414 batting average, and excellence in the field.

Yet Stargell had one more growth spurt in his emergence as a leader. Throughout and after the World Series, he showed his teammates how to be about the team and not personal accomplishments. He was not one to sulk over his personal disappointments. After rain had delayed Game Two, Stargell calmly answered pointed questions from reporters about his lack of hitting in the NLCS and his 0-for-3 in Game One

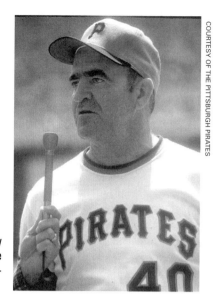

Pirates Manager Danny Murtaugh had a close and trusting relationship with his players.

COURTESY OF THE PITTSBURGH PIRATES

against the Orioles. He refused to snap at reporters. "When I was going good, I didn't get excited, so when I'm going bad, I'm not going to hit the bottom of the barrel," he said, "I'll be able to say I did my best."[17] Wrote Kansas City writer Joe McGuff, "He never tried to hide from writers. He knew he was having a bad Series, but he always gave the impression that team winning was more important than any personal gains he could have in the Series."[18]

Stargell was delighted to have scored the crucial second run in the 2–1 win in Game Seven. He led off the eighth with a groundball single and scored on Jose Pagan's double to the left-center-field wall. "I must have looked like a runaway beer truck going around the bases," Stargell said. "It was a hit-and-run and I had to stop at second to make sure the center fielder wasn't going to catch the ball. Once I got going again, though, I thought to myself, 'There's nothing that's gonna stop me from making home plate.'" Then, with a Stargell smile, he added, "Of course, a guy with my wheels can afford to take chances. I stole 40 bases this year."[19] The center fielder bobbled the ball on his original throwing motion and Stargell—who really had stolen zero—slid home without a play.

The mature Stargell put his highly tuned skills and leadership to good use in 1972. It was another solid All-Star year for him. An injury limited him to only 138 games but he still batted a robust .293 with 33 home runs and was third in RBIs, driving in 112. He finished third in the MVP award voting.

In the offseason, tragedy was then thrust upon the Pirates. On New Year's Eve, Clemente died in a plane crash shortly after takeoff as he tried to help get relief supplies to earthquake victims in Managua, Nicaragua. His body was never found. With the retirement of

Stargell had the first of five straight Top-10 finishes in the National League MVP voting in 1971, finishing second twice. He would eventually share the MVP award with Keith Hernandez in 1979.

Mazeroski at the season's end, and now the loss of Clemente, a void needed to be filled on the field and in the clubhouse. Leadership would fall to Stargell. Replacing Clemente as the team leader was not a role he actively went searching for, but he was ready.

When spring training 1973 opened for the mourning Pirates, Stargell in particular was barraged with questions about who would fill Clemente's shoes as the team leader. Stargell grew weary of the question, but stayed on the high road, claiming he was not seeking to replace Clemente, no one could, but as the elder statesman of the team, he'd help all those seeking advice from him. When Murtaugh asked Stargell to be the team captain a year later, he agreed only if he could lead his own way. He could not be Clemente. Murtaugh told him he understood and wouldn't want it any other way.[20]

Stargell responded to the loss of Clemente with one of the best seasons of his career. He batted .299 with 44 home runs and a league-leading 119 RBIs. He also led the league in doubles, slugging percentage, OPS, and OPS+. It still was not enough to win the league's MVP, finishing second again, this time to Pete Rose.

At season's end, Stargell learned he would be receiving the award he really wanted: The Roberto Clemente Award, given out to the player who exemplifies the late star on and off the field. "Of all the awards this ranks number one with me," Stargell said, "because it identifies with Clemente, who always tried to help people."[21] He also won the Lou Gehrig Memorial Award as the player who best exhibits the character and integrity of Gehrig on and off the field.

Stargell remained one of the dominant players in the decade of the 1970s. He walloped 296 home runs, more than any other player. He capped that decade off in 1979 with a magical season at the ripe old age of 39. He won three MVP awards—for the regular season, the NLCS, and the World Series. His Series performance had similarities to Clemente's. He batted .400 with seven extra-base hits and seven RBIs as the Pirates again beat the Orioles. This time the Bucs rose from a 3–1 deficit to win it. And it was Stargell's home run that put the Pirates ahead for good in the seventh game.

So the 1971 season will long be remembered as the year Clemente showed the world why he was "The Great One," and the year the Pirates changed baseball by starting the first all-minority lineup. It was also the pivotal year for Willie Stargell emerging as a complete hitter, establishing himself as a superstar for years to come, actively becoming a team leader, and helping lead the Bucs to a world championship. And in doing so, Stargell accelerated his journey to the Baseball Hall of Fame. In 1988, he was voted in on his first ballot. ∎

Notes

1. Charles Feeney, "Willie Stargell Puts It All Together," *Baseball Digest*, September 1971.
2. Willie Stargell and Tom Bird, *Willie Stargell: An Autobiography* (New York: Harper & Row, 1984), 140–41.
3. Bruce Markusen, *The Team that Changed Baseball* (Yardley, PA: Westholme Publishing), 2006, 19–20.
4. Jim O'Brien, "Willie at the Front," from Baseball Hall of Fame files, April 26, 1971.
5. Feeney, "Graveyard Strolls Keep Slugger Stargell Slim," *The Sporting News*, May 22, 1971.
6. Dick Young, "How Stargell's Saigon Visit Made Him a Better Hitter," *New York Daily News*, June 24, 1971.
7. Markusen, *The Team that Changed Baseball*, 41–42.
8. Lester Biederman, "Willie's 3 Homers, Cardwell's Pitching Spark Rout, 13–3," *Pittsburgh Press*, June 25, 1965; Biederman, "Stargell Raps for Attention with Three Homer Salute," *Pittsburgh Press*, June 8, 1968.
9. Feeney, "Willie Stargell: A Superstar At Last?" *All-Star Sports*, September 1971.
10. Markusen, *The Team that Changed Baseball*, 81.
11. Stargell and Bird, *Willie Stargell: An Autobiography*, 146–47, 155.
12. Roy Blount, "On the Lam With the Three Rivers Gang," *Sports Illustrated*, August 2, 1971.
13. Stargell and Bird, *Willie Stargell: An Autobiography*, 144–45.
14. Stargell and Bird, 145.
15. Jim O'Brien, *Remember Roberto* (Pittsburgh: James P. O'Brien Publishing, 1994), 234.
16. Markusen, *The Team that Changed Baseball*, 74.
17. Markusen, 140.
18. Markusen, 181.
19. Bill Christine, "Clemente Drives Pirates to Title," *The Pirates Reader* (Pittsburgh: University of Pittsburgh Press, 2003), 214.
20. Stargell and Bird, *Willie Stargell: An Autobiography*, 159.
21. Feeney, "Clemente Award Given to His Ex-Mate Willie," *Pittsburgh Press*, April 27, 1974.

The Annual Forbes Field Celebration

Pirates Fans Relive Mazeroski's Moment

Richard J. Puerzer

On October 13, 1985, a Pittsburgh resident by the name of Saul Finkelstein decided to personally commemorate the 25th anniversary of the seventh game of the 1960 World Series. Finkelstein went to the corner of the University of Pittsburgh's campus where Forbes Field was once located to listen to a tape recording of NBC's broadcast of the game by Chuck Thompson and Jack Quinlan. On his way there, he bought a couple of hot dogs for his lunch from the Original Hot Dog Shop a few blocks away. Finkelstein sat down next to the flagpole that was once in deep center field, a few feet from the remnants of the center-field wall. He began the recording at 1:00 PM.

The recording of the game concluded, just as the game and the 1960 World Series had 25 years earlier, at 3:36, when Bill Mazeroski hit one of the most famous home runs in baseball history.[1] This solitary act by Saul Finkelstein of celebrating that game began a unique annual celebration, a tradition that would grow to include hundreds of people gathering annually at the vestiges of Forbes Field, listening to that World Series game, and celebrating one of the great moments in the history of baseball.

From 1985 to 1992, Finkelstein made this an annual event for himself. A quiet, wispy-haired, somewhat disheveled guy from Squirrel Hill, a nearby neighborhood, he obviously loved the Pirates. At a PiratesFest in January 1993, he told Jim O'Brien, who had just written the book *Maz and the '60 Bucs*, about his annual pilgrimage. O'Brien was intrigued by the idea and spoke about it as a guest on a radio sports-talk show.[2] Others read or heard his description and they too decided it would be a good idea to go celebrate Mazeroski's home run and the 1960 World Series.

In October of that year, a number of others joined Finkelstein at the Forbes Field wall. After 1993, it became an annual event for many to go to the Forbes Field wall each October 13, listen, and celebrate. The event grew organically—there was no involvement on the part of the Pirates, no sponsorships, just baseball fans coming together each year to celebrate the 1960 World Series, the Pirates' victory, Bill Mazeroski, and baseball.

Of course, the annual celebration would not take place if not for the event it recalls, the Pirates' victory in the 1960 World Series, and specifically their dramatic win in Game Seven. The 1960 World Series was an unexpected gem. The Yankees, who finished the season with a record of 97–57, were World Series regulars, making their 10th appearance in 12 years. The Pirates, on the other hand, with a record of 95–59, were in their first World Series since 1927, when they were swept by the "Murderers' Row" Yankees. The Yankees were managed by Casey Stengel and featured Mickey Mantle, Yogi Berra, Whitey Ford, Roger Maris, and Elston Howard. The Pirates were managed by Danny Murtaugh and their roster included Roberto Clemente, the double-play combination of Mazeroski and Dick Groat, and pitchers Vern Law and Roy Face. The Series was as tremendous as it was unusual. The Pirates won Game One, 6–4, then got blown out in Games Two and Three by scores of 16–3 and 10–0. The Buccos came back and won the next two games, 3–2 and 5–2. Games Six and Seven were played in Forbes Field. The Yankees came back with another blowout win in Game Six, winning, 12–0. Going into Game Seven, the Yankees had outscored the Pirates, 46–17.

Game Seven of the 1960 World Series was one of the great games in the history of baseball. Not one batter struck out in the game, an oddity even in that era. The Pirates got out to a 2–0 lead in the first inning on a Rocky Nelson home run. They scored two more in the second and chased Yankees starter Bob Turley from the game. The Yankees tallied a run in the fifth inning on a Moose Skowron home run, and scored four more in the sixth, three of them on a home run by Yogi Berra. In the top of the eighth, the Yankees scored two more to make it, 7–4, but the Pirates answered with five runs in the bottom of the inning, including a now-underappreciated three-run homer by Hal Smith, to take a 9–7 lead. The Yankees answered back with two more runs in the top of the ninth inning to tie the game, 9–9. The Pirates came to bat in the bottom of the ninth with Mazeroski leading off. At 3:36 PM, with a 1–0 count, on a Ralph Terry slider, Bill Mazeroski, the Pirates' 24-year old second baseman batting eighth in the order, hit arguably the most important home run in the history of baseball—or at least in the history of the Pirates. He pulled the ball to left-center field, over Berra's head and over the ivy-covered brick wall. Mazeroski rounded the bases, batting helmet in hand, to the roar of the crowd. The jubilant fans at Forbes Field and throughout Pittsburgh were delighted.

The aftermath, like the World Series itself, was unique and substantial. The Series MVP was Bobby Richardson of the Yankees, the only player on a losing team ever to win it. Mantle wept following the seventh game, and later said it was the only loss that affected him that much. Stengel was fired as manager of the Yankees and said, "I'll never make the mistake of being 70 again."[3] In 1961, the Yankees, now managed by Ralph Houk and led by Maris, had a tremendous season, winning 109 games and the World Series. The Pirates, on the other hand, fell to sixth place and did not win another pennant until 1971.

Among the most important reasons the annual commemoration occurs is that one can still make the pilgrimage to the former location of Forbes Field and see parts of the great old ballpark, which remain almost as sacred grounds today. While the location of most former ballparks is evinced by little more than a historical marker, a portion of Forbes Field's brick center-field wall still stands, alongside the base of the original flagpole. Home plate itself still remains near its original location, encased in glass in the floor of an academic building on the University of Pittsburgh campus. These relics provide visitors with the ability to see, touch, and celebrate the great old stadium.

Forbes Field, to some, was the perfect ballpark. Built in 1909 by visionary and influential Pirates owner Barney Dreyfuss, it was among the first steel and concrete stadia. It was located in the then-affluent Oakland section of Pittsburgh, bordering the University of Pittsburgh, Carnegie Tech (later Carnegie Mellon University), and Schenley Park. The Cathedral of Learning, the University of Pittsburgh's iconic 42-story Gothic building, was just a few blocks away and provided a location for some Pirates fans to watch games. Like most fields in that era, Forbes was asymmetrical, and it had a huge, triples-inducing outfield. In addition to being the home of the Pirates, it was also the location of a number of prominent events. It was at times home for the Homestead Grays and Pittsburgh Crawfords of the Negro Leagues. The Pittsburgh Steelers played football at Forbes Field, as did all of Pittsburgh's college football teams. Several boxing title fights and political rallies took place there, and the 1951 version of the movie *Angels in the Outfield* was filmed there. No no-hitters were ever pitched at Forbes Field, but Babe Ruth hit his last three home runs there. Rickwood Field in Birmingham, Alabama, which was built in 1910 and is still standing today, was modeled after Forbes Field.

By the late 1960s, the park was showing its age. It had very little parking and was not easy to get to—the same issues that led to the demise and replacement of many other ballparks in the era. It was decided that Forbes Field would be replaced with the multi-use Three Rivers Stadium, to be built downtown. The final games at Forbes Field, a doubleheader, were played against the Cubs on June 28, 1970. Two years later, the stadium was torn down to make way for several University of Pittsburgh buildings.[4] Home plate is now located in Posvar Hall. Some of the land on which Forbes Field sat remained the property of the city of Pittsburgh, and the city presciently allowed segments of the outfield wall to remain. The brick wall was built in 1946, when wood walls were replaced. The city also added a small baseball field adjacent to it, appropriately named Mazeroski Field.

In his book *Baseball as a Road to God*, author and New York University President John Sexton states: "When Pirates fans congregate at the remaining piece of the Forbes Field wall, they see the monument as much more than slabs of brick, and they arouse the deeper perception that religious man has brought to many sacred spaces through the ages."[5] If these relics of the field were not standing today, it is unlikely that the annual

RICHARD J. PUERZER

The center-field wall of Forbes Field, as it still stands today.

celebration of 1960 would exist. Mazeroski serves as something of a patron saint for the annual celebration. Not only was he an unexpected hero of the 1960 World Series, he had a long, blue-collar career with which many Pittsburghers could readily identify. Mazeroski was born relatively close to Pittsburgh in Wheeling, West Virginia, and grew up just on the Ohio side of the border. He is considered by many to have been the greatest fielding second baseman of all time, winning eight Gold Glove Awards and turning more double plays in his career than any other second baseman in the history of the game. Mazeroski was named to 10 All-Star teams during his 17-year career, all of which he spent with the Pirates. He retired following the 1972 season and was inducted into the National Baseball Hall of Fame in 2001. On September 5, 2010, his 74th birthday, the Pirates unveiled a 12-foot-tall statue of Mazeroski outside PNC Park, depicting him running around the bases after hitting his momentous home run.[6]

The annual celebration continued on through the 1990s, with attendance steadily growing each year. Mazeroski made an appearance at the event in 2000, celebrating the 40th anniversary with about 400 other attendees. Steve Blass, who was signed out of high school by the Pirates in 1960 but did not debut with the team until 1964, has attended several times. Another former player who has attended more than once is Frank Thomas, who was one of the players traded by the Pirates to the Reds in 1959 for Harvey Haddix, Don Hoak, and Smokey Burgess—a move that helped the Pirates a great deal in 1960. Other former Pirates have also attended over the years.

Saul Finkelstein passed away in 2004. But by this time there were others who had followed in his footsteps and attended each year. In 2006, some of these regulars formed a group known as the Game 7 Gang, dedicated to continuing the annual celebration. Herb

The author at the wall.

Soltman, de facto leader of the Game 7 Gang, was at the game in 1960. Soltman has served as the master of ceremonies for the event for several years. George Skornickel, another Game 7 Gang member, has made the event a multi-generational family celebration. His daughter has joined him at the celebration each year for decades, and his granddaughter has joined the two of them every year of her young life.[7] For the members of the Game 7 Gang and all of the other attendees, the event reflects what is best and what is to love about baseball.

L–R: George Skornickel, Joe Landolina, John Urso, Herb Soltman, Dan Schultz, Steve Neumeyer.

Each year, the crowd acts as if they are not just listening to the game, but playing the part of the fans who were there in 1960. They sing the national anthem, applaud as the game goes along, lament when the Yankees score, cheer when the Pirates do, sing "Take Me Out to the Ballgame," worry as the game goes to the ninth inning, and, of course, cheer when Mazeroski hits his home run. One rule that is followed by all attendees is that no one celebrates with high fives, as the gesture was not in use in 1960.

In 2010, the 50th anniversary was celebrated in a special way. The Pirates organization joined in helping to organize the event and invited every living member of the 1960 team to celebrate at the wall. Players who attended included Groat, Smith, Law, Face, Bill Virdon, Bob Friend, Joe Christopher, George Witt, Joe Gibbon, Bob Oldis, and of course Mazeroski. Vera Clemente, Roberto's widow, and their son Luis also attended. They were joined by more than 1,000 fans who came to listen to the game and celebrate. Since 2010, the celebration has returned to normal. In 2016, no former players were among the roughly 75 people who attended.

Every October 13, in a corner of the baseball world in Pittsburgh, you will find a special celebration of the history, love, and joy of baseball. Each year, a group of baseball fans, and this event itself, are able to turn back the clock, if but for a few hours, and celebrate a great baseball game. One can only hope that this celebration of Bill Mazeroski's home run, Forbes Field, the Pirates, and victory in the 1960 World Series continues on as long as people are playing, and loving, baseball. ∎

Sources

David Finoli and Tom Aikens, *Forbes Field* (Charleston, SC: Arcadia Publishing, 2013).

Pittsburgh Pirates, *Forbes Field 60th Birthday, 1909–1969: Pittsburgh Pirates Picture Album* (Pittsburgh: Pittsburgh Pirates, 1969).

Len Martin and Dan Bonk, *Forbes Field: Build It Yourself* (Oakmont, PA: Point Four, 1995).

Jim O'Brien, *Maz and the '60 Bucs: When Pittsburgh and Its Pirates Went All the Way* (Pittsburgh: James P. O'Brien Publishing, 1993).

Baseball-Reference.com, https://www.baseball-reference.com.

Notes

1. Jim O'Brien, "Relive the Pirates' Wonderful World Series Victory Over the New York Yankees in 1960," Valley Mirror, October 9, 2014; O'Brien, "Saul at the Wall," in Forbes Field: Essays and Memories of the Pirates' Historic Ballpark, 1909–1971, ed. David Cicotello and Angelo J. Louisa (Jefferson, NC: McFarland, 2007), 150-154.
2. O'Brien, phone interview, May 9, 2017.
3. Marty Appel, Casey Stengel: Baseball's Greatest Character (New York: Doubleday, 2017), 277.
4. The School of Law, School of Business, and Posvar Hall.
5. John Sexton, Baseball as a Road to God (New York: Gotham Books, 2013), 27.
6. Mazeroski's statue joined statues of all-time great Pirates players Honus Wagner, Roberto Clemente, and Willie Stargell.
7. George Skornickel, email correspondence with author, May 24, 2017.

Contributors

RON BACKER is an attorney who is an avid fan of both movies and baseball. He has written five books on film, his most recent being *Baseball Goes to the Movies*, published in 2017 by Applause Theatre & Cinema Books. A long-suffering Pirates fan, Backer lives in Pittsburgh, Pennsylvania.

DR. JOHN J. BURBRIDGE, JR. is currently Professor Emeritus at Elon University where he was both a dean and professor. He is also an adjunct at York College of Pennsylvania. While at Elon he introduced and taught *Baseball and Statistics*. He has authored several publications and also presented at SABR Conventions, NINE and the Seymour meetings. He is a lifelong New York Giants baseball fan. The greatest Giants-Dodgers game he attended was a 1–0 Giants' victory in Jersey City in 1956. Yes, the Dodgers did play in Jersey City in 1956 and 1957. John can be reached at burbridg@elon.edu.

MATTHEW M. CLIFFORD is a freelance writer from the suburbs of Chicago, Illinois. He joined SABR in 2011 to enhance his research abilities while helping to preserve accurate facts of baseball history. His background in law enforcement studies and forensic investigative techniques aid him with historical research and data collection. He has reported several baseball card errors and inaccuracies of player history to SABR and the research department of the National Baseball Hall of Fame. He is also a contributing writer for SABR's BioProject. Feedback is welcome at his email address: matthewmclifford@yahoo.com

ALAN COHEN has been a SABR member since 2011, serves as Vice President-Treasurer of the Connecticut Smoky Joe Wood Chapter, and is the datacaster (stringer) for the Hartford Yard Goats. He has written more than 40 biographies for SABR's BioProject. He has expanded his research into the Hearst Sandlot Classic (1946–65), an annual youth All-Star game which launched the careers of 88 major-league players. He graduated from Franklin and Marshall College with a degree in history. He has four children and six grandchildren and resides in West Hartford, Connecticut, with his wife Frances, a cat (Morty), and a dog (Sam).

ROB EDELMAN offers film commentary on WAMC Northeast Public Radio, and his byline has appeared in *Base Ball: A Journal of the Early Game* and dozens of other publications. He is a longtime Contributing Editor of *Leonard Maltin's Movie Guide*; his books include *Great Baseball Films*, *Baseball on the Web*, *From Spring Training to Screen Test: Baseball Players Turned Actors* (co-edited with Bill Nowlin) and (with Audrey Kupferberg) *Matthau: A Life* and *Meet the Mertzes*, a double biography of *I Love Lucy's* William Frawley and Vivian Vance. He teaches film history courses at the University at Albany.

ED EDMONDS is Professor Emeritus of Law at the University of Notre Dame. He is the former law library director at William & Mary, Loyola New Orleans, St. Thomas (MN), and Notre Dame. He is a frequent speaker at the NINE Spring Training Conference and the Cooperstown Symposium. With Frank Houdek, he is the co-author of *Baseball Meets the Law* (McFarland 2007). He has taught a seminar on sports law for over 35 years and written numerous law review articles on the legal aspects of labor and antitrust law and baseball. Edmonds first encountered SABR when he bought a copy of the *Baseball Research Journal* during his first trip to Cooperstown in 1975 while on his honeymoon.

CHARLIE FOUCHÉ is a native of Jacksonville, Florida. He received a Bachelor of Science in Journalism from the University of Florida. He has also earned a Master of Divinity, a Doctor of Theology, a Doctor of Christian Education, and a Doctor of Biblical Studies. He has written and edited for several publications, and written several theological works. He teaches in an alternative high school in Dalton, Georgia.

GORDON J. GATTIE serves as a human-systems integration engineer for the US Navy. His baseball research interests involve ballparks, historical records, and statistical analysis. A SABR member since 1998, Gordon earned his Ph.D. from SUNY Buffalo, where he used baseball to investigate judgment/decision-making performance in complex dynamic environments. Originally from Buffalo, Gordon learned early the hardships associated with rooting for Buffalo sports teams. Ever the optimist, he also cheers for the Cleveland Indians and Washington Nationals. Lisa, his lovely bride who also enjoys baseball, continues to challenge him by supporting the Yankees. Gordon has contributed to multiple SABR publications.

FRANCIS KINLAW has contributed to 18 SABR convention publications (matching the number of Max Surkont's pitching losses in 1954, Ron Kline losses in 1956, Bob Friend losses in 1957, and Roy Face and Vern Law victories in 1959). He has attended 22 SABR national conventions, equaling the number of Bob Friend's mound victories in 1958. A member of SABR since 1983, he resides in Greensboro, North Carolina, and writes extensively about baseball, football, and college basketball.

HERM KRABBENHOFT, a SABR member since 1981, is a retired organic chemist. He is a lifelong fan of the Detroit Tigers. His baseball research endeavors have included ultimate grand slam homers, leadoff batters, quasi-cycles, and ascertaining accurate records for runs scored and runs batted in by players of the Deadball Era.

DAVID KRELL is the author of *Our Bums: The Brooklyn Dodgers in History, Memory and Popular Culture* (McFarland, 2015). *Our Bums* received Honorable Mention for SABR's 2015 Ron Gabriel Award. In addition to *The National Pastime*, David has written for the *Baseball Research Journal*, *Black Ball: A Negro Leagues Journal*, and *Base Ball: A Journal of the Early Game*. David is also a contributor to SABR's Biography Project, Games Project, and Ballparks Project. David often speaks at SABR conferences and the Cooperstown Symposium on Baseball and American Culture.

TED KNORR has been a baseball fan since infancy, when his grandma gave him a Brooklyn Dodgers jersey. A few years later, an aunt introduced him to baseball via Ladies Nights at Forbes Field. Later still, a childhood friend—Martha—introduced him to the APBA Major League Baseball Game. Ted has been a SABR member since 1979 and, in 1998, founded and hosted the initial Jerry Malloy Negro League Research Conference. This is his first article for *The National Pastime*.

WILLIAM E. McMAHON is professor emeritus of philosophy at the University of Akron. Born in Chicago in 1937, he is a lifelong Cubs fan. In the early 60's (the era of Bob Prince and Rege Cordic) he lived in the Pittsburgh area and became interested in the Pirates. He has been a SABR member for about 30 years, active in the Jack Graney Chapter, and he has contributed several articles to SABR publications.

RICHARD "PETE" PETERSON—a Pittsburgh native and professor emeritus of English at Southern Illinois University—is the author of *Growing Up With Clemente*, *Pops: The Willie Stargell Story*, *Extra Innings: Writing on Baseball*, and co-author, with his son, Stephen, of *The Slide: Leyland, Bonds, and the Star-Crossed Pittsburgh Pirates*. He is the editor of *The Pirates Reader* and *The St. Louis Baseball Reader*, and co-editor, with David Shribman of *Fifty Great Moments in Pittsburgh Sports*.

RICHARD J. PUERZER is an associate professor and chairperson of the Department of Engineering at Hofstra University. He has contributed to several SABR Books, including *Mustaches and Mayhem: The Oakland Athletics: 1972–1974* (2015), *When Pops Led the Family: The 1979 Pittsburgh Pirates* (2016), and *Bittersweet Goodbye: The Black Barons, The Grays, and the 1948 Negro League World Series* (2017). His writings on baseball have also appeared in: *NINE: A Journal of Baseball History and Culture*, *Black Ball*, *The National Pastime*, *The Cooperstown Symposium on Baseball and American Culture* proceedings, *Zisk*, and *Spitball*.

JOHN RACANELLI is a Chicago lawyer with an insatiable interest in baseball-related litigation. When not rooting for his beloved Cubs (or working), he is probably reading a baseball book or blog, planning his next baseball trip, or enjoying downtime with his wife and family. He is probably the world's foremost photographer of triple peanuts found at ballgames and likes to think he has one of the most complete collections of vintage handheld electronic baseball games known to exist. John is a member of the Emil Rothe (Chicago) Chapter of SABR.

BLAKE W. SHERRY is a lifelong Pittsburgh Pirates fan who resides in Dublin, Ohio. A retired Chief Operations Officer of a public retirement system, he has been a member of SABR since 1997. He co-leads the Hank Gowdy SABR Chapter in Central Ohio, and currently runs that chapter's quarterly baseball book club. He contributed to the SABR book *Moments of Joy and Heartbreak: 66 Significant Episodes in the History of the Pittsburgh Pirates*.

GARY A. SARNOFF has been an active SABR member since 1994. A member of the Bob Davids and Goose Goslin SABR chapters, he has also contributed to SABR's Bio and Games Projects, to the annual *National Pastime* publication, is a member of the SABR

Negro Leagues committee, and is the chairman of the Ron Gabriel Committee. In addition, he has authored two baseball books: *The Wrecking Crew of '33* and *The First Yankees Dynasty*. He currently resides in Alexandria, Virginia.

MARK SOUDER served as the US Congressman for northeastern Indiana 1995–2010. He was a senior staff member in the US House and Senate for a decade prior to being elected to Congress. He was one of the primary questioners in the hearings on steroids abuse in baseball. He has contributed articles to the last two issues of *The National Pastime* as well as several recent SABR book projects including *Boston's First Nine*, *Puerto Rico and Baseball*, and *From Spring Training to Screen Test*. Souder is retired other than occasional political commentary and meddling. He lives in Fort Wayne with his wife Diane and his books.

GEORGE SKORNICKEL is a retired educator who has been a Pirates fan for over 60 years. He is the president of the Forbes Field chapter and has presented at SABR 44 and 45, Malloy Negro League Conference in 2012 and 2014, The Frederick Ivor-Campbell 19th Century Baseball Conference in 2017, and the Cooperstown Symposium on Baseball and American Culture In 2017, 2018. He has been published in the *Baseball Research Journal* and *Sweet '60*, and is the author of *Beat 'em Bucs: the 1960 Pittsburgh Pirates*. He lives outside of Pittsburgh in Fawn Township with his wife Kathy and two Labs, Maz and Dexter.

ROBERT C. TRUMPBOUR is Professor of Communications at Pennsylvania State University, Altoona College. He recently served as co-author of *The Eighth Wonder of the World: The Life of Houston's Iconic Astrodome* (University of Nebraska Press), recipient of SABR's Seymour Medal in 2017. Trumpbour also served as author of *The New Cathedrals: Politics and Media in the History of Stadium Construction* (Syracuse University Press). Prior to teaching, he worked in various capacities at CBS in New York for the television and radio networks. Trumpbour periodically does freelance production work on live sports broadcasts.

THOMAS E. VAN HYNING, US correspondent for the Puerto Rico Professional Baseball Hall of Fame, 1991–96, presented at SABR 25 in Pittsburgh (1995). He authored *Puerto Rico's Winter League*, *The Santurce Crabbers*, Rubén Gómez and Dick Hughes SABR bios, and others. Tom saw Roberto Clemente and Carlos Bernier play in Puerto Rico's Winter League. He is a Tourism Economist and Data Analyst in Mississippi, and member of Arkansas's Robinson-Kell SABR Chapter. His BBA degree is from the University of Georgia, and Masters' degrees are from Southern Illinois-Carbondale and a Puerto Rico university.

DAN VANDEMORTEL became a Giants fan in Upstate New York and moved to San Francisco to follow the team more closely. He has written extensively on Northern Ireland political and legal affairs, and his Giants-related writing has appeared in San Francisco's *Nob Hill Gazette* and SABR's *The National Pastime*. An investigation into the shooting of a fan at the Polo Grounds will appear in a Polo Grounds anthology to be published this year. He is currently researching and writing articles on the 1971 Giants and their time period. Feedback is welcome at giants1971@yahoo.com.